THE CURSE OF NEMUR

Illuminations: Cultural Formations of the Americas

John Beverley and Sara Castro-Klarén, Editors

THE CURSE OF NEMUR

IN SEARCH OF THE ART, MYTH, AND RITUAL OF THE ISHIR

Ticio Escobar

Translated by Adriana Michele Campos Johnson

Foreword by Michael Taussig

UNIVERSITY OF PITTSBURGH PRESS

Published by the University of Pittsburgh Press, Pittsburgh, Pa., 15260

Copyright © 2007, University of Pittsburgh Press

Manufactured in the United States of America

Printed on acid-free paper

10 9 8 7 6 5 4 3 2 1

0-8229-4293-3 / 0-8229-5937-2

Library of Congress Cataloging-in-Publication Data

Escobar, Ticio, 1947-

   [Maldición de Nemur. English]

   The curse of Nemur: In search of the art, myth, and ritual of the Ishir / by Ticio
Escobar ; translated by Adriana Michele Campos Johnson ; foreword by Michael Taussig

      p. cm. — (Illuminations: cultural formations of the Americas)

   Translation of La maldición de Nemur.

   Includes bibliographical references and index.

   ISBN 0-8229-4293-3 (cloth: alk. paper) — ISBN 0-8229-5937-2 (pbk.: alk. paper)

   1. Chamacoco mythology. 2. Chamacoco Indians—Religion. 3. Chamacoco Indians—
Rites and ceremonies. I. Title.

   F2230.2.C5E8313 2007

   398.2'08998—dc22

                  2006025144

CONTENTS

ILLUSTRATIONS

FOREWORD

If you want to learn something about color and feathers—from an Indian point of view—read this book. It also happens to be of service to literature, to art criticism, to the comparative study of religions, to shamanism, the practice of anthropology, and above all to the rethinking of the role of Native Americans in shaping the self-understanding of the Americas. It is a precious document, an extension of the delicacy and uniqueness of the thought it treats. It is as valuable for the way it goes about its task—an anthropology of anthropology, if you will—as for what it says.

Working his way through stories of how the world came to be, Ticio Escobar goes on to describe the art of featherwork, body painting, and ritual in the densely detailed shamanism that exists among the Ishir of the Gran Chaco of Paraguay. The subject matter is exotic, which is to say true, in this case, to the reality depicted. It is also unique. I know of very little written on featherwork and body painting in the ethnographic literature—let alone integrated so honestly and hence beautifully into myth, ritual, and native aesthetic theory. As regards the latter, Escobar provides the reader with copious and stupendous material on the use of color, and for that alone the book deserved to be translated. A final chapter offers a series of random documents intended to give a sense of the book's origins and the recent history and physical health of these native people. It is a shocking history, especially in regards to the role of the Paraguayan army in the Chaco War of the 1930s, and the role over several decades of the U.S.-based New Tribes Mission.

The Ishir have evaded the missionaries hell-bent on destroying their mythic and ritual life. Some worked for a tannin company. Others cut down trees to sell to logging companies. From the stories collected here we learn of non-Indians using the promise of measles vaccine to lure Indians into working for them while dying from measles. Priests do the same. Alcohol was a means of payment and prostitution of Indian woman to Paraguayan soldiers was a supplementary form of income.

In *Tristes Tropiques,* Claude Lévi-Strauss bemoaned the fate of the modern ethnographer equipped with powerful theories regarding society and heir to lively philosophical debates, yet confronted with so-called primitive societies that seemed mere shadows, even parodies, of their former selves. Fate has decreed, however, that with the Ishir of the Gran Chaco, Ticio Escobar has to some extent circumvented this cruel paradox.

He began his inquiries in the mid-1980s, and although the people with whom he spent most time are among the most resistant of Paraguay's indigenous peoples, they have suffered mightily. It thus seems miraculous that so much of their culture is intact, although I use the word "intact" with reservations, because no culture is truly intact but is open to influences on all sides and is always, so to speak, negotiating the terms of influence. And if I think of Colombia, a country in which I have lived on and off since 1969, there are plenty of indigenous societies that have preserved a good deal of autonomy. There, for example, the Kogi Indians of the Sierra Nevada de Santa Marta, along with the Ica and Arahuaco, have maintained their language and spiritual beliefs as well as their economic forms against a rapaciously destructive non-Indian culture, as have the Paez and Guambiano Indians of the Cordillera Central. In Ecuador, Peru, and Bolivia, indigenous culture is gaining political ground hand over fist. Of course this can lend itself to a mean-spirited and ignorant ethnic nationalism. It can be exaggerated and even phony, especially as what might be called a pseudo-Indianness under conditions of extreme self-awareness is cultivated for political gain—but then the line between the authentic and the phony can be a very hard one to draw and cultures are always in a process of continuous becoming.

His book bears comparison with two others that constellate the South American anthropology of indigenous people whose societies have no state or chiefs: Martin Gusinde's marvelously interesting ethnographies of Tierra del Fuego of the 1920s, and Pierre Clastres's recently published *Chronicle of the Guyaki* (also of Paraguay). Ticio Escobar's book offers a nice moment of similarity and difference with these classic works in terms of subject matter and originality of style.

Yet it is not merely the loving attention to detail that makes this book stand out. Rather, what brings life and spirit to the work is the author's relation to writing, and to the travail of fieldwork mediating the white man's world with that of the Indians. In this sense the book is the sheer antithesis of the exotic. It is prosaic, which, when combined with the exotica of feathers and color, amounts to a "profane illumination." It is prosaic in that it sets forth its own "featherwork," which is to say its own means of production. You can see how the author became interested, how the pre-fieldwork occurred, step by step, and then witness the subsequent meanderings of his own discoveries and epiphanies. It even has something of the detective novel.

You sense, in a thoroughly relaxed and unforced way, the trial runs, the shifting gaze, the tumbling of thought. You simultaneously sense the shifting human and personal relationships that develop between the Indians and this anthropologist, art critic, and politically sensitive Paraguayan. Land-locked and isolated, Paraguay is the country Escobar and the Ishir share; it has been home to countless dictators—hence Roa Bastos's famous novel, *Yo, el Supremo* —and fugitive Nazis, such as Joseph Mengele.

The book eludes definition thanks to its unorthodox yet relaxed manner of presentation beholden, in the gentlest and least pretentious ways, to what came to be called "postmodernism." Take Escobar's opening: a long list of his Indian friends and informants—perhaps discussants and storytellers are better terms here—page after page of them. Take his use of different persons' accounts of the same event or story so as to present the reader with different points of view. He sets forth his "theory," as in the chapter on ritual; intersperses extracts from his fieldwork diary, a brief commentary, then notes on what he has described; produces fragments from a letter to Roa Bastos, where he explains the origins of this book as lying in his fascination with the featherwork he saw in an art gallery in Brazil; lists vocabulary; reproduces taped interviews like theater scripts or courtroom records; and so forth. You always know where you are, yet it is never the same voice. As with all fieldwork, an effervescent touch of chaos intersperses and disperses the narrative, and this is what makes the work fun and light. The soft voices of his storytellers flow through the text no less than through each other. And the drawings are electrifying.

Early on he announces his theory of interpretation as one he derives from art criticism, not one of pinning down a meaning so much as a practice of initiating a conversation that allows for a cascading multiplicity of perspectives forming a chain or even a network of ideas displacing one another and going who knows where. Readings provoke other readings, like witchcraft, as I understand it, a process of continual deferral, playing and teasing with the holy grail of a final answer. In Escobar's rendering (in the wonderful translation by

Adriana Johnson): "For this reason it is wise to distrust the innocent arrogance that swoops down on a discourse, claiming to reveal the secret of its key. This key will always lead to another key and so on in an unending displacement. Art gestures towards a radical absence whose trace bobs in the wake of this displacement."

In his discussions of shamanism the author explores the ways that dream, song, and body painting work together to potentiate shamanic flight and intervene in meteorological crises, sorcery, and ill health. These practices are of fundamental importance, I think, in shaking up Western ideas of art. Assuredly Escobar is not the first to have stumbled across this place of the dream in song and of both song and dream in opening out visions and "art" so as to act magically on the world. Gusinde is full of it, too, as is some of the ethnography of Native North America and of indigenous Australia. But Escobar is in a league of his own here. He has so much wonderful material and lays it on thick, but *never* succumbs to the cloudy realms of New Age mysticism.

Although Escobar writes as someone fascinated by art, rather than as a "professional" anthropologist, his approach has much to teach anthropology as a critique of Western civilization. His resolutely nonfunctionalist way of understanding ritual is intellectually fascinating. Indeed, one of the reasons for publishing this work would be to show North American and European audiences what a local intellectual does in South America without the carapace of a PhD and other body armor. It is refreshing, to say the least.

The book differs from most ethnography in its focus on art—but this is hardly surprising, given the author's activities as a curator and art critic. What is surprising, perhaps, is that Escobar fulfilled these artistic occupations alongside his committed work as a lawyer defending indigenous people in Paraguay. This mixture is somewhat reminiscent of the late Geoffrey Bardon, who studied law for three years in Australia and then taught art in a racially segregated school for the indigenous people of Papunya, in the red desert of central Australia, in 1971. He was there for a mere two years, but this was sufficient—before his breakdown in that most racist of situations—to trigger the extraordinarily successful Aboriginal art scene, changing white Australia's conception of itself. (See Geoffrey Bardon and James Bardon, *Papunya: A Place Made after the Story: The Beginnings of the Western Desert Art Movement,* Carlton, Victoria: University of Melbourne, Miegunyah Press, 2004.) Bardon realized that the art the old people were showing him in sand drawings was that of body painting for ceremony. His presence translated that into two-dimensional visual art on paper, wood, and cardboard, and something profound snapped in Australian identity and imagination such that the political horizon was changed overnight in favor of indigenous rights.

Escobar sticks to the body, to its colored painted designs, to its feathers, and to ceremony. The artwork of the Ishir has not yet been translated into media other than his wonderful book—but who knows where it could lead? Read, and participate.

Michael Taussig

TRANSLATOR'S INTRODUCTION

This book is a reflection on the art forms of the people who call themselves Ishir, and who are commonly known within Paraguay as the Chamacoco. Despite Ticio Escobar's many years as an advocate for indigenous rights—he served as president of the Asociación Apoyo a las Comunidades Indígenas del Paraguay (ACIP) from 1989 to 1991, wrote *Misión: Etnocidio* (1988), and was recently recognized for such efforts by the Premio Bartolomé de Las Casas, awarded by the Casa de América in Madrid—this book was not conceived as an ethnographic project. Escobar baldly states this in his first sentence and later describes himself as an art critic, not an anthropologist.

The incredible force and importance of the book derives from this original perspective. Suspicious of any intent to peel back language to reveal a hard secret kernel of truth, Escobar's labor in art criticism is shaped by the structuralist and post-structuralist approach to signs as a shifting, sliding chain of meanings. Rather than pretending to clarify and explain the Ishir for those outside their world, Escobar engages in a dialogue with the aesthetic forms and theoretical propositions of the Ishir. These are more conceptual and performative than strictly material, and this is why the book dwells not only on body paintings and featherwork but on myths and rituals. In doing so, Escobar is as attentive to the unruliness of form among the Ishir as he is when he analyzes, for example, the poetics of absence and residue in the avant-garde art of Osvaldo Salerno (*Obra de Osvaldo Salerno: La Cicatriz,* 1999).

Escobar is no stranger to such mixed territories, since he is not only an activist and art critic but also curator, cultural promoter, and theorist. Escobar's theoretical inclinations also explain why he chooses to transcribe, as he says, rather than strictly translate the Ishir myths. While plots and narrative sequences have been rigorously followed, he says that he sought to express what the myths had evoked in him according to his cultural tradition, and in a language that was the cultural equivalent (more or less) of that employed by the Ishir. Any translation of Ishir myths is already a reading of them, has already changed them inescapably, and Escobar chooses not to fight such unavoidable alterations.

I have tried to follow Escobar's lead in my translation of his book, but would like to briefly glance back and gesture to the differences between the original Spanish edition and this translation. The stark but dynamic, ever-changing dualities of Ishir logic and the complicated, twisting architecture of their forms drove Escobar to excavate the most baroque possibilities of the Spanish language (to the great pleasure, perhaps, of Alejo Carpentier, who claimed that the baroque was the true expression of the American continent). These dense forms, which often weave archaic and little-used words with contemporary theory, only to dip into oddly relaxed colloquial stretches of text, produce a complicated and fluctuating beauty, which I have tried to conjure up in English, although it is a language with lesser baroque reservoirs than Spanish. In the Spanish edition, this fluctuation in tone and register has a visual counterpart in different forms and formats for the field notes, observations, analyses, and complementary details. The field notes, for instance, are italicized, and the theoretical considerations of myths in the first chapter are indented. Escobar notes in his introduction to the original text that such differences in format are not always consistent, and sometimes overlap and blend as an echo, perhaps, to Chamacoco reflections on permutations of identity and difference. He also cautions that such textual indicators should be understood neither as literary devices nor responses to a necessary schema, but as signposts through precipitous terrain. These typographic variations have not been reproduced in the English text.

The density of Escobar's prose is augmented by the constantly surfacing layer of words in Ishir, as well as the occasional presence of the Guaraní language, seams that alert us to the fact that the Spanish text is itself already a text with multiple layers of translations and transfers. Some comments are perhaps in order regarding the relationship of Ishir to Guaraní and Spanish, to indicate the dimensions of this undercurrent. Paraguay is an officially bilingual country (Spanish and Guaraní), although in truth, according to the 1992 census, 50 percent of Paraguayans are bilingual, 88.6 percent are Guaraní speakers, 38 percent are monolingual Guaraní speakers, and 7 percent are monolingual Spanish speakers. This bilingualism has contributed to one of the reigning myths of a deep homogeneity in Paraguayan society posited in both linguistic and racial terms (its bilingualism being the linguistic counterpart of a profound racial *mestizaje*, and vice versa), often attributed to the integrating effects of the famed Jesuit missions. The reality is of course a little more complicated, and a little less rosy. In spite of its widespread use, the appreciation of Guaraní has not always been favorable or even consistent. Looked down upon in the Liberal Era, when the country was largely run by elites that had come from Buenos Aires, Guaraní was valorized in the moments of war, and used as the language of the army on the front. The Ishir/Chamacoco, however, belong to an ethnic and language group that is very different from the Guaraní ethnic group that entered into negotiation and contact with the Spaniards during the colonial period, and are thus perhaps doubly marginalized from mainstream Paraguayan culture.

This chain of relationships between Ishir and Guaraní and Spanish is evident in the transcription of Ishir words and in references to the region's particular flora and fauna. Escobar explains in the introduction to the Spanish edition that he endeavored to use the simplest possible phonetic transcription of Ishir words. Thus, *i* indicates the guttural sixth vowel in Guaraní (y). *J, sh,* and *h,* he wrote, should be pronounced as they are in English and Guaraní (at present it is more common to use *x* instead of *sh* in Guaraní); and the dieresis over the vowels indicate nasal sounds. (Other scholars have transcribed Ishir words differently: for example, *ebidoso, tomáraxo, axnábsero*. See *Folk Literature of the Chamacoco Indians*, edited by Johannes Wilbert and Karin Simoneu, Los Angeles: University of California at Los Angeles, 1987.) Escobar also explains that he has maintained the convention of not pluralizing indigenous names, since the Ishir have their own system of pluralization, one that he used for certain recurring words like *konsaha* (shaman) and *konsaho* (shamans). While certain Ishir words were emphasized in the original text in Spanish, Escobar did not italicize the names of different ethnic groups, like those of the clans, that function as tribal or national designations, and my English version follows suit. Fauna and flora in the original text can appear under Ishir, Guaraní, or Spanish names. Some of the equivalents he used do not correspond strictly to the animals referred to, but he chose them in the interest of simplifying a text that was already overpopulated with indigenous terms (for example, *avestruz* [ostrich] and *cigueña* [stork], instead of *ñandu* or *tujuju*). Similarly, I chose to use the word "ostrich," for example, instead of "rhea"; but the Ishir world is intensely and inextricably knotted into a singular environment and such options were not always available. Where equivalent Spanish or Guaraní names did not exist, Escobar sometimes gave scientific names or took pains to describe local species, both bridging and underscoring the gap between the Ishir world and an archive of references that would be more common to non-Paraguayan Spanish speakers. I have followed his lead and introduced some additional footnotes to describe flora and fauna that could be unfamiliar to non-Spanish speakers. I have given both scientific names and English names when available.

The book has been changed in other ways. Escobar reduced the size of the published Spanish text for this translation. Some of the original footnotes have been excluded, and some illustrations are not reproduced in this edition. Finally, two appendices, which meticulously detailed different featherwork artifacts and examples of shamanic paintings, are not included here.

Adriana Michele Campos Johnson

ACKNOWLEDGMENTS

I want to express my gratitude to all the Ishir men and women who allowed me a much desired glimpse into a remote world. Thanks as well to Meme Perasso and Hugo Duarte Manzoni, who corrected the original manuscript meticulously; to Osvaldo Salerno, who laid out its structure; to Jorge Escobar Argaña, who skillfully identified the animals that inhabit the skies, rivers, and hills of the Chaco and that as yet lack names in Spanish; to Edgardo Cordeu, who generously provided me with his unpublished but indispensable texts; to Adelina Pusineri for unconditional support; to Miguel Chase-Sardi for his patience, friendship, and open library; to Eduardo Galeano, whose *Memory of Fire* allowed me to remember the words of the other; to Carlos Colombino, exemplary writer and first reader; and to Dr. Branislava Susnik, teacher, with admiration and nostalgia.

THE CURSE OF NEMUR

INTRODUCTION

SETTING THE STAGE

THIS book was conceived not as an ethnographic project but as a reflection on the art of the Ishir of the Great Chaco region of Paraguay. In indigenous cultures, however, the aesthetic manifests itself not only in art, but in myth and ritual. For this reason, the project quickly acquired multiple intersecting dimensions whose boundaries often—but not always—blurred. This book moves through this unpredictable terrain without staking out spaces or setting down clear limits: it considers the artistic through its desire to affirm the rhetoric of myth and emphasize the effects of ritual. The artistic act should not be approached in terms of an integrated event, explainable in and of itself, but insofar as it intersects with other kinds of acts and doings, lighting their way ever so briefly.

I do not pretend however to account for all forms of art among the Ishir (such an enterprise would be futile), nor to provide an inventory of the boundless patrimony of mythical tales and ritual procedures. This book follows instead certain specific cultural practices only inasmuch as they illuminate the intricate spaces traversed by form.

In order to correctly render the complexity of such spaces, I have had to introduce several concepts whose function is primarily operative and pragmatic. Each of the aforementioned dimensions (art, myth, and ceremony) can be approached from three different angles: religion, shamanic magic, and history. Just as form is the protagonist in a variety of performances, it is also the object of a plurality of gazes. Yet this variety of positions and points of view is not crystallized in an ordered scheme in this book: they establish references rather than rigorous variables. The chapters of this book, therefore, are not organized around systematic encounters with these concepts whose ductility, in any case, prevents them from being forged into fixed and exact contours.

THE FIGURES

Although this book resolutely insists on referring to art, it will also linger on subjects that exceed the domain of art. Its point of departure is necessarily the place occupied by the author: the confused site of art criticism. One should recognize, in any case, that it is a field driven less and less by hermeneutics, since the project of interpreting artistic production and revealing hidden meanings is on the wane. The art critic confronts the work of art and ventures a reading that, in the best of cases, does nothing more than incite other readings and suggest other possible points of entry. Faced with the urgent presence of the work of art the critic erects his own reading: for such a task his point of view is necessary. He does not set out to decipher the work of art, to describe it objectively, or to judge it; instead his gaze confronts it, intersects it, and seeks to shake it, frame it, and turn it into the focal point of other gazes. And in this, art criticism coincides with certain positions in contemporary anthropology that no longer pretend to dissipate the mists of barbarous languages but face them in their differences. The Other is no longer an object of study that needs to be explained and illuminated under the authority of one universal Reason. The Other is a subject who interpellates me as a subject, who opposes his truths to mine, who refutes my forms with his forms and returns my gaze. The anthropologist's subjectivity enters into a transitive relation that bleeds his discourse of "scientific objectivity" but compensates for this loss by preventing its closure, by unsettling and enriching it with new problems.

The paths of form are wild and unruly and it is not my intention to set them straight. I do not intend to disentangle the forms with which the Ishir conceal the real in order to reveal it in all its nakedness. Nor do I seek to push aside veils, tear off masks, or dismantle theatrical artifices. The truth of the referent is best exposed through the very ruses of representation. Myths, rituals, and poetry always express more through what they conceal than through what they reveal. For this reason it is wise to distrust the innocent arrogance that swoops down on a discourse, claiming to reveal the secret of its key. This key will always lead to another key and so on in unending displacement. Art gestures toward a radical absence whose trace bobs in the wake of this displacement. Myth and ritual, like art, are founded on a profound misunderstanding: the shadows of a truth in withdrawal can be glimpsed in the rift between what is said and what is left unsaid. Since myth, ritual, and art eschew prose, only their heterogeneous figures offer signs of a message, which always lies elsewhere.

All that remains is to name these figures. How to do it? The might of the mythic word and the power of ritual action, as well as the beauty they both advocate, transpire between the saying and the showing. The phrase "to translate is to betray" is not only a commonplace in literary theory but also an obsessive theme in a contemporary anthropology that is not free of such guilt. How to repeat the speech of the Other when this speech is based, in great part, on unknown codes, alien atmospheres, other scenes? The question is especially complicated in the case of mythic narratives; we are all too familiar with what happens when they are literally transcribed in the broken Spanish employed by the indigenous translator or in the precarious indigenous language accessible to the myth collector. And this does not even take into account the rhetorical and argumentative subtleties that are incomprehensible to alien cultural horizons. The drive to expression withers in the face of these impoverished translations.

Thus, insofar as this book attempts to suggest—rather than display or unveil—the complex richness of Ishir culture, and in the absence of any satisfactory option, I have chosen to freely transcribe the myths. That is, I have scrupulously respected plots and narrative sequences but have conveyed the myths in a language that is, according to my possibilities, more or less equivalent, culturally speaking, to the language employed by the Ishir. It is obvious that I do not pretend to measure up to their original flashes of brilliance—such a task exceeds me—but attempt to present a narration that preserves what these myths have evoked in me according to my own cultural tradition and language. In a certain sense, such an appropriation is the task of the critic who prowls around and through an alien discourse, usurping themes in order to expose them to different gazes. The critic does not offer up the work of art, but simply a reading of the work, hoping it will stimulate new approaches and new appropriations.

OTHER RIGHTS

This brings us to another goal of this book, one we could call political. My interest in emphasizing the power of indigenous cultures is driven less by the requirements of scientific rigor than the desire to promote respect for ethnic differences. I want my interpretation of a culture other than mine to suggest that its forms are as complex, intense, and vulnerable as those of my culture and that we should value them as much as our own. There are two ways to make this argument. One is to denounce the ferocious violation of indigenous cultural rights; this was the option I took in the text *Misión: Etnocidio* (1988). The other is to underline the value of indigenous culture and to present it not only as a site of dispossession and marginality but also as a place of creativity and ethnic self-affirmation, to reveal it as the center of one of the most original and intense projects of heterogeneous culture produced in Paraguay. Indigenous people are not only the most exploited and humiliated inhabitants of this country: they are also great artists and poets, creators of worldviews, inventors of alternative ways of feeling and thinking in this world.

Not only is it necessary, then, to condemn the oppression of these men and women and repudiate the ransacking of their natural resources; we must also recognize the rights of their symbols, these strange forms that stubbornly survive the siege of a national Paraguayan society, resisting its attacks or negotiating with it for space. The latter was the approach I took in *La belleza de los otros* (1993) and the one I take here. While the ominous presence of neo-colonial ethnocide is an oft-remembered presupposition of this book, I will not insist on it and prefer to emphasize instead the expressive possibilities of a culture that has been persecuted, mutilated, and deeply wounded but that even so continues to imagine a common path and to daily heal the lesions of a desecrated history.

THE LEVELS

The complexity of this book's themes requires a writing that can traverse more than one register. The first register comprises notes taken while in the presence of the ceremonies and other cultural acts I observed directly. Some of these take the form of the field notes in which they were first written down. The second register consists of the accounts and tales of the Ishir. As indicated above, while I respect the plot and sequence of these tales, they have been rendered according to my own expressive possibilities and those of my language. Finally, there are theoretical considerations evoked by the material.

THE ACTORS

The indigenous peoples whom Paraguayan national society calls the Chama-coco but who call themselves the Ishir (although they do not refuse the other name) dwell in the northeast of the Paraguayan Chaco and comprise, along with the Ayoreo, the Zamuco linguistic family. Their traditional economy is one of subsistence based on hunting and gathering; at present it alternates with new forms, which include light agriculture, craftsmanship, and intermit-tent labor in neighboring establishments and villages. The current Ishir pop-ulation is estimated at approximately one thousand people divided into two groups: the Tomáraho, who live in the forests, and the Ebytoso, who populate the banks of the Paraguay River. Although today both groups are experienc-ing similar processes of *mestizaje* and transculturation, historically the Ebytoso were submitted to greater missionary pressure and have consequently suffered a greater loss of rituals and myths. The Tomáraho, on the other hand, maintained themselves apart from missionary circuits at the cost of near extinction and were thus able to systematically preserve a body of myths and ceremonies. These myths and ceremonies both have made possible their strong cultural cohesion and have contributed to various movements among the Ebytoso to regain their culture.

While this book briefly touches on the history of the current Ishir, especially the Tomáraho, in the last chapter I refer readers to the work of specialists cited in the bibliography—such as Alfred Métraux, Edgardo Cordeu, Branislava Susnik, and Miguel Chase-Sardi—who have studied the ethnohistory and current situation of the Chamacoco with greater competency and depth.[1]

THE SOURCES

This book is based fundamentally on facts and experiences from my relations with certain groups of Ishir since 1986. Driven by the interest to understand a disquieting culture and to support their demands for land and freedom of worship, Guillermo Sequera and I established contact with the Tomáraho of San Carlos and the Ebytoso of Puerto Esperanza in April 1986. Some of the Ebytoso helped the Tomáraho to abandon the sawmill where they lived in squalid conditions and move to a part of the Ishir territory of Puerto Esperanza.

In San Carlos, and later Puerto Esperanza and Potrerito, I interviewed various men and women of these communities and produced a copious list of ceremonies and other cultural practices I saw performed. Through the years I also worked with Tomáraho and Ebytoso informants who traveled sporadically to Asunción for a variety of errands. Given the enviable capacity of the Ishir to quickly learn other languages and speak them easily, many interviews were conducted directly in Guaraní and Spanish and did not require translators. Other accounts, however, especially the narrations concerning essential mythic events, took place in Ishir and required the participation of skillful Ebytoso translators (Bruno Barrás, Clemente López, and Flores Balbuena). Some of these tales were based on drawings, a few of which are published here.

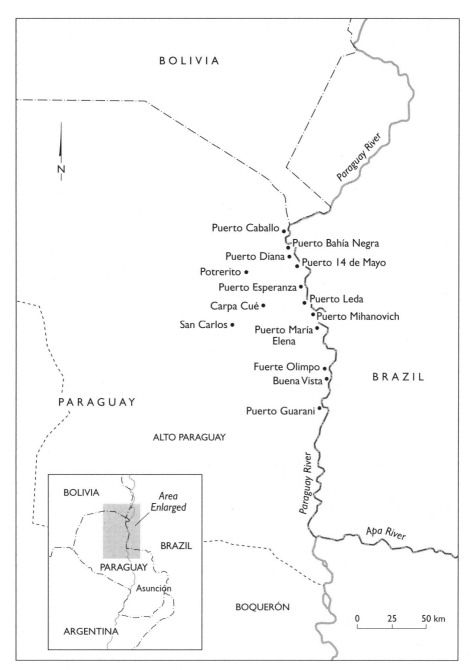

Area of distribution of the current Ishir settlements. (Information provided by Jorge Escobar Argaña. Map by Bill Nelson, derived from a drawing by Félix Toranzos.)

THE INFORMANTS

Emilio Aquino
Born in Pitiantuta in 1945, Emilio is Tomáraho, affiliated with the Posháraha clan. His Ishir name is Opserse. He was the leader of the community of Potrerito (Peishiota). He is an expert in Ishir culture and a scrupulous narrator of its myths, which he shared with me in Tomáraho (Bruno Barrás translated).

Daniel Aquino
A son of Emilio Aquino, born in 1971. His brother Crescencio, whose Ishir name is Apytal, was leader of the community of Potrerito. Daniel, whose Tomáraho name is Wulud, is a member of the Posháraha clan. I began working with him after he emerged from the seclusion that is part of the initiation into Ishir culture, and he provided accounts of this process from the point of view of a recent novice. In addition, he has given me valuable accounts of ritual games.

Gregorio Arce
One of the few Ishir better known by his indigenous name, Wylky, than by his official Paraguayan denomination, he is a shaman of the category "of the far ends of the earth." He was born in Puerto Casado in 1935 and briefly served as leader after Emilio Aquino. When an epidemic decimated nearly all of his family, Wylky sought refuge in the woods and sang until his mouth bled and his vocal cords were almost completely shattered. Despite his ruined voice and his melancholy, he has a delicate and genteel character and is one of the most precise Tomáraho informers.

Flores Balbuena
Born in 1937 in Puerto Caballo, near Bahía Negra, his Ebytoso name is Ogwa and he is a member of the Posháraha. He is one of the best transmitters of Chamacoco culture due to his wisdom and erudition, his talent in drawing, and his mastery of Spanish and Guaraní. Initiated in Puerto Diana at the age of twelve, he worked from 1959 to 1969 as a Bible translator for the New Tribes Missions. This work, so foreign to his history and convictions, has given him detailed knowledge of Spanish and Christianity, but without detriment to his own knowledge and wisdom. Since leaving the Ishir community he has lived

with his family in Itá Anguá, Nueva Colombia. He makes a living selling his drawings and wood sculptures in Asunción. He is an expert in shamanic mythology.

Bruno Barrás

Bruno is Ebytoso, of the Tahorn clan. Born in 1947, he embodies one of the many strategies of coexistence (survival) that the Ishir have developed in their contacts with Paraguayan national society. He is a prestigious leader of the Puerto 14 de Mayo community, Karcha Balut, and moves in the white world with great ease and tact. He is practically fluent in six languages and possesses both extensive knowledge of his own culture (in which he was initiated in 1960) as well as an understanding of the codes, beliefs, and weaknesses of Paraguayans. His insight and magnanimity make Bruno a remarkable inform-ant and privileged translator.

Ojeda Benítez

Ojeda is Ebytoso, of the Dosypyk clan. He was born in Puerto Leda in 1935 and lives in Puerto Esperanza, where he works as a picker of heart of palm, a day laborer, and shaman. He is well versed in the *debylyby*, the Great Ishir Ceremony, as well as the mythology of the *anábsoro* (Chamacoco gods).

Aligio Estigarribia

Tomáraho, of the Dyshykymser clan, he is a *konsaha porro* (shaman in the pre-liminary stages) and great singer. He was born in 1940 and answers to the Ishir name Ikyle. He provided useful information on shamanism, but his knowl-edge of the Ishir religion is basic and superficial.

Aparicia Estigarribia

Born in the 1940s into the Kytymáraha clan, her Tomáraho name is Chikíe Oula or Dichéhe. Like her husband, Aligio, she is a shaman singer. She has in-formed me of an emerging feminine shamanism and of certain aspects re-garding the current situation of the Chamacoco woman.

Jazmín Gamarra

Jazmín is an Ebytoso shaman. He was born in 1954 and lives in Puerto Espe-ranza, where he works as a carpenter specialized in manufacturing oxen-pulled carts that are used to transport logs. He has provided me with information on the themes of shamanic singing.

Clemente López

Clemente is Ebytoso; his Ishir name is Cháaro. He was born in 1932 of mestizo origin but participates in the culture of the Kytmáraha clan. He lives in Puerto Esperanza and is married to the mother of Bruno Barrás. If Bruno, his stepson, represents a certain model of Ishir relationship with the national society, Clemente embodies the opposite and complementary model. The cunning required by the Ishir in order to traverse alien white territory takes on a thoughtful, subtle tone in Bruno. Clemente, on the other hand, is impulsive and direct and acts through the charm of his simultaneously energetic and vulnerable character. Bruno negotiates with the prudence of the ancient masters of the word. Clemente persuades and tricks with his splendid generosity and constant enthusiasm; he pressures and lays siege with the snares of the hunter and the aggressive authority of those who remember battle. Clemente also expresses all the ambivalences of the ties that unite and divide the Ebytoso and Tomáraho. On the one hand, he enthusiastically assumed the cause of the Tomáraho. He facilitated their contact with Paraguayan society, helped them obtain solidarity, and disinterestedly supported them in their settlement in Puerto Esperanza. On the other hand, he harassed and frequently attempted to subordinate them. Clemente is a good storyteller and is well acquainted with shamanic and religious myths, minor fables, and tales nourished by his own imagination.

Marcos Maciel

His Tomáraho name is Kaiuhé; his clan is the Namóho. He was born in 1955 and dedicates himself to growing vegetables in the family garden, hunting iguanas, and occasional jobs on farms and timber yards. He lives in María Elena and has provided accounts of the history of the Tomáraho, hunting, initiation, and ritual games.

Luciano Martínez

Born in 1952, his Tomáraho name is Tybygyd and his clan filiation Tahorn. Luciano lives in María Elena where he grows small crops and works at various temporary jobs. He is also a sky shaman. Some of his versions of the

Great Myth have proved especially rich in new details and suggestive commentary.

Vicenta Mauro

Her Ishir name is Mbolué. She was born in Puerto Casado in 1956 and married Feliciano Rodrígeuz (Túkule). She lives in María Elena. She is one of the great weavers of her community and has provided valuable information on weaving with the fibers of the caraguata plant.

Enrique Ozuna

Ebytoso, of the Tahorn clan, Enrique is also called Auteke. He was born in 1932, and lives in Puerto Esperanza where he dedicates himself to small-scale agriculture. His accounts of Ishir religious mythology, which he knows in depth, have been invaluable. His list of the *anábsoro*—the characters that appear in ceremonial representation—is one of the most complete.

Clotilde Pajá

Called Ña Cortita by Paraguayans and Tyrymyr by the Ebytoso, she was born in Puerto Guaraní in 1931, daughter of a Spanish father and Chamacoco mother. She lives in Puerto Esperanza. Despite her mestizo origins she speaks only Ishir (Bruno translated her accounts), and does so with a profusion of gestures and incomprehensible grace. Her husband was the great Beshá, the powerful shaman Molina, and she has given me an important account of his deeds. She is also a skillful artisan who works with palm leaves and the fibers of the caraguata plant.

Eligia Ramírez

Nyerke is her Tomáraho name; her clan is the Tahorn. She was born in the 1930s and lives in María Elena. She claims to have inherited from her father (a powerful sun shaman) the power of singing to bring rain and accelerate the growth of various plants, especially of the carob tree. With an energetic character and dramatic expressivity, she is an expert on principles of auspicious magic and the great themes of female shamanistic song.

Feliciano Rodríguez

Born in Puerto Casado in 1951, he belongs to the Tomáraho and is called Túkule. He was leader of the Tomáraho during their historic migration from their settlement near sites of tannin production in San Carlos to Puerto Esperanza. He is an artisan (he makes feather ornaments), iguana hunter (he sells their skins in Bahía Negra), farmer, and day laborer. He has proved especially useful in informing me of techniques of featherwork and body painting.

Faustino Rojas

Faustino was called Lokurixto in Ebytoso. He was born in Puerto Guaraní in 1907 and died in Puerto Esperanza in 1993. He was the shaman of Pfaujata, a fearsome figure of Ishir mythology. He informed me on various occasions regarding shamanism, especially processes of apprenticeship, revelation, and trance.

Pabla Romero

Ebytoso, Pabla dedicates herself to auspicious magical chanting and weaving bags from caraguata fibers as well as baskets of palm leaf, which she barters for provisions in the community warehouse. She was born in Puerto Olimpo in the 1950s. Her information on the classification of objects woven with caraguata was fundamental.

Ramona San Diego

Her Ishir name is Tanishé, and her clan is the Namoho. She was born in Puerto Casado during the Chaco War (1932–1935) and lives today in María Elena. She lost all of her family: her husband and four sons died at the hands of soldiers or in the devastation caused by chicken pox among the Tomáraho. She inherited shamanic song from her father. Along with Eligia Ramírez she has informed me on the range of auspicious magic and the themes of female shamanic song.

Neri Sánchez

Born in 1985, he is Tomáraho and belongs to the Dyshykymser clan. He is an artisan (he makes bows and arrows) and helps his grandfather, Bruno Sánchez, on the orchard. He was initiated in the María Elena community in 1998. He has given me useful details on the teachings and myths learned in the *tobich*, the space where the masculine initiation ceremonies take place.

Bruno Sánchez Vera

Called Tamusía by the Tomáraho and affiliated to the Posháraha clan, he was born in Puerto Sastre in 1941, and works on the family orchard in María Elena.

He has given me facts and drawings on the costumes and choreography of some characters of the Great Annual Ceremony.

Palacio Vera

His Ishir name is Nintyke, and his clan the Kytymáraha. He was born in La Estrella in 1934, and lives in María Elena. He is a shaman of the category "of the far ends of the earth." He is one of the best experts on Ishir mythology, and his reports (proferred in Tomáraho and translated by Clemente) have been indispensable. He has remarkable narrative talent; his stories are calm and deliberate and go on for hours.

Pedro Vera

His name is Mbochana, but he is known as Peíto. He is Kytymáraha. Born in 1964, he is the leader of the Tomáraho community of María Elena. He is considered a good intermediary and efficient spokesman for the interests of his people before national authorities (he has obtained deeds for the community lands). His reports on the order of the clans and the general situation of the Tomáraho have been used in the book.

Benjamín Vierci

Of the Kytymáraha clan, he is the cacique of the Ebytoso community of Potrerito. He was born in the 1940s. Based on his reports, as well as those of Emilio Aquino and Pedro Vera, I have been able to draw up a map of the current Ishir settlements in the Chaco. He has broad knowledge of the Chamacoco population and an enviable memory for names and personal histories.

ALTHOUGH this text considers the general panorama of Ishir culture, the experience of the Tomáraho is emphasized over that of the Ebytoso. There are two reasons for this emphasis. On the one hand, I have established stronger ties with the Tomáraho and have thus had greater access to their rituals, myths, and artistic forms. On the other hand, as previously indicated, many of these forms are only observable among the Tomáraho: they conserve the Great Annual Ceremony and an important corpus of expressions that the Ebytoso have abandoned. I should note that after contact with the Tomáraho, some of the Ebytoso from Potrerito have embarked on the project of reviving various ritual practices.

Tomáraho man representing an *anábser*, against the backdrop of the Paraguay River. María Elena, 2001. (Photo by Nicolás Richard.)

THE GREAT MYTH

field notes

Puerto 14 de Mayo, 6 October 1989

Today I decided that I will organize the Great Ishir Myth according to the version narrated by the conjoined voices of Clemente, Bruno, and Emilio (the first two men are Ebytoso; the last is Tomáraho). Although I have in the past three years already collected dozens of versions—whole, fragmented, and overlapping versions—this one strikes me as the fullest and most complete. I will use it as the foundation of my own narration and confront it with other versions I, or other authors, have come across, filling in the blanks and interspersing (my own or others') commentaries throughout its dense discourse.

    Correction: I do not know if this is one of the most complete versions. Perhaps the circumstances in which the Great Myth is now being presented to me—intense oral performances on the very ground on which the events of the myth supposedly took place—accentuates its thick atmosphere and its intricate architecture. Jorge, my brother, and I take down whatever notes we can in Karcha Balut, open to the Paraguay River and lodged atop enormous mounds of old snail shells, the fearsome remnants of ancient divine banquets. We arrived this afternoon via a motorboat from Bahía Negra and are awaiting a group of Tomáraho who will bring us horses tomorrow morning and take us to Potrerito (Peishiota), the current location of the Tomáraho settlement.

As he stokes the fire, Bruno speaks about the forces that inhabit this strange place. Clemente and Emilio sing at length, shaking their maracas to scare off shadows, mosquitoes, and who knows what other evils. The river has become an enormous mass of pure dark presence. The dry rustle of the rattles has spread a pool of silence over our campsite. Now the men sit back on their heels and begin to say the true words.

THE GREAT MYTH, ACT ONE

The Birth of the Gods

I WILL begin before the beginning. It is afternoon in the brutal Chaco summer. A small group whose number varies, according to different versions, between seven and ten women, have fallen behind as they follow the tracks of a nomadic group that is moving the village to which they belong. They make jokes and laugh; they are young and unmarried. "They are jútoro,"[1] says Bruno. "Whores," Clemente translates with little hesitation, offering the semantic equivalent of a term that lacks negative connotations in his culture. One of them, the narrator continues, feels the caress of a plant stem between her legs. She shivers and comments, pleased, that the sensation reminds her of a lover's touch. Intrigued and still laughing, her companions begin to pull on the stalk only to find that an enormous force holds it firmly in place. They do not however lose heart, and turn to the *alybyk*—the stick used by women to dig for food —and remove the dirt until they find an *ahpora* (wild watermelon).[2] Terrified, they discover that it is being held by a monstrous being. This being rises out of the ground with awful cries, accompanied by clouds of smoke and deep earthly rumbles (according to the tale told after, or before, by Flores Balbuena).

Bruno interrupts him. "I don't want to contradict my father," he says slowly, trying to avoid the unforgivable discourtesy this would imply among the Ishir. "I hope he corrects me if he considers that I am wrong, but according to Chypyló, the wisest of the five teachers that I had in the *tobich* (the site where the initiation of young men takes place), the women were thirsty and stopped to look for a wild watermelon. When they found one while digging with the *alybyk* they saw that it was swelling before their very eyes to unnatural proportions. The *jútoro* cracked open the fruit with their sticks and the ferocious stranger emerged from inside the watermelon, amidst a violent fountain of water quivering with fish that poured from the broken fruit." Although he respects the erudition of Chypyló, Clemente prefers the Tomáraho version.

Both groups agree, however, that a creature emerges from the earth and that though its features are humanoid, it also exhibits clear evidence of its exceptional nature. It is an *anábser*, a demon-god, a monstrous and somewhat brutal superhuman. The identity of the first anábser varies according to the informants. Most of them, especially the Ebytoso, insist that this first anábser is none other than the terrible Wákaka, the cannibal; but others, especially the Tomáraho, maintain that it is the one-eyed Houch Ylybyd, or even the healer Wioho, one of the generous *anábsoro* (plural of *anábser*). Regardless of who emerges first, it is immediately followed by a group of other anábsoro (as many of them as there are women in the story) that burst from the ground amid deafening shrieks.

The appearance of these beings is imposing and the women cower in terror. They lack facial features. Their bodies are covered with protrusions that resemble dense feathers, copious furs, multicolored scales, or patterns of drawings and colors never before seen by the human eye. Although it is impossible to locate their eyes or mouth, these beings can see through the densest fogs and breathe and scream through their ankles. Their knees are backwards ("like the ostrich," say the Tomáraho) and this gives them a peculiar gait. According to Cordeu, female anábsoro's genitals are located in the same place as the human navel (1984, 213).

Aside from these common characteristics, each one possesses unique features. Wákaka bears the sharp fangs of the giant piranha. Pohejuvo lacks arms but his prodigious virility more than compensates for this serious defect. Pfaujata fires deathly glances of frozen yellow flames. Purt is a dwarf. Manume is lame. Holé has feathers instead of fingers. Okío has unusually large ears.

Each of them possesses a particular excess or lack that sets them apart from each other and from humanity. The costumes that the women and, later, the men, will use to represent the deities simulate their idiosyncrasies. Ashnuwerta's head is crowned in tongues of fire; the flaming crest radiates from the occipital bone only to burst into a shivering beam of many colors. A thicket of fog that shakes with the whitest of tremors sprouts from Nemur's head. Apepo's body is covered in thick hair and frizzy fur. Almost all anábsoro have temples, necks or napes, waists, and wrists or prickly ankles of uncertain thickness that resemble multicolored manes. Each one of these dense appendices will be represented in performance through feathers, just as the spots, textures, and drawings that brighten and darken, calm and agitate the different divine bodies are reproduced through corporal painting.

Each demon-god emits its own cry: intense, stuttering whistles, dismal howls, hoarse bellows, or disquieting whispers that forever perturb the fields and distant woods. Each one, finally, has his or her own way of walking: some hop swiftly, others rush aggressively; some prance proudly or glide slyly, others can walk with a measured pace or wander hesitantly; some move with dignified long strides, others trace spirals and crazy cross-steps that, briefly, fill the scene with light whirlwinds of feather and dust.

References on the Anábsoro

Rudolph Otto's studies regarding religious experience, published in 1917, have contributed to a richer understanding of the sacred in different cultures, especially in so-called "primitive" cultures (Otto 1958). Human beings sometimes face situations that exceed them, and realize they stand before unknown powers that point to the existence of supernatural realms. Otto speaks of a "numinous" (*noumen* = god) feeling regarding the uncanny or the markedly different. This feeling, which promotes more intense and dramatic visions of reality, does not exhaust itself in what is simply natural, but is animated by forces and traversed by transcendent powers and complex meanings that fill the human horizon with concerns, defining it against the backdrop of death.

The experience of the sacred begins with situations that elude the ordinary, with moments saturated with significance, with moments that concentrate power. The Chamacoco name this extraordinary power, this overflowing and strange energy that can both help and harm them, *woso*. *Woso* is the impulse that perturbs certain moments or places, beings or things, tearing them from their banal facticity and bringing them face to face with the thresholds of meaning. The numinous operates on the basis of such an experience of power, much like the aesthetic, which accentuates the object's form so as to name obliquely the unattainable secret of its doubled meaning and its ancient lack. Both the numinous and the aesthetic appeal to the cunning recourses of artifice and the errancy of poetry in order to challenge the obviousness of the object, its ordinary presence, its innocence and calm. This is why both the numinous and the aesthetic re-present the object: they place it onstage, under a new light; they veil and mask it; they reflect and elude it. They seek to reveal the object through what it is not, through the intimate absence that lurks beyond it and opens it up to limitless articulations, to foreign powers that seize it.

Like the aesthetic experience it closely relates to, the experience of the numinous requires images and figures that start from sensory experience and mobilize the impression it awakens. This experience provokes contradictory and shocking reactions: on the one hand, its uncanny terror is repulsive; on the other, the fascination for the profoundly unknown is attractive. Human beings want to flee the dark forces of numinous power but are simultaneously seduced by the enigma's dangerous beauty. They want to participate in its strange aura.

The anábsoro are the essential Other. They condense numinous potency and overflow with extraordinary powers. They are radically opposed to mortals. Their strange features are the inverse of human ones, and the few anthropomorphic aspects they present only establish a common ground from which to digress in their differences. Thus they are supremely divine beings who tear apart secular time; powerful figures who forcefully expand human horizons; superior beings who regulate and condemn, distress, and redeem; who, for one instant, soothe.

The Secret

When the anábsoro emerged from their subterranean world, the women were struck down by their strength and overwhelmed by the power they exuded, the *woso*. According to Luciano's account, Wioho brought them back to life by blowing into their ears. Then the terrible strangers surrounded them.

"Do not fear us," one of them said, "we don't want to harm you, we only want to talk." And so they talked. The anábsoro promised to show them unknown things and give them new powers, and the women agreed to take them to their village to establish a *tobich*, the center for initiation where they would receive divine instruction. Since the women wanted to be the only ones to profit from the new alliance, they denied the existence of men and took the gods to a secluded part of the village instead of to the *lut* (where the houses were concentrated).

Digression on Deceit

The decision to hide the existence of men and the anábsoro from each other constitutes the first deception. Every symbolic system is built on pacts of silence, trickery, concealment, hoaxes, and simulacra. But for hunting cultures, the practice of the ruse that confuses and distracts is especially valuable: the hunter faces the animal's cunning and whoever is better at deception wins. The survival of the forest community depends on the use of tricks, baits and traps, camouflage and decoy. But survival also depends on the indigenous people's capacity to deceive the white man's invading arrogance: in his presence they simulate and dissimulate, trick and elude, mimic and mask. Words are powerful weapons in the difficult relations humans maintain among themselves and with the gods: through words silence and norm are imposed, battles fought and negotiations reached. It is with words that people deceive.

No one knows how, but when the group of anábsoro and women arrived at a clearing amid the carob trees, Ashnuwerta was already waiting for them. The Great Goddess of Red Splendor, the Lady of the Anábsoro was surrounded by her female retinue and by a large group of new anábsoro, gleaming in their unknown textures and red, white, and black colors; quivering in their supernatural manes and plumes; resplendent in their pure strange power. They were now submerged in a silence laden with an infinite clamor that disquieted the plains, the river, the mountains, and the swamps.

They immediately began to prepare the space where the original initiation would take place. According to Luciano—who told this story on another hot, mosquito-filled night in San Carlos—the *tobich* was established toward the west, in Nymych-wert (etymologically, "red earth"). This place is located about twenty kilometers south of Bahía Negra, on the great Paraguay River in Karcha Balut, known today as Puerto 14 de Mayo. Karcha Balut literally means "the great deposit of shells." There the anábsoro used to bathe and eat piranhas and snails (do they still?). The ceramic and bone fragments found there, as well as the millions of large shells that cover the ground, speak of divine banquets and preserve, even today, the dangerous aura of their excesses.

The first *harra*—ceremonial circle where the sacred dances are represented—was set up in a clearing in the woods. According to some Tomáraho narrators this original *harra* was located forty or fifty kilometers west of the first *tobich*, in a place called Nahyn. According to the Ebytoso, the place was called Moiéhene and would correspond today to Caacupé, located 120 kilometers from Bahía Negra.

Aided by the anábsoro, the women cleared a straight path from the secret initiation grounds (*tobich*) to the site for ceremonial acts (*harra*). They hoed the scrubland and laboriously ripped out roots with their newly acquired tools. The strangers did it effortlessly with their hands and feet; pushing weeds, herbs, and spiny bushes; knocking down palms and carob trees; using their hardened fingers to dig and fill the *depich*, the secret path that would unite the Ishir with the gods and that would render them fully human.

The *tobich* is the house of words, the center of myth, but also the antechamber of image. In its hermetic space the Ishir prepare the re-presentations that are to take place at the *harra*. Teaching and discussion, control and regulation happen in the *tobich*. There, the shamans endlessly sing and pray and the masters of ceremonies meticulously organize scenic details. There, one only fasts and eats ritually; one learns the methods of purification and the value of silence. In the *tobich* one works on memory and forgetting, suffers severe tests to temper the spirit and body, and listens with an open mind to attain wisdom—or at least brush up against it, no small task if one is still maturing.

The mythical *depich*—path between the first *tobich* (located on the river) and the original *harra* (cleared in the middle of the jungle)—was very long and hard to travel. Because of this, the anábsoro invented a mechanism to abolish distance: by blowing hard on the earth, they installed a powerful spring at both ends of the trail. Thus, to get from one end to the other, it was enough to jump on the contraption and be propelled by it through the air. The passage was sudden and instantaneous: the anábsoro and the women effortlessly appeared at one end or the other.

Commentary on Dualities

The forest/river duality plays an important role in Chamacoco thinking inasmuch as it clearly illustrates two of its basic figures. On the one hand, it marks a difference: the sophisticated mechanisms constructed by society to elaborate pairs of identity/alterity. On the other hand, it is an axis to various sets of intersecting or counterpoised positions. These opposing positions confront one another but they can also reach agreements, enter into association, and even neutralize each other through various leveling and balancing mechanisms. In principle the other is my "opposite," but I can negotiate with him by "exchanging words" and we can agree to provide each other with companionship and aid, thereby converting us both into *ágalo* (associates). For Chamacoco thinking, therefore, contradictions are not resolved through synthesis (in the western, Hegelian sense of the word); opposites can become allies or eternal adversaries. But they can also compensate for the asymmetries generated by difference through a complicated system of social, ritual, aesthetic, and mythical codes that generally combine all the above variables (agreement, clash, and equilibrium). In addition, difference can be negated, but not abolished, through efficient cultural mechanisms. One of the poles in tension can (temporarily or not) assume the powers of the other, identify with it, and take its place—or some of its place—although it never completely dissolves into the other. This relationship is a figure called *cet*.

The basic scheme of Chamacoco logic is certainly binary, but its movement complicates this model to incredibly refined levels through astute mechanisms of pacts, confrontations, compensations, and counterbalanced intersections. Chamacoco thought, myth, and social organization are constructed through intricate ascending spirals of successive moments that aim to resolve the controversies generated by the twisting movement itself. It is difficult to label such a complex culture as simply "dualist," first, because of the complexity produced by the above-mentioned interplay of opposites. Also, there are so many axes of antagonism and so many possible diagrams of equivalence and contradiction that can be traced, that they end up blurring into one another in a web of connections so dense that it is difficult to define the place of the desired postures. For the sake of orientation, we can consider these dichotomies to be formal ones, but only if they are not granted stable or definitive places nor assigned an essential function.

The disjunction established between the river (*tobich*) and the woodland (*harra*) is related to the difference between the Ebytoso, who consider themselves river people, and the Tomáraho, who consider themselves forest dwellers. In many of the Ishir ritual games and encounters, as well as in the classification of the anábsoro and shamans, the distinction between "those of the forest" and "those of the river" defines the occasional challengers, the enemy, or simply the inverse term of any conflictive relationship. Once *tobich* and *harra* are organized in terms of contrary signs, their difference is emphasized. Once a path and mechanism that enables such distances to be crossed is established, mediation with other men and the gods becomes possible. Today, says Emilio, the white man has reduced the map of the Chaco: *tobich* and *harra* are located less than a kilometer from each other and the secret of the springs has been forgotten, though some sky shamans frequently use it still.

field notes

Puerto Esperanza, 16 August 1986

We are sitting on a tree trunk in the San Carlos *tobich*. In the seemingly distracted presence of Palacio Vera, Emilio Aquino traces the ritual map on the sand: a small circle is the *tobich*, a bigger one is the *harra*; between the two circles he carefully draws two parallel lines that represent the *depich*, the Path of Knowledge and Silence that is now shortened because the springs that catapulted the anábsoro and the women no longer exist. A noisy flock of birds glides above us and settles on a tree that trembles and quivers for an instant. "*Kuréeky* [parrots]," my informant comments laconically, without raising his eyes. "Long ago the parrots were soothsayers; they belonged to the Tahorn clan. Their cries announce that a moment has ended and another begun: something special happens to time when a flock of *kuréeky* screeches like that," he says, and then falls silent. He continues his story. His non-story. The figure traced on the sand has been shadowed by the early nightfall of the harsh Chaco winter.

On the Power of Beauty

One night something special took place. The *wyrby*, the spring that facilitated the movement between both extremes of the ritual space, was already in place and the women, who had crossed the distance without the travails of a long march, now found themselves standing around the *harra*, the ritual scene. "Something special happened then," Emilio repeats.

For the first time the anábsoro perform their ceremonial circle in front of human eyes. The spectacle is terrifying. The women are first frozen by fear and then, later, enthralled and excited. The men, who spy on the scene in the darkness behind thorny fronds, are too scared to consider approaching. They hear, from an increasing distance, the burst of the numinous bubble that concentrates all the possible sounds of the universe and intensifies all essential colors until they are but ciphers of fire and blood, of the deepest darkness and of absolute silence.

Bruno affirms that the first performance was that of the terrible Wákaka, followed by the benevolent Wioho in counterpoint. Clemente and Emilio insist that Ashnuwerta was the one who erupted first in the ceremonial circle amidst a trail of red flashes, unleashing a chorus of cries that tore primeval time in two, much like the flock of parrots. Whoever came first, he or she was escorted by their respective retinues and followed by the women, the first human beings to participate in the dark secret that renews time.

In the following days, this participation opened up various possibilities to the women. On the one hand, the great anábsoro mothers taught them the use of techniques and tools that would, from then on, be characteristically theirs. Kaiporta taught them the art of gathering food and provided them with the *alybyk*, the stick women use to dig. (The men, who use larger versions of this instrument, make the ones the women use with the hard wood of the guayacan, or palo santo tree,[3] but once given to the women, the men can never again touch the wood. And so, symbolically, the distributions of tasks intersect and compensate for each other.) Pfaujata, the fearsome Chamacoco Arachne, gave them the caraguata[4] and taught them how to use its fibers to fashion the cloth used in everyday domestic use and ritual dress. On the other hand, the male anábsoro seduced the women with the power of their voices, the beauty of their colors, and their alien forms. And so the furtive visits undertaken by the women to their husbands and children under the pretext of bringing them food became less and less frequent until they settled definitively in the *tobich* and became lovers to the gods.

On Knowing the Divine

Cordeu argues that the mythical women were at a disadvantage regarding their access to knowledge of the divine (1991a, 117). The men reached the divine through *eiwo,* intellectual reflection, while the women experienced the sacred through the most superficial aspects of perception (image, color, shine, and physical appearance of the anábsoro). However, it is probable that for the Chamacoco culture (and I suppose, for culture as such) the aesthetic experience, sensible perception, is as important as reason in the search for a superior knowledge of things (form is an essential instance of access to the numinous). Perhaps Ishir culture assigns men a more discursive relation to the divine, while women are given a more figural relation. The gleam of a verb is as important as the concept it shelters from any direct assault, from any attempt to get to the bottom of what is bottomless. The gods dispose of an imposing repertoire of images comprised of contrasts, textures, and tones of skin; the terrible lightness of feathers; and the explosion of cries that knocks down birds and unleashes a chorus of subterranean, aquatic, or celestial thunders that echo to the very limits of the Chaco.

All these dramatic figures the anábsoro pass on to the Chamacoco are as important for their human plenitude as is the clear path opened up by knowledge. For this indigenous group, myth does not contradict logos; it provides essential arguments that logos lacks. The women's bedazzlement by form and their consequent sexual relations with the gods provides access to another moment, one that is necessary in the creation of the alliance: the moment of the *imitatio dei*. The women identify with the gods and convert themselves into their image and likeness. The Chamacoco call this rhetorical mechanism in which a being takes on the powers and features of another being *cet*. *Cet* names a play of identifications, which keeps the extreme difference between the two positions visible.

Deceits and Discoveries

To resemble the anábsoro and acquire their supernatural powers, the women were taught to disguise themselves in their likeness. Thus, when they entered the ceremonial circle, they painted their bodies with stripes, circles, spots, and various figures. They created different colors from ashes, coal, vegetable juices, and minerals of bloody tones. In order to simulate the strange divine skins they covered their bodies with the feathers of ostriches[5] and parrots, malicious ducks, storks, flamingos, and spoonbills, and with coarse fabrics made of caraguata and the thick furs of the anteater. They used masks to hide their human faces, and hung wild seeds and animal hooves from their wrists, ankles, and waists to ape the creaking sounds made by the dancing gods. They also learned to shout.

At this time the anábsoro did not know the men existed; nor did the men know the truth of the event that would change their lives. But they could feel that something was different. They thought the women's actions strange. It is likely that they also found the women themselves different, since they had surely changed in their intercourse with the divine. One day a young man, intrigued when he discovered the vermin a widow carried (to feed the supernatural appetite of the foreigners), decided to follow her in secret. Susnik doesn't discard the possibility that the spy was Syr himself, the first Ishir leader (1995, 189). What is certain is that a Chamacoco discovered the deceit and informed his companions. Neither he nor they ventured into the lands occupied by those uncanny strangers they had discerned from afar. And not only did the men not take action to dismantle the fraud but, in their sheer terror before these unknown beings, they became accomplices of those who swindled them. According to Emilio, the men secretly passed on meat, honey, and fruit to their wives as the women spent their days absorbed in the initiation and pleasures of ritual splendor and Olympic love.

But harmony does not last long, even in myths. In the village, unbeknownst to the gods, a man found himself in trouble: his wife, absorbed in her godly affairs, had forgotten her prosaic obligation to return every so often to breastfeed her child. Since the man could not reach the tobich he asked his wife's sister to find her, remind her of her maternal duties, and bring her back to the village. But neither the child's hunger nor the husband's pleas moved her in her enthusiasm to see Kaimo preparing to enter the stage. The motley colors of Kaimo's skin made him one of the most impressive anábsoro. "She was enamored of his colors," Clemente explains. And bewitched by the complicated interplay of tones that stretched across his powerful body, she imprudently demanded that her child be brought to her. ("I won't budge," she told her sister.) Not even the anxious sucking of the child, delivered to her with frightened urgency, distracted her from her rapture: she carried him in her arms, tilted awkwardly, not noticing that the *pypyk* (a diaper made of caraguata) was sliding until it fell to the ground and exposed his small genitals to the astonished eyes of the anábsoro. Thus it was that the gods learned of the existence of the Ishir men, and of the first deceit. Bruno's version (that of the Ebytoso of Puerto Esperanza) differs little from this one: the anábsoro discovered the fraud because the child urinated; the arch traced by the liquid in the air clearly indicated that it was produced by a male.

The anábsoro were furious. After holding various long and heated discussions at the center of the *tobich*, they summoned the women and forced them to reveal the existence of the men. From this moment on in the tale, Ashnuwerta begins to take center stage. She orders all the *nagrab* (adult men) to present themselves that very night on the sacred grounds.

The men were so terrified that only the prodding of the women could make them obey. They arrived one by one in silence, their eyes lowered to the ground. (Luciano says that the men were grouped in twos and threes each night during the ritual.) Another act begins at this moment, as if the afternoon had been torn in two by a noisy flock of parrots.

On the Divinity of the Anábsoro

I have been referring to the anábsoro as divine. Yet what kind of deities are they? Jensen (1963) defines three ideal types of gods that predominate in traditional societies: the "Masters of the Animals" in hunting and gathering societies, the sky gods of pastoral societies, and the Dema-deities of agrarian societies. The Chamacoco forests and plains are populated by Masters of the Animals, but these belong to a different dimension than the anábsoro, though they can sometimes intersect. Considering Jensen's classification in its formal scheme, Cordeu estimates that the Ishir gods blend the last two divine prototypes. "One can speak," he says, "of a typical modality that is in part similar to the sky-gods . . . and of a dema modality that closely resembles the Dema-deities." Although they lack the cosmological and anthropogenic responsibilities of the sky gods, the anábsoro resemble them "in their coarse and terrible nature, [as well as in] the morality of their actions and commands" (Cordeu 1984, 257).

According to Jensen (1963), the essential traits of the Dema-deities are that their activity develops at the end of a primeval time and produces cultural gifts and the consciousness of death; that they are sacrificed at the hands of the men of the time; that they are distant deities, active only through the order they impose on mortal beings; and that human beings are morally obliged to remember their divine actions by ritually performing the events of this primeval time. The similarities of these traits with those of the anábsoro are evident.

field notes

Puerto Esperanza, 18 August 1986

Today Palacio Vera tells me about the moment when Ashnuwerta begins to acquire a more distinct profile. It seems that the relationship with the men requires the entry of this Super Woman; in fact, she ends up intimately linked with a Chamacoco leader called Syr. Palacio speaks at length in an expressionless voice. His gaze is absent. The fact that my translator, Clemente, lets so much time pass without intervening in the flow of narration worries me. But when he does translate I am reassured by Palacio's brief nods of agreement and small corrections and notes. (Palacio seems to understand Guaraní well, although he refuses to use it when speaking the "heavy words.") After all, I know the Chamacoco have an incredible facility with words: they remember easily and speak with enviable ease. Now the nearby forest throbs with heat and confused sounds. Now the shadows of the trees grow. The two men fall silent and look at me. Courtesy impedes them from getting up before their guest but they are waiting for me to leave. In any case, soon I won't be able to write.

The Time of Ashnuwerta

"The Ebytoso mix things up," Palacio Vera said in the San Carlos *tobich*. (The old shaman refuses to speak of the essential if he does not do it in the *tobich*.) In reality it wasn't the women who brought the Ishir to the anábsoro. It was Ashnuwerta herself who went out to meet the most valiant of men, who was called Syr, and demanded that he bring the others. Syr was a *pylota*, a warrior-hunter of strong and clear words. On his forehead he bore a wreath of jaguar skin, the arrogant insignia of chiefs respected for their boldness and lucidity. Syr encouraged the frightened men and together they presented themselves before the anábsoro.

"From now on and forever you will occupy the place of the women, who will be expelled from the *tobich*." Ashnuwerta's words did not and do not allow for the possibility of a response because they are the original words. "*Ishir poruta uholó*," Luciano says. "Words of those that come before the humans." Without objections, therefore, the women retire to the village and yield their privileged places to the *nagrab*.

Note on Ashnuwerta

Ashnuwerta represents the exemplary model, the quintessence of the anábsoro. Like all superior deities, she condenses various paradigms and articulates different, intense meanings. She incarnates the Chamacoco concept of opposition as a difference between two terms that can be resolved through words (and produce an alliance), or through collision (leading to conflict). However, as noted, there are other possible outcomes to any encounter: mediation and doubling, displacement, identification. Ashnuwerta condenses all these possibilities. On the one hand she acts as an ally: she is the Great Mother who favors the Ishir, the Teacher, the Giver of Words, she is the one who institutes the cultural order, who establishes the symbol. And she is in fact a powerful ally: she plays the part of the Anábsoro Lata, that is, the mother, matron, or master of the anábsoro. They are considered her *ebiyo*, her children or subalterns. Cordeu criticizes Baldus's and Susnik's translation of *lata/ebiyo* as "mother/child," and their references to Ashnuwerta as the Ishir proto-mother (Cordeu 1990, 167). But it is indubitable that, though it is not the only meaning, there is a strong sense of filiation in these terms: the Chamacoco translate *lata* as "the greatest," "the principal," but also as "the mother." What is important is to emphasize the figurative sense in the use of the "great words." I do not believe that the Chamacoco include the biological connotations of maternity when using this term. But without a doubt their rhetoric is meant to emphasize her superiority and power as well as the protection and respect associated with mothers.

Ashnuwerta, however, can also be terrible. As the Mistress of Water and Fire she can, and does, bring on plagues and catastrophes. (Such were the floods of what is today called the Paraguay River, provoked to avenge the anábsoro. This disaster led to the death of young novices during the first initiation ceremony of the new times.) Ashnuwerta is the Mother of the Birds of the Benign Rain, but also Mistress of the Dark Blue Storm (Susnik 1995, 197–98). It is she who, before abandoning the earth, gave Nemur the mission of punishing the Chamacoco for not following her prescriptions, cloaking them forever with a tragic shadow.

This dual character of the deity, which prompts Cordeu to consider her a summary of the positive and negative qualities of the anábsoro, is expressed in the doublings of her figure. Sometimes she becomes an animal or human, seeking to attain experiences or dimensions that surpass her own divinity. While she is associated with the color red, Ashnuwerta can turn into her opposite, into Ashnuwysta the dark: both are opposite sides of the same entity and mark the counterpoint between the mythic and ritual, gift and punishment; between the naked brilliance of the numen and its nocturnal side; between the luminous force of the image and the somber power of cries. (Ashnuwysta, in her Hopupora phase, appears only on ritual occasions, in darkness, and only through sounds.)

Thus Ashnuwerta signifies the universal nexus: she acts as the prototype of mediation. Through her complicity with the Ishir, her union with the human Syr, and her metamorphoses into Arpylá, the woman / doe, she links feminine and masculine, human and divine, symbolic and natural. She connects the earthly and celestial from her relationship with the Milky Way (in whose vicinity she eventually establishes her dwelling, and with which she is ritually identified, as will be seen). The brief intersection of her path with that of certain shamans knots the greatest divine power with maximum human potential: she is the protector of certain konsáho of the rain and her celestial abode shelters the "invincible shamanic souls" (Susnik 1995, 200).

OBEYING the orders of Ashnuwerta, men begin to participate in the debylyby, the Great Ceremony through which each day the gods renewed the ties that unite all beings, called upon elusive favors from the sky, earth, woods, and waters, and affirmed the permanence of the goddess's words and the timeless value of her commandments. Men began to accompany the anábsoro in their rounds through the harra and to learn their calls, movements, and gestures.

Depiction of Nemur and Ashnuwerta. Drawing by Bruno Sánchez Vera. Potrerito, 1998.

They also learned to copy their appearances: now it is the men who cover their faces and paint their bodies, covering it with furs, feathers, and fabrics in order to imitate the sacred features.

The entry into the ceremonial circle does not only presuppose the identification (*cet*) of men with gods through performance. It also sets in motion a complex process of apprenticeship that promotes the growth of human faculties. For this reason, men were also initiated into the mysteries of the *tobich*. And thus they learned the names of unknown things and beings and were instructed in how to manipulate the forces that animate them and on how to reach *eiwo*, understanding, the faculty prized by the Ishir as one of the gods' precious gifts.

Note on Knowledge

Analytical capacity promotes a discriminating knowledge of the world. Now the Ishir know how to distinguish, classify, and oppose. These differences entail rules. Ashnuwerta introduces the canons and codes that govern community life, taboos and prohibitions, rites, rules of social etiquette, and the order of sex. Desire emerges from the restrictions. And with this desire, comes art: the symbol, culture in its entirety. Now things carry meanings: they bear enigmas and opacities; they are linked by arbitrary relations; they point to memory and dream; they are filled with powers, promises, and threats; they become beautiful, feared, desired. The Ishir theory of knowledge presupposes a long path toward the comprehension of the mystery of things. Every object, every being, insofar as it belongs to a symbolic order, harbors a potential, a hidden dimension that can be revealed and assumed. For this reason, the world is populated by unknown forces, which can be either allies or adversaries depending on whether or not one knows how to grasp their deeper meanings. Many secrets can be accessed by observation and the efforts of patient study; some through the interchange of words or revelations (which are generally dreamed). The wisest are the most powerful: they know how to use, neutralize, or divert the power of things. Shamans are wise by definition: they are the ones who know the depths of men, things, and natural phenomena and can, therefore, appropriate their energies.

Gifts

Knowledge, however, also applies to the practices and norms of subsistence. If the goddesses taught the women the art of gathering, the gods instructed the men in the use of instruments for hunting. The primitive Ishir killed animals at random. They had no system to organize a hunt, select animals, or govern their ingestion. In the new time, men and anábsoro paired up to go into the woods. If the men learned about the "superior words" in the *tobich*, they began at the same time to penetrate the secrets of ordered survival in the woods. The Ishir learned to identify the confused tracks of the turtles and the terrible scent of the jaguar; they were trained to summon the delicate meat of the anteater; they learned how to skin silky iguanas and bristled peccaries and to catch slippery eels by grabbing them from the warm mud of certain swamps.

The anábsoro enjoyed qualities that allowed them to catch whatever animal they wanted without the necessity of strategy or weapon. Their powerful shouts, fired like bolts from their ankles, knocked down their prey instantaneously. Susnik writes that they knocked down birds, sauroids, and beasts simply by pointing and screaming. But Bruno insists that this act was intended simply to disorient the humans who could not know that the gods' power (and weakness) lay in their ankles.

Brief Commentary on Primitive Life

At the beginning of time, or before it—before the arrival of the gods, at least— humans lived a colorless, grey existence, an undifferentiated life without markers or direction. They did not know methods, techniques, rites, or social forms. They did not dance or sing. Their hunting was random and disorganized. They lacked adequate tactics and instruments; they did not organize hunting expeditions or have any taboos on consuming the prey. They gathered plants without knowing which fruits they should eat or how best to use them. Life was purely organic, a second-class existence. For the *os póruwo* (primitive men) life, love, and death were neutral physical processes that held neither enigma nor mystery, neither beauty, flash of astonishment, nor desire. The Ishir gods do not create anything in nature. What they do is create meaning. They introduce words, law, and symbols: they introduce the necessity of ordering life in order to face death.

THE use of weapons and hunting strategies that the gods had recently passed on to the Chamacoco could have caused great ecological damage. Ashnuwerta therefore instituted prescriptions, methods, and figures to prevent ecocide by rationalizing the distribution of food and regulating hunting. Both the eating taboos as well as the complex rules of social etiquette, ceremony, and clan institutions wisely and rigidly restrict what animals can be hunted and eaten, and under what conditions. (There is another mythical institution that promotes the balanced use of natural resources: the figure of the Master of the Animals. Every animal has its master—its balut, "spokesperson," or *cabezante* as the Ishir translate today—who simultaneously facilitates hunting and severely sanctions its excess.)

"Initiates and teachers went off into the woods in teams composed of one man and one god," Palacio repeats. He was referring to the fact that the initiation / warfare / hunting / ritual camaraderie had been established between men and gods. They had become *ágalo*: that is, they became mutual counterparts of a formalized masculine socialization; they are companions, allies, ac-

Depiction of an *anábser* teaching an Ishir to hunt. Drawing by Flores Balbuena.

complices. (The figure of the *ágalo* has important weight in Ishir culture. The pact implied by this institution was sealed in myth not only with the presence of the men in the ceremonial circle but also with the exchange of foods and the participation in the Great Game. This alliance in spite of, or thanks to, the difference and opposition between men and gods, is well expressed in their encounter in the ceremonial ball game. The *póhorro*, as the game is called, signifies both companionship and rivalry, link and opposition, a recreational moment and sacred time, and constitutes a passionate metaphor of the Chamacoco ideal of compensation—if not conciliation—between opposite terms.)

According to Ebytoso informants, it so happened that men and anábsoro had opposite diets. (Again we see the resurgence of the basic frame of oppositions, so dear to Chamacoco logic.) While men ate fish, meat, and fruit, the gods fed off of snails and various poisonous vermin. Thus when an Ishir hunted tarantulas, snakes, or scorpions he gave it to his supernatural *ágalo;* and when the god snatched a wild boar or a found a swollen honeycomb he passed it on to his human partner.

Adversities

Even in myths, ideal moments are brief and quickly disrupted by conflicts. The harmony between such different beings could not last long, and many factors intervened to break that idyllic relation and initiate another time. On the one hand, the men had crossed the categorical threshold of the terrain of symbols and had thus lost forever the innocence of those who do not see the dark side of things. They were irreversibly located in the new times of norms, of "words" as they say. And for the words to be sanctioned and fixed, their givers had to retire. The possibility of return had to be cancelled. Bruno takes up the thread of the story like this: "The Ishir had already learned everything the anábsoro had to teach them, and the gods were now nothing but a nuisance."

On the other hand, the daily coexistence of men and gods generated the inevitable friction, competition, and tension that arise when different groups share a crowded story. Things become even more complicated when one considers that the anábsoro had the same desires, virtues, and defects as the humans. The coupling between the women and the gods had produced hybrid offspring who inherited certain features from their divine fathers, but not their powers; they were mere mortals (with the possible exception of Pfaujata, as we shall see later). The love affair between Ashnuwerta and Syr also complicated the coexistence of gods and men, as the Chamacoco chief had in effect two women: the mortal one lived in the *lut* and the divine one in the *tobich.* (Bigamy is considered perturbing and is rejected by the Ishir social order.)

Parenthesis on Myth

The time of myth has no time: it takes place in a dimension that does not compute its moments in terms of duration nor count its phases according to a single measure. Some aspects of a mythic event can last years while other aspects last but a few instants. It is therefore impossible to know how long the stage of female deception, and subsequent moment of male ritual hegemony lasted. Neither, therefore, do we know how long it took to establish the Ishir Olympus in the first *tobich*. But the various informants agree that when the next generation reached adolescence it was necessary to initiate them into the mysteries of men, gods, animals, and woods.

ASHNUWERTA ordered that the pubescents be brought to the site of first knowledge. Then one night a group of adult males invaded the village, forcefully grabbed the boys amidst the frightened cries of the women, and herded them through the dark path leading to the place of mysteries. There the *wetern*, as the novices are called, were submitted under the personal instructions of Ashnuwerta to the hard training that would turn them into *nagrab*, adult custodians of the words.

The inclusion of the youth in the *tobich* generated new problems. For one, jealousy and competition arose among the different generations. Susnik writes that the process of the first male initiation "displeased the anabsonic children" (that is, the hybrid descendents of the anábsoro and humans) because Ashnuwerta did not treat them any differently than the human children (1995, 191). In addition, the novices inevitably failed some of the several difficult tests or committed mistakes in the observance of the ceremonial etiquette governing the *tobich*. These failings exacerbated the impatience of the anábsoro and led to unfortunate excesses. There were cases in which some *wetern* could not resist the exaggerated rigors of the initiation and fell to the ground, literally dying of exhaustion. In other cases some youth were sacrificed because they violated dietary taboos or other restrictions. Wioho, the anábser healer, brought them back to life by blowing on them or caressing them softly with the powerful feathers of his strange body. But the death of the *wetern* woke Wákaka's cannibalistic impulses and he began to devour some of the initiates as soon as they died.

"In these cases," Luciano explains, "the *wetern* could also be resuscitated through Wioho's intervention, but once they were brought back to life they were changed. In the process of being swallowed by Wákaka their bodies had lost too much blood, which is the liquid that completes them as human beings." Depending on the quantity of recovered blood, the revived *wetern* could either closely resemble their former selves or be reborn as faded, weak copies. In extreme cases, some *wetern* were brought back as mere ghosts of their original selves.

Achilles' Ankle

The Ishir did not react until Syr's son became one of the victims. There are different versions of the manner of his death. Some say that Jolué died because he could not bear certain "tests of endurance" required by the stoic ideal of the Ishir. In other versions he was sacrificed for eating the flesh of eels (taboo for the initiates), or because he violated rules on the exchange of food (he did not return a gift to Kaimo). Others, finally, claim that he was killed in punishment for tempestuously abandoning the *tobich*, an action that is prohibited by the strict norms of ritual courtesy that reign during the meals of the anábsoro. It is said that Kaimo killed him and that he was devoured instantly by Wákaka. Either because he was charred as soon as he was thrown into the banquet fire, or because Wákaka drank all his blood as he was eaten, or because the good doctor Wioho was delayed, Jolué could not be saved. Wioho anxiously dug into the wet earth trying to recover the youth's blood, Luciano continues, but could only gather a fistful of the sticky and bloodied mud. He could do little with it; a spectral body appeared and then instantly dissolved into nothingness.

Syr vowed to avenge his son. He would kill his son's assassin's himself, he said. One of the signs of Ishir mourning are the grooves cut by tears on a painted face. The warrior decided to conceal his son's death in order to better plan his revenge, and he wiped his face clean as he entered the village. He appealed only to the complicity of his Ishir *ágalo* (or his brother, in another version). Early the next morning, he and his companion went out hunting with Wákaka and Kaimo. At a site far away from the village both Ishir cut off the heads of the gods with their clubs (*noshikó*). When they returned to the *tobich*, however, they were terrified to find the anábsoro alive and well.

The arrogant chief fell into a profound depression. (Chamacoco depressions acquire ontological proportions and, one could say, a Heideggerian brilliance: they are dark disturbances on the edge of nothingness.) Syr could no longer conceal his pain and, abandoning political and conjugal duties, he wandered alone in the woods for days. Ashnuwerta found herself in a difficult situation: if she helped Syr she betrayed her numinous race. Yet, both the nature of her relations with him, as well as the possible fact—in some versions—that Jolué was her own son, prompted her to reveal the secret of anábsoro vulnerability to her lover.

Emilio and Clemente perform before me the indirect method used by the great goddess to reveal the secret to Syr. Emilio takes off the anklet of plumes he had put on to dramatize the tale and covers his hardened bare foot with dry palm leaves. "This is what Ashnuwerta did in front of Syr," he says. The lower part of anábsoro legs are covered with dense hair so that they resemble a feathered anklet; Ashnuwerta lifted the feathers on hers and bared her ankle, quickly covering it with a small pile of leaves. When these began to quiver rhythmically, Syr discovered that the beat was produced by the hidden, divine extremity. Ashnuwerta gives him instructions: "You need to strike the exact place indicated by the pulse, and then bring me back to life by blowing in my ears." Some Tomáraho versions maintain that Ashnuwerta indicated another procedure for resurrection: after killing her, Syr had to spit on the ground around her in order to revive her. Clemente offers another variation at this point in the story: the goddess ordered that Wioho be brought to resurrect her. Emilio and Clemente agree (and demonstrate through a performance) that Syr killed Ashnuwerta by kicking her in the ankle and then, following her instructions, immediately brought her back to life and to her powers.

Syr thus discovered that the ankle (*diorá*), the place from which the anábsoro breathed and let out their imposing cries, also harbored their only weak point.[6] The Chamacoco chief gathered the men of his village and, after revealing the secret to them, plotted his vengeance. After the ritual representation of every killer anábser, one Ishir will go off to hunt with him and kill him in the woods. In principle, only the killers of the young novices would be killed in turn, but in their enthusiasm the *nagrab* began to indiscriminately strike down every anábser they found, even those that had been their benefactors, as many had in fact been. Realizing they were under attack, the anábsoro reacted and confronted the humans with their supernatural powers. A terrible battle ensued between gods and men, one that took place between the *tobich* at Karcha Balut and the *harra* at Moiéhene. Although both sides experienced ruin and devastation, the combat was unequal: the knowledge of the secret gave the humans a tremendous advantage and they aimed directly at the ankles of the gods (the anábsoro were stronger and more powerful, but the humans were more agile). Worried that the anábsoro were losing and faced with extermination, Ashnuwerta decided to intervene. She ordered the men to stop the slaughter, but they were out of control and—for the first time ever—they did not heed her command.

At this point, the Tomáraho and Ebytoso versions part ways. I will follow the Tomáraho tale, basing myself primarily on one long and unexpected session with Luciano as we plied the Paraguay River on a particularly still night. My Tomáraho informant assures me that there were three basic kinds of anábsoro: the *nymych-ut-oso* (literally, "those that come from the depths of the earth"), the *eich-oso* ("those that come from the forest"), and the *niot-ut-oso* ("those that come from the bottom of the river"). Those under Ashnuwerta's power were subterranean anábsoro. When this group was on the verge of extinction at the hands of the Ishir, the goddess telepathically pleaded for help from the wood gods, and these promptly appeared to aid their threatened kin. The Ishir, in turn, asked for reinforcements of warrior armies from other nations so as not to lose the equilibrium in the numbers of men and gods (yet another example of the importance of the symmetry of opposites for Chamacoco thinking). But since the wood gods displayed the same weakness as their subterranean kinsmen, the massacre soon recovered its enthusiastic rhythm. Then Ashnuwerta warned the men that she would be forced to call on the terrible aquatic beings, and that this would imply the extinction of the human race: for these were *huwyrö*, implacable cannibals. There is no defense against them because their "place of breath and death" is concealed under their armpits, under small stumps in place of arms, which they hold tightly against their body to protect their weaknesses. The greatest of all horrors was that these anábsoro were mute, which for the Ishir signifies a perversion of alterity. Since they are mute it is impossible to negotiate with them through words, an essential avenue for dealing with otherness. But the threat of Ashnuwerta was too late: aside from herself and Nemur, all the anábsoro had been eliminated.

Luciano's tale ends here and the Ebytoso narrations I could collect on this incident are confused and extremely poor. In order to confront Luciano's version on these incidents my reference point is the sequence written down by Cordeu (1984, 242), which is based upon various Ebytoso versions that essentially coincide. According to the versions Cordeu refers to, once Ashnuwerta's orders to stop the killing are ignored, the anábsoro seek reinforcements under the earth. The Ishir do likewise, and militias of subterranean men appear to fight against the anábsoro that emerged from the depths of the earth, thus reestablishing the balance of oppositions. Ashnuwerta warns about the unspecified danger of the aquatic cannibals, but this warning does not stop the battle either. She attempts therefore a reconciliation through ceremony, the mechanism that compensates for differences. Arrayed in pairs symmetrical in number and appearance (feathers, bodily paints, cries, and movements) both armies need to proceed together to Moiéhene to perform a rite to repair the conflict. But, determined to eliminate the anábsoro, the Ishir once again disobey the divine mandate. In the *tobich* of Karcha Balut, they use the *wyrby*, the spring that allows them to reach the *harra* instantly. Once they are there, they deactivate the machine in order to prevent the anábsoro from using it to escape. In this way they are able to surround and exterminate the threatening invaders, their teacher-gods, their allies and opponents, their other faces.

Notes on Nemur

The final act of the first part of the Great Myth waxes on the persecution of Nemur, the last of the anábsoro, and his exemplary dialogue with Syr. The plot of this episode articulates both the Tomáraho and Ebytoso versions and coincides essentially with the versions collected by Susnik and Cordeu. Nemur is the complement and counterpart to Ashnuwerta: the other, the counterweight to the great presence of the goddess. Although he thus occupies a fundamental place in the Chamacoco pantheon, strangely enough it is only at the end of the tale that he makes an appearance. He is only present in the Great Myth for this brief, albeit intense, incident. Ashnuwerta represents the benefactress, the "Great Teacher" and "Giver of Words." Although she delivers the Law, the figure of Ashnuwerta stresses the moment of mediation, alliance, and even complicity with humans. Nemur, however, signals the severe moment of punishment for the violation of the norm: for this reason he is called the "Great Prosecutor," "The Avenger," "The Punisher," "The Vigilant," "The Patron of Tóbich," "The Bringer of Sadness," and even "The Exterminator" (see Susnik 1995, 201–2).

For Cordeu, Nemur represents the prototype of the terrible dimensions of the sacred inhabited by the essence of these deities: his prophecies are as inexorable as the apocalyptic commandments of Ashnuwerta, with whom he shares the highest of powers. Nemur's power is represented through his capacity to metamorphize into a serpent or jaguar and identify with the great ostriches and a certain kind of sparrow hawk, which implies not only vigilant control from on high but also permanent communication with Ashnuwerta. This link is what bestows on him the title "Lord of the Birds of the Wind" (Cordeu 1992b, 224ff.).

But—it is important to insist—although Chamacoco thought works in dualities, these dualities are not frozen into place and are not conceived in Manichean terms. The ties between opposites are quickly complicated and often their functions are bartered, their positions interchanged. This is why if Ashnuwerta is the paradigmatic bringer of cultural goods, her positive features coexist with terrible threats (destruction through plague, water, and fire). And this is why, though Nemur is assigned severe judicial and sanctioning missions, he also ensures order and guarantees social and existential stability for the Chamacoco (whenever the norms are respected, of course). Nemur's scepter, the *ook*, which is sumptuously covered in somber feathers, represents the bastion of rule and punishment as well as the staff of equilibrium.

The Nemur/Ashnuwerta antinomy therefore presupposes a complicated nexus built on the basis of affinities and discrepancies. Between norm and sanction, between the poles of a shared power, a web is woven of tensions, encounters, disagreements, antagonisms, and reciprocity. In order to differentiate between them in appearance, Nemur's trappings are characterized by their dark color, the somber *wys*, which marks his patterns. The goddess bears the reddish tones of *werta*, the color that dyes her name and that signifies the symbolic antithesis of the Nemurtian black. As the counterpoint to Ashnuwerta's relation with an Ishir, Nemur is conjugally linked to Pfaujata, a figure of mortal origin who ascends to divine status. (Pfaujata, in turn, is opposed to the god with whom she is paired: hunter/gatherer, black/red, large ostrich/middle-sized ostrich.) In order that his powers be comparable to those of Ashnuwerta, Nemur also transcends at some point the space of the Great Myth and crosses over into distant celestial and shamanic spaces. Thus, as the goddess is a tenant of the Milky Way, Nemur dwells in the Third Sky (from which he grants powers to the sky shamans) and is Master of the Highest Sky. Just as Ashnuwerta bears the status of the Mother of Water, Nemur displays the rank of Master of the Terrestrial Species: using the sparrow hawks as vehicles, he brought down from the sky all the models that gave rise to zoological differences (Cordeu 1992b, 231–32). In this episode Nemur encounters (challenges/cohabits with) Debylybyta, Mistress of the Aquatic Species.

Both the fluctuations in Ishir logic and the observations and commentaries of certain informants allow me to venture the hypothesis that Nemur belongs to a different group than that of Ashnuwerta. The fact that the power of the Great Prosecutor is as strong as the Mistress of the Word leads to the suspicion that he is the chief of some of the anábsoro armies she summoned, say Clemente and Enrique Ozuna. The possibility that Nemur does not belong to Ashnuwerta's lineage can be reinforced by an incident noted by Susnik (1957, 26): the only effect produced by the lance that Syr sinks into the ankle of the persecuted god is a trickle of honey. The hypothesis of the two castes was not explicitly confirmed by any of the informants I spoke to; only Faustino Rojas affirmed that "Nemur was of a different kind."

The Last Dialogue

When Nemur finished his performance in the *harra*, all the other anábsoro had already been exterminated. Syr tried to reach him but the anábser, who bounded away like an ostrich, was much too quick for the human. Syr was able to rope him as he fled, but the god was so strong that he could not stop him: the rope burned his hands and his arms fell numb. Nemur easily escaped. Syr, a fast and well-trained runner, followed him quickly but the anábser used his powers to place obstacles between them: estuaries boiling over with piranhas, trenches covered in thorns, fences of fire, pastures infested with serpents, clouds of maddened hornets, sands bristling with sharp stones and scorpions. Susnik says that Nemur is able to call upon the help of the North Wind, which brings "pain and exhaustion," according to an Ishir expression. But the fury of Jolué's father permits him to dodge the pitfalls. When Nemur felt the human drawing up on him—they were already in Karcha Balut—he scooped up a snail from the soil or pulled it from his body's thick plumage (depending on the versions) and with an extravagant gesture produced a raging river that sprouted out of its shell. In Luciano's version, Nemur made the river spring forth by striking the ground with his right foot. The man and the anábser, separated by the river known today as the Paraguay River, "exchange words" for the last time.

"You can run, but your destiny is to remain forever alone," pronounces Syr, standing on the riverbank. "Your people are numerous," replies Nemur from the opposite bank, "but they will be forever obliged to follow the words. If they fail, sickness, hunger, and enemies will decimate then until the last Kytymáraha [name of the clan of Syr] is extinguished." The man voices the

A representation of Nemur. María Elena, 2002. (Photo by Nicolás Richard.)

price of immortality: solitude. The god the price of the symbol: death. (And with it desire and guilt, and the forms of myth and art.)

The Ishir had rid themselves of their gods but the curse of Nemur subjugated them eternally to the representation of these same gods. From this moment on they were required to occupy their places and supplant them in the ritual so as to not forget the dark reasons of the social pact, nor lose the uncertain path of meaning. (Culture turned them into slaves of the image.)

field notes

Potrerito, 10 October 1989

When the sun sinks, the village lights up with small fires and stories whose whispers blend with the night noises. Ebytoso and Tomáraho, united in a new common space, exchange minor tales, *mónene*. Although these are not part of the central mythic corpus and cannot match its gravity or brilliance, they enliven and enrich it. They also entertain the audience, compensating for the excess of night brought on by winter. These small tales can be told by anyone, before anyone, and in any place. They do not therefore require the sententious intervention of the wise: the authentic transmitters of the "heaviest words," as the Chamacoco translate into Spanish with the light-hearted freedom with which they so quickly appropriate foreign tongues. ("The gift of illiterate peoples," Susnik used to say.)

To the delicious terror of the children, some say that although the anábsoro no longer exist on the earth, their threatening presence forever haunts men from the depths of the water, earth, or woods. Faustino says that when Syr spoke of Nemur's solitude, he simultaneously (as if contradicting himself) pointed to the eastern hills, seething with obscure sounds, signaled the reeds lifting out of troubled waters (the aquatic anábsoro use them to breathe) and struck the ground forcefully, setting off, in response, the dull echoes that announced the presence of the earth's sullen inhabitants. One Tomáraho narrator maintains that when the Ishir first attempted to kill off the gods (before they knew the secret of their ankles) some of the anábsoro were set on fire and, instead of dying, turned into animals that speedily fled to the nearest trees.

Many beasts, birds, and reptiles that populate the surroundings are, in fact, anábsoro that have become *ymasha*, adversaries, as a consequence of man's attempt to assassinate them. Luciano affirms that Ashnuwerta recommended that the Ishir cut off the heads of the anábsoro after they had killed them and place them, still warm with life, over their own in order to appropriate the powerful wisdom contained there. Not all of them remembered the advice; only the ones who later became the most prudent shamans and the valiant leaders followed it.

It is the hour when buzzing clouds of mosquitoes harass the sleepless village. There is no protection against them other than the asphyxiating proximity of smoke and heavy ponchos or thick mosquito curtains (when they're available). According to Baldus, the ancient Ishir used to bury themselves up to their necks at night to escape the biting Chaco torment or use thick blankets of caraguata as little awnings. Even now, women and men use square cloths of this vegetable fiber to fan themselves constantly and keep away the implacable *nenyr*, *kytybe*, or *asykyporo*. An enigmatic old man affirms suddenly: the mosquitoes and other plagues are also a consequence of a forgotten divine commandment. Ashnuwerta had ordered that the bodies of the anábsoro be burned once they were dead. In the midst of the excitement, however, the men forgot to do so and the great corpses filled with venomous power released vapors of sicknesses and swarms of mosquitoes, which until then had not existed. The mosquitoes, Clemente says, without contradicting the old man, are a product of a lover's snub. The moon (male in the myth) loved a woman but she, finding the spots on his face repulsive, rejected him. The spiteful moon sent her a fan crafted from the feathers of various birds that turned into mosquitoes after the first rainfall. These same waters washed off the spots on the face of the moon, and he was then able to conquer his beloved. The mosquitoes, however, were here to stay.

Other Deceptions

After failing to capture Nemur, Syr returned to the Moiéhene *tobich*. He bore with him the frustration of his fruitless chase and the profound anguish caused by the last god's curse. He knew that his people, who had until then lived a calm and unperturbed existence, would soon know the disquiet and anxiety bequeathed them by the "Bringer of Sadness." Gloomy moments of collective depression, apocalyptic anguish, and unease afflict the Chamacoco: they remember an ambiguous guilt and sense an ancient punishment. (It is possible that the devastation wrought on them by the whites is a facet of the fugitive god's punishing sentence.)

Ashnuwerta awaited him in Moiéhene. She could no longer remain among the humans: her cycle was ending. She still had to proffer her last words, her most serious words, those on which human destiny would hang. She gathered all the Chamacoco in the *tobich* and spoke thus: "You have killed the anábsoro; now you must occupy their ceremonial places. And just as the women deceived you, hiding from you the existence of the anábsoro, now you will deceive them, denying the death of the anábsoro and taking their place in the *harra* until the end of days. This is the Great Secret, which can never be revealed. Now you know their cries and movements, their appearances and patterns. Imitating them in the rites you can use their powers and guarantee the survival of the Chamacoco people and the observance of the words." Ashnuwerta lay down exhaustive rules concerning the attire, corporal paints, choreography, rites, and performance of each of the assassinated anábsoro. Negligence would bring down upon them the doom prophesied by Nemur (now transformed into the Great Guardian of the Tobich).

Comments on Missionary Acculturation

The acculturation of the Ebytoso at the hands of certain fanatical, evangelical Christian groups is visible in certain changes in their store of myths. The most notable example of such a group is the New Tribes Mission.[7] Driven by messianic fundamentalism and an intolerant creed, the missionaries of this sect are convinced that theirs is the only truth and that it must be imposed over and above any other belief in order to redeem the heretics (who hold other beliefs). Any religion other than theirs implies a satanic deviation that must be abolished at any cost. The cross has been, from the first days of conquest, the other side of the sword. Despite its declared high principles, the missionary ethnocide to which I now refer (insofar as it affects the Ebytoso) is part of an essentially pragmatic system of colonization. On the one hand, it clears the land of indigenous peoples, concentrating them in missionary reductions. On the other, it promotes their subsequent integration as cheap labor into the establishments built on those very lands. The New Tribes missionaries installed themselves in Bahía Negra, Chamacoco territory, in 1954. They began a systematic campaign of pressure, repression, intimidation, and various kinds of blackmail to force the Chamacoco to abandon the "festival of clowns" as they called the Great Ceremony, the *debylyby*. (The name of "clowns," divested of its derogatory connotations, was subsequently adopted by the Ebytoso to designate their gods.)

It is obvious that the missionaries act in historical situations that favor ethnocide. These are complicated conditions that I will not delve into here, and that I have addressed elsewhere (Escobar 1988). It is obvious that these acculturative processes are not solely due to missionaries, and neither are they infallible. In many cases indigenous peoples elaborate a complicated synthesis between their beliefs and Christian beliefs, or adopt superficial Christian elements that allow them to survive and accommodate themselves to new conditions. The Tomáraho were not affected by the missionaries and continue to practice their rituals. Many Ebytoso, in contact with the Tomáraho, are now recovering their traditions. They are no longer the same, of course, and betray the presence of vital processes of adaptation and transculturation; processes that signal a possible antidote to the siege of an intolerant Paraguayan society.

Susnik says that the doubts fostered by the various processes of acculturation have produced an opposition between older men, who are more attached to Ishir tradition, and the youth who are seduced by new truths (1957, 69; 1995, 202ff.). In order to combat the loosening of bonds of identity, the former emphasize the figure of Nemur as vigilantly watching over the faithful performance of rites. The Guardian of the Tobich makes his rounds through the villages to control and sanction the Ishir. But the missionaries use Nemur's threatening aspects to encourage conversion to Christianity. The fear of extinction and punishment, the collective anxiety and sadness (figures associated with the role of the Great Prosecutor) are contrasted with the promise of eternal Christian delight, the idea of salvation, and the image of an indulgent protecting god. Nemur is Satan. Not only does he harm the Chamacoco, but he has deceived them as well, the missionaries insist. In 1957, a group of Ebytoso living in Puerto Diana decided to set up a Great Test. Fearfully they decided to forego the *debylyby* for one year. When they confirmed that they have not been visited by the terrible curse of the Exterminator, they abandoned their ritual and converted to Christianity. (The echoes of Christianity, which do not displace the *debylyby* of the Tomáraho, provoke other associations for them: Ashnuwerta is vaguely linked to the Virgin Mary, and Nemur to a strange synthesis between Christ and the devil.)

The Canon of Ashnuwerta

After Ashnuwerta gave her instructions on the forms of the *debylyby*, the Great Ceremony, she established the taboos, norms of initiation, severe codes governing the *tobich*, and, in general, all norms regarding the many other rites that rule communal life. Next, the goddess of flamboyant splendor began to structure the society that had hitherto been amorphous. She established age, sexual, and professional distinctions, and the delicate norms of sociability that articulate, compensate, and balance the different segments. The complex scaffolding that orders ethics, rights, love, leisure, religion, aesthetics, and power sprang from her words, converted forever into figures, images, and ideas; converted also into obsessions that would mark every act and dream of those men and women, redeemed and condemned by the pressures of memory and the imposition of silence.

Ashnuwerta finally organized the system of clans based on the deicide. From her place in the *tobich* of Karcha Balut, the goddess asked each group of men which group of gods they had killed. "We killed Kaimo and his retinue." "Well then, you will belong to the Posháraha. You are linked to the anteater and will wear a cap made of the skin of the ocelot. In the ceremonial circle you will fight with the Kaimo but will end up blessed by them, and your descendents will be protected by the Kaimo Lata, the Great Mother of the lineage of the Kaimo. Your offspring will have the ability to manipulate words and thus penetrate deceit and understand the secrets of things. They will be decisive and vindictive. They will be silent and will move somewhat slowly, like the anteater. But in the word games their insults will be mordant, their replies as subtle as the dragonflies whose name they bear. In the ritual they will be responsible for controlling the dress and adornments of those who will represent the anábsoro."

Ashnuwerta then called the killers of Wákaka. "You and your children will be the Kytymáraha, protected by Hoho Lata. You will have the privilege of wearing a hat wrought from the skin of the jaguar; the hat of the most valiant warriors and hunters. The duck, which represents you, signifies the wisdom, prudence, and virtue of deceit this lineage will display. Your clan will be serene, their words severe. They will defend the interests of your people: they will negotiate in instances of conflict and will know how to persuade adversaries and obtain advantageous positions. They will be responsible for the annual realization of the Great Ceremony. The last man, according to Nemur's curse, will be a Kytymáraha, and will guard until the end the weight of the words that make the Ishir Ishir, and that enable them to die with their memory intact."

And in succession the goddess classified the assassins of the anábsoro and established other groups. The Tymáraha, the clan of the monkey, is protected by Wawa Lata, identified by headgear from the ocelot, and recognized for their strong and stubborn nature, their jokes, and quarrelsome disposition. Those who killed Wioho are the Tahorn; they are friendly and gentle and are represented by the parrot. The silent Namoho of the lineage of the jaguar came next; they were given the right to wear a crown of wolf skin and given the protection of the Great Mother of the Kaiporta. The symbol of the Dosypyk is the ostrich; they wear the coati on their head and are known for their happy nature, a breath of hope in the somber moments of collective anguish.

Those who killed Pohejuvo are the Datsymáraha. Little is known about them because that line is extinct. They were guardians of myth and counselors of the Ishir. They used words to resolve conflicts and were known as conciliatory, impartial, and prudent.

When Ashnuwerta asked the last group of men which anábsoro they had killed they answered that they had not killed any. According to the Ebytoso this was because these Ishir belonged to Syr's group and could not kill any anábsoro because he was pursuing Nemur. The Tomáraho deny this. Syr belongs to the Kytymáraha: he is a bold leader, a cautious negotiator, an authentic guardian of words. But the versions coincide in the fact that Ashnuwerta, disconcerted because she could not connect these strange men to any anábser, decided to assign them their own clan family. From then on, the group of people who did not participate in the anábsoro massacre belonged to the

Dyshykymser clan, represented by the figure of the carancha bird[8] and protected by the sinister Pfaujata. It is the only endogamic clan, the dark organizer of the most cryptic and most essential moments of the Great Ceremony: its members are entrusted with imposing the secret names. But it is also the only clan that does not participate in any dramatic representation (for they cannot supplant someone they did not eliminate), nor in the ritual ball game (*póhorro*) that expresses the elaborate system of reciprocal interactions between different social segments.

Ashnuwerta complicated the system of classification even further by introducing a new variable. The groups that were protagonists in the battle are considered "strong clans" and occupy a hegemonic position; the clans who distinguished themselves less in battle are known as the "weak clans" and occupy a subordinate position. The first are composed by the Kytymáraha, Tymáraha, Posháraha, and Tahorn; the latter by the Namoho, Dosypyk, and Datsymáraha. The lineage of the Dyshykymser, in spite of its marginal role during the battle, is considered a powerful clan, due to its mysterious weight during the ceremony.

The interplay of particularities and interclan ties are completed by the rules of marriage and attire that Ashnuwerta established for each group, along with the prescriptions on social etiquette and performance during ritual dramatizations and athletic competition. Each group received, in addition, a style of song (Boggiani [1894, 56] mentions the existence of singing competitions between clans that no longer seem to exist.) Lastly, Ashnuwerta sealed the institution of clans with a banquet that established the tradition of great ritual feasts among the Ishir. These symbolize both community cohesion and the community differences from which the larger unity is articulated. Susnik details how the meat of the anteater was distributed in this "first mythic feast" (1995, 138). The lineage of the sacrificed animal (the Posháraha) ate the hair on its tail; the clan of the monkey (the Tymáraha) ate the lungs; the head was given to the group of the jaguar (the Namoho); the liver to the parrot clan (the Tahorn); and the entrails to the ostrich-people (the Dosypyk). The members of the carancha clan, the solemn Dyshykymser, participated only with their silent, stoic presence.

Now the Ishir were definitively tied to their gods/victims not only through ritual representation but also through the destinies of the clans they share. Order was consummated, and the circle was now closed. Ashnuwerta

no longer had a place in the circle. In truth, she no longer had a place anywhere, Bruno comments, because she could no longer return to the underground with her kin since she had betrayed them by revealing the secret of
their mortality. So Ashnuwerta retreated to an unknown place in the south.
The wind that blows from that direction is so strong and cold that not even
the sun can resist it.

Commentary on the Clans

The system of clans is the spine of Chamacoco society. It is the efficient regulating mechanism of unity and difference, an obscure poetic trope conjured
up to explain the inexplicable relation between men, nature, and gods. For a
society of hunter-gatherers such as the Chamacoco, the daily confrontation
with nature needs to be worked out meticulously. Nature is subjected to a
careful rhetorical process that simultaneously traces frontiers between different kingdoms and facilitates traffic between those domains. Displacements,
free associations, identifications, substitutions, and sleights of hand enable
free circulation, rapid passage and, above all, the provisional nature of this
movement between the human and the natural. Scientist ethnographic readings neglect the metaphoric level of these transactions, which is why I find it
necessary to emphasize that the associations of hunters with their prey (and
gatherers with their fruit) are better understood metaphorically than in terms
of strict causality.

At the same time, the figure of the clans processes the nexus among
humans, and between humans and deities. They weave a formalized web of
cultural progenies over a frame of natural filiations, which is touched up symbolically and located in a dense field of social forces. The clans, therefore, pro-
pose an intricate and dynamic model of sociality: a totality that is structured
and mobilized through an interplay of segments that are opposed or allied
continually on different levels that seek compensation (only provisionally, of
course). The clan system emphasizes the idea of difference and consequently,
that of rivalry, reciprocity, and exchange. The clans instill a precise mechanism
that regulates the combination of familial, sociocultural, religious, and economic relations among the Chamacoco. The clans demarcate social positions
and distribute movements on the cultural chessboard. The strong dualist slant
that traverses Chamacoco social order is well expressed in this system where

places are so clearly assigned. Matrimonial ties, the exchange of economic favors and ritual performances are ruled by categorical figures created by the system. Their distinct forms are stamped with a rhythmic and controlled movement. Trading insults (called *enehichó*) between clans, for example, can compensate for the asymmetries produced by banquet invitations: the hosts insult their guests to repair the imbalance produced by the gift (the roles are later reversed). These insults are metaphors for the rhythmic to and fro of complementary tasks. Moreover, the clans, who are all patrilineal and exogamic (except the Dyshykymser) determine the conjugal compatibility of their filiations according to the classic mechanism of binary oppositions and intersecting equilibriums. Lastly, the clan structure manifests itself in the ritual ball game and in the plot of the *debylyby*, the Great Ceremony (not only in its performance, but also in the organization of the scene and the ceremony's libretto).

Given these functions of the clans, it is understandable that an Ishir is considered a pariah if he or she doesn't have an affiliation with a clan. Susnik writes that one of the great attractions offered to the Ebytoso by evangelical Christianity lay in the idea of having a place reserved in the sky, a concept akin to the assigned positions of clans in the ball games played in the Land of Death (1995, 134).

While the clan structure is practically extinct among the Ebytoso, it survives falteringly among the Tomáraho. The brutal population decline they have suffered upset the balance in the relations between the segments and diminished the number of members in each clan. For this reason, the Ishir today need to make dramatic internal adjustments to adapt their cultural dynamics to the new realities abruptly imposed by the alteration of the traditional modes of survival, the devastation of their lands, and the invasion of strange clanless gods. In fact, some severe restrictions have been reformulated, adapted, or simply abandoned. For one thing, many marriages now ignore the laws that govern clan affiliations. For another, some ceremonial performances need to overlook the requirements of clan functions: many anábsoro who appear onstage accompanied by their large entourage could not be represented if the Ishir rigorously followed the rules, which determine that only actors from certain clans can represent certain gods.

Contemporary Chamacoco society must, therefore, take on the challenge of repairing its symbolic articulations with increasing speed. It is an important challenge, but not the only one they face. Just as any indigenous group in

Paraguay, and in South America, the Chamacoco know that their ethnic survival depends on their capacity for rhetorical maneuver. They are experts in this. Meanwhile, they proudly preserve their enigmatic animal names and the stubborn hope that, aided by the Great Mothers, their clan descendents will increase.

THE GREAT MYTH, ACT TWO

Sweet Deception

Ashnuwerta imposed the Great Secret, according to which the women would believe that the men who danced in disguise in the ceremonial circle were really the anábsoro, who still lived among them. However, as soon as the men appeared in the *harra* wearing masks, feathers, and paint, the women did not accept the simulacra. Doubled over with laughter, they ridiculed the actors, mocking their attempt to supplant the gods.

The Tomáraho explain this humiliating failure as follows. I rely on Luciano's version (confirmed by Wylky). When the women learned of the existence of honey from the Great Mothers they decided to hide this delicious discovery from the men and enjoy the sweet secret of the honeycombs by themselves. The men were suspicious of the women's frequent and apparently pointless incursions into the woods and decided to send one of their children to spy on them one day. Aware of the youth that followed them, and in order to slip away from him, the women changed the path they usually took to reach home. As they walked through a part of the woods they had never before seen they found the rotting bodies of their ancient divine allies. And so they discovered that the anábsoro had been assassinated. Surrounding the bodies, they mourned the death of the gods. When they reached the settlement, the men saw their reddened and tearstained faces. "The sun burned our skin," some said. "The nettles made us cry," others lied. "It was the wasps," an older woman affirmed with authority.

Thus it was that the women discovered that the supposed anábsoro were their own companions in disguise. And this discovery made them even more jealous of their golden secret and its lively sweetness and, in revenge, they increased their excursions for honey and redoubled their efforts to hide it from the men. But the men decided to send another agent to discover the secret: this was an astute *wetern* who managed to follow them unnoticed. The youth saw the women gathering the swollen honeycombs, gorging themselves on the nectar and filling pots with the golden honey to carry back to the village to share with the old women or to feast on when the men were off hunting. Following the women further, he also discovered their secret daily ritual of mourning for the dead anábsoro. The youth assembled the men who were off fishing for eels and communicated his grave findings. As proof, he made them taste a pot of the unknown elixir he had managed to steal from the women.

Emilio's version has a number of small differences. Although the women had decided to keep the honey secret from the men, they had decided to justify their continued incursions into the woods by offering the men empty honeycombs to eat (they kept the thick syrup hidden in ceramic jars). When the men put the supposed delicacy in their mouths they tasted nothing but larvae and dried husks. Not only were they disappointed at the bitter and withered flavor of those emptied honeycombs, but they soon began to vomit and suffer from diarrhea. From then on, they decided to avoid the indigestible banquet and left the honeycombs to the women without understanding why they derived such apparent pleasure from it. Following the tortuous path of deceptions and revelations that leads to knowledge, a *wetern* accidentally discovered the wild ambrosia and the cries of the women over the lifeless bodies of those who had been their masters, allies, and occasional lovers. The adolescent's discovery is in turn discovered: his mother, who was among the mourners, pleads for his silence but the *wetern* runs off and reveals the double secret to the men.

The Sentence

The Tomáraho and Ebytoso coincide in the account of the following episode. Ashnuwerta still lingered in the *tobich* giving instructions and preparing for her departure. The *nagrab* approached her and informed her that the women knew the truth of their fraudulent costumes (and, according to the Tomáraho, also informed her of the honey hoax and the women's secret discovery of the divine corpses). To their shock, Ashnuwerta decreed that the women had to be killed. Although the men knew that they could not ignore the divine words and felt humiliated by their wives' deception, they were not prepared to sacrifice them. Ashnuwerta calmed them down by assuring them that if they followed her instructions, step by step, they would recover their families. "So that no one has to assassinate his own wife, each man will kill the wife of his *ágalo* and in turn his *ágalo* will kill his wife." Afterwards, the goddess designated one woman as the wife of the *pylota*, the leader (Syr, in some versions): through her, the men would have their wives again. She told them thus: "Tomorrow, the one I choose will prepare a *kobo* (a ceramic vase). This will serve to identify her so her husband can recognize her and avert her death."

The Ebytoso affirm that the woman charged with the rebirth of the Ishir women was a daughter or godchild of Ashnuwerta. But according to the Tomáraho, that woman was the goddess herself transformed into a human called Hopupora. Some who know the myth even believe that Ashnuwerta had already turned herself into Ashnuwysta, who then became Hopupora in order to announce the first ritual in which the men participated after the death of the anábsoro (the *debylyby* begins with the calls of Hopupora). Therefore, according to this version Hopupora was the one who decided the death of the first women (*tymycher*) and who, in her human form, offered herself up as the origin of the new women (*tymycher aly*).

On Metamorphosis and Other Conversions

This episode touches on one of the most obscure and complicated moments of Chamacoco mythology: the doubling of beings according to a logic of dualistic oppositions (which are also bifurcations, displacements, and identifications achieved despite or through differences). Ashnuwerta of the Red Splendor is opposed to Ashnuwysta of the Black Brilliance, her opposite and adversary (the black/red antithesis is the paradigm of radical opposition). But she is also Ashnuwysta herself, expressed in all her contradictory aspects: her most somber and negative aspects, linked to sickness and terrible collective punishment. She is her own dark side. The Ashnuwerta/Hopupora opposition speaks to the link between the divine and human that is named through the mediation of myth. Hopupora is the hidden mistress of ceremonies: she is Ashnuwerta—or Ashnuwysta—present in the ritual form that reconciles the order of the gods with that of the Ishir. Finally, the Ashnuwerta/Arpylá relationship (which we will get into shortly) also signals the constant rivalry between the divine and the human. In this case, it does so by using the organic natural as intermediary: the goddess passes briefly through an animal state (woman/doe) in order to connect the conflicting terms.

AFTER the discussion of the identity of the chosen woman, the versions coincide again. Based on collective hunting techniques, the men began to erect a giant circular enclosure made of tree trunks, surrounding the village so that no one could escape once the sacrifice was under way. Some say that the women, astonished at such unusual activity, asked for explanations. "We are preventing a possible enemy attack," the *nagrab* are said to have responded. Well before dawn (and to the right of the fence), the massacre of the women began. In one corner of the *lut* a woman quietly molded strips of clay to make a pitcher. This activity identified her as the woman chosen to renovate her gender, the one who should be spared from the holocaust. However, in the midst of the confusion of shadows and dust, cries, terror, and disgust, the brother (or *ágalo*) of the chief destined to be her husband lunged toward her brandishing the *noshikó*, the mortal mallet made of palo santo wood. As he was about to reach her he saw her turn into a doe and leap effortlessly over the wall of palm trees. She disappeared among trees, barely outlined in the misty light and early murmurs of the morning.

It was still dawn when the chief (some say it was Syr) and his brother (or *ágalo*) set off to find her. They were accompanied by a large group of strong men. They found the light tracks left by the doe as she rested on the ground, but found no other indication of where she had gone. They sought her in the thickets of caraguata plants, the pasture and swamp lands, under the monotonous palms, the thorn-infested undergrowth and distant lands where the carob trees end, unknown fruit trees grow, and strange beasts prowl. They did not find her. Arpylá, turned back into her human form, was hiding in the branches of a guayacan tree, and from her high perch she blew a wind that erased her tracks and produced strange sounds that confused the men and led them astray.

On the second night, the exhausted trackers returned to the village, which was still sleepless with the mournful song and tears of the widowers. When Arpylá noticed that only her husband was still searching for her she blew in the other direction to orient him. Without knowing exactly how, the man reached the foot of the tree. At that moment he felt the throbbing pain of a thorn that had punctured his foot. He sat down and bent over to extract it when he felt something cold on his neck. Lifting his head he saw Arpylá, who had spit the cold saliva that is the gift of Ashnuwerta.

The woman taunted him from above. "Come and take me," she said. Either because, as the Ebytoso say, she was a stranger sent by Ashnuwerta or because, as the Tomáraho insist, she was the goddess herself in human form, their marriage had not yet been consummated. (In the versions of those who insist that Syr was the chief of the story, he had supposedly never lived with her in human form.) It seems that the chief, incited by the woman's invitation, was anxious to obey her. He tried to climb up to the object of his desire, but his sexual excitement was such that he ejaculated prematurely, smearing the tree trunk—polished and slippery in itself—with his chaste marital sap, rendering the task impossible.

In Ashnuwerta's grave voice, Arpylá showed him how to overcome the obstacle. He had to climb up the vines hanging from a nearby tree and then swing over to where she sat in the guayacan tree. Following her advice he reached her and lost himself in her amidst the restless rustle of the leaves. Afterwards, in Ashnuwerta's wise voice, Arpylá gave him disconcerting instructions he could not refuse: "If the men want to recover their women they have to do what you just did. After that they will kill me and distribute my body in as many pieces as there were families, take my flesh to a new village, far away from the old one, and wait there until nightfall when the resurrection of the women will take place. Keep my genitals for yourself."

One after one the Ishir attempted to climb the tree and reach the woman (the goddess, the doe). Each man suffered the same fate as the chief: the anticipation of possessing Arpylá excited them so much they could not control themselves, and with each avid attempt the trunk of the tree became more and more slippery with their semen. Just as she had with her husband, Arpylá showed each of them how to reach her. And following her instructions they reached the top of the tree and copulated with her. When the last man had finished, Arpylá climbed down from the guayacan and lay down over a *pypyk*, a shawl woven out of caraguata fibers. Her husband's brother, or companion, killed her with the *noshikó*. Then, using their *ybykúú* (small sharp knives), all the men cut her body into pieces they then distributed and carried off in their *boná* (hunter's bag made of caraguata). Although they had decided to cut the body into equal parts, inevitably some of the men grabbed bigger parts. Others had to content themselves with simply cradling some blood in their hand. Dazed by the situation, Syr, the husband (*abich*) of Ashnuwerta, forgot to follow her instructions and did not keep for himself the essential part appointed to him. He was never able to recuperate his wife. "From that moment on, Ashnuwerta never again appeared among men," says Wylky, emphasizing the Ishir obsession with those who forget the divine precepts and receive exemplary sanctions.

Commentary on Arpylá

Arpylá's tale is a tight mythic nucleus whose greatest effect is the intense poetry, obscure brilliant metaphors, and suggestive complexity of impenetrable designs. Like other figures whose symbolic weight exceeds them, it emits a beam of meanings that can not be fastened to any vertex. And yet the expressiveness of its fertile mayhem suggests a variety of readings: its own rhetorical generosity makes it the ready accomplice of multiple interpretations and of attempts to reveal a nonexistent key. It is not the function of this book to profit from such attempts or to venture its own hermeneutic gestures. Yet it is evident that many interpretations, despite their failure to account for the whole myth, touch on some of its nerves. They can, if not unveil its structure, enrich its reading, signal its densities and echoes, ambiguously indicate its intricate paths. For this reason I'll mention (and simplify) some suggestive figural or conceptual associations tied to this dense mythic episode.

Arpylá consummates the mediating destiny of Ashnuwerta, whom she represents, supplants, or simply continues. The figure of the goddess / woman / doe fixes an axis of oppositions between the sacred and profane, between the numinous and the merely organic. It confronts human beings with the gods, on the one hand, and with animals, on the other. It works the differences, quarrels, and coincidences between male and female. It elaborates the difficult nexus between reproduction and death, between accomplished time and the present. It establishes instances of mediation, connections through rule and ritual, through the idea of a death that orders and restricts all human industry.

The figure of the men's climb toward the goddess is fairly expressive. It signals, among other things, the elevation required by the craving for the sacred. Human beings need to rise and climb to communicate with deities. They need to overcome difficulties, including their own impatience and clumsiness.

And they must learn: reaching a higher level requires knowledge. (In this case revealed knowledge: the goddess teaches them the steps needed to reach her.) If the guayacan alludes to the cosmic column—the axis mundi, the connection between the earthly and the celestial—the vines suggest the indirect and necessary path of mediation. The desired object can only be reached through laborious detours. Truth is reached at a slant, if it can be reached at all.

The copulation between Arpylá and the men points to and reinforces a notion of unity in the Chamacoco social body. The men identify with each other through their identical effort to reach the goddess, through a single way of climbing up to her, possessing her, and later killing her. The social pact is renovated on a backdrop of eroticism and death, sealed with the collective semen spilled on the guayacan and the precious blood of the last/first woman. Arpylá's instructions reinforce the image of a feminine source of normativity and meaning: she institutes the technical procedures for achieving what is desired, she regulates sexuality, codifies the forms of death, and installs the proportional distribution of goods under the oscillating sign of chance and the uncertain rubric of human justice. She rolls out before their eyes the essential utopia: the ancient dream of a renewed society.

If the men identify with each other through their sexual intercourse with the goddess, the women identify through the common flesh out of which they are reborn. And if the men attain the sacred by rising to the numinous, the women participate in a superior dimension by the very material that comprises their bodies and makes them apt for new progeny. Bearers of divine stock, ephemeral dwellers of Osypyte, the Kingdom of the Dead, they give birth to the generations that will comprise the new Ishir people under the sign of word, silence, and secrets.

AFTER Arpylá's tragic sacrifice and the distribution of her body, the men abandoned the village and established a new provisional settlement not too far away, as commanded. They carefully guarded the valuable bits and pieces of the deity. In order to pass the restless hours remaining before nightfall and to calm the hunger produced by such fateful, intense activities, they went in search of eels in a nearby stream. They fished, but the anxiety of knowing whether or not the miracle had taken place drove them crazy. Finally, at the limits of desperation, they decided to send Tetís, or Pytís, a nephew of the chief (Syr for the Tomáraho) to the village to spy on what was happening and bring back news. The youth was a *konsaha porro*, that is, a shaman-apprentice who already had certain powers. Converted into an *ave-sastre*, a small swift bird which bears his name to this day, Tetís flew low over the settlement and was chased by a noisy group of women who wanted to capture him. These were, he realized, the new women.

Back in human form, the youth returned to where the men now rested. He lay down on the ground by his uncle on a caraguata mat and informed him of the good tidings. (Here is a minor episode, a *mónene*, which has nothing to do with the dramatism of the narrated events, but which expresses a trait of Ishir culture: the value assigned to cunning and deceit, considered resources to obtain advantages, and the relation of deceit to a certain, often crude sense of humor that is not lost even in the most serious circumstances.) Syr, or whoever the chief was, and his nephew decided, whispering, to hide the news from their companions. "Carrion birds, or perhaps wasps, ate up Arpylá's flesh. There is no way to recuperate the lost wives," they said solemnly. Desperate, the men abandoned their *boná* brimming with eels and decided to disperse: some returned to the settlement, others wandered deep into the forest with no destination. The chief gathered the bags and sent Tetís to gather the men again and tell them it had been a joke. When the men run to the village shouting for joy, they find their wives who—ignorant of all that has happened, and ravenous, since they have not yet eaten in their new life—only demand the slippery products of their husbands' fishing endeavors.

Final act: the chief enters with the bags of caraguata filled with eels, and after reserving the best pieces for himself and his nephew (and attributing to himself the merits of the fishing expedition), he distributes the eels among the carefree *tymycher aly* (new women). The men observe them: they are and are not the same. The unequal distribution of Arpylá's flesh has made some of them reappear fatter and others skinnier than they had been before. Those who were formed with only the blood of the goddess came back slightly more somber and sad, as if they were faded copies of themselves.

There is one other fundamental difference between the old and new women. Their memories have been erased: they do not remember their encounter with the gods, nor their death and substitution by the men. From then on, when the Ishir reappear in the ritual circle, tearing the depths of the Chaco with their ferocious cries, upsetting the peace of the village with the agitation of their feathered, painted bodies, the women believe they are in the presence of supernatural beings, of gods who can, like all powerful beings, be either generous or harmful. Then men and women will reverently, fearfully, and even joyfully watch this performance that seeks to reestablish the origin and renovate time, cast away death and reaffirm desire. This is the Great Secret. The day in which the Ishir forget to imitate the gods, and the women stop officiating as guarantors of the profound truth of fiction, the curse of Nemur will fall upon their heads. Then the stage on which the Ishir represent, justify, and reproduce themselves will cease to exist. "Then," says the old shaman Faustino Rojas, watching a fixed point on the horizon, "the Chamacoco will die, or will cease to want to live, which amounts to the same."

Notes on Myth

Myths do not have a meaning, a univocal truth that can be unraveled. They are the vertebrae of different constellations of meaning that a society generates in order to anchor its origin and conjure away the absurdity of death; in order to name its depth, its beyond, and its forever; in order to redesign its profile according to a choice that overlays and counterbalances a natural organic model.

To defend the secret of myth and question the idea that it transmits an exact and decipherable truth does not mean conceiving it as a text that is beautiful but mute, or as a mere arabesque of fantasy. Myth opens up a terrain of knowledge that would otherwise be inaccessible. It lodges the real in another scene whose artifices reveal new flanks of understanding.

The difficulty of assuming the rhetorical level of myth is a problem common to the social sciences, which find themselves bewildered in the face of a fact that grounds its truth in fiction. They can not comprehend certain oblique strategies through which society recognizes itself and dramatizes itself, through which society subtracts and justifies itself. To consider myth (as one often considers ideology) a deceptive mechanism that skirts "true reality" is to lose sight of the revelatory potential of figurative language, which conceals and deceives in order to intensify meaning and bring to light dimensions invisible to the prudent gaze of the concept.

Amidst the simulacra and performance of drama, in the very confusion of shadows and reflections, myth smuggles in dark unanticipated forces such as unknown actors or events and dialogues that took place elsewhere.

Myth's lack of clarity is offset by a gain in vigor and vehemence, in the generosity of excess. The complicated wandering of myth recovers lost ground through the shortcuts of poetic detours.

The mechanisms of knowledge of myth begin to operate where those of discourse fall silent. The question of meaning, the theme of the unconditional, the desire for transcendence, and the necessity to grasp the multiple dimensions of the real, exceed the possibilities of reflection and leave behind an excess that cannot be captured through analysis and definitions but only alluded to through suggestions. It can only be broached indirectly through circumlocutions, deflections, and slanted approaches.

Myths address the radical questions of a community: the unanswerable ones. From their obscure narrations, the silhouette of the absolute, the place before the origin and beyond the limit (the event that takes place outside time), is illuminated intensely, if briefly, so that humans can orient themselves. They are furtive reference points through which to glimpse or imagine the direction of essential paths. There can be no clear, definitive resolution. (The wise old Ishir have a saying, translated roughly, that the secret is the guarantee of meaning.)

Notes on the Great Ishir Myth

The Great Ishir Myth is an efficient filter regulating Chamacoco society and a powerful storehouse of meaning. Its vigorous figures pose a central question that orders society and grounds its thought: the links between the same and the other. The elaboration of difference (gender, age, personality, profession) translates into different positions and traces the intricate maps of interpersonal relations. Men and women; the uninitiated, adults, and the old; members of different clans and families; warriors, hunters and gatherers, leaders and shamans assume places endorsed by the power of the "great words," urged and anointed by the obscure work of metaphor.

The great webs of meaning are woven by fastening uncertain figures and masked ideas; by weaving desires and fleeting signs created by fear, engendered by imagination and the delirium of ecstasy, or revealed in dreams. They are also produced by manipulating clear reasons, and by borrowing or stealing alien forms that are then plaited into the plot of the tales.

It is true that myth allows the Ishir to tie, explain, and legitimate social order. It is true that myth produces the great arguments through which a collectivity ensures its own continuity, explains itself, and elaborates its own image. It is also true that the Great Myth does not close off the large questions, but constantly renews them. Challenged by historical situations, myth creates conflicts and unravels crises. It requires change. It destabilizes. The Chamacoco anguish—this restless affliction of the soul that mimics the boredom of palm trees or the threat of white men—is as much the child of myth as is tranquility. Myth wards off chaos on the razor's edge: it molds order out of nothingness. It is only in the language of myth that death can be named.

Clemente López, Ebytoso shaman, crowned with a feather headdress and large neck-guard. Puerto Esperanza, 1986. (Photo by Ticio Escobar.)

FEATHERS AND FEATHERWORK

field notes

Potrerito, 7 October 1989

Clemente's niece Elena is a lovely and vivacious fifteen-year-old. Her proud grandfather assures me that she has shamanic gifts and will one day be a great *konsaha*. For now she sings, maraca in hand, in accompaniment to her teacher. Since Emiliano, the director of the Spanish TV crew, arrived, Elena has not taken her eyes off him. Her gaze is so direct, so natural that the Spaniard, more curious than uncomfortable, asked her one day: "Why do you stare at me like that?" Elena's dark eyes did not look away from his blue ones. "What is the color of the world for you?" she asked him. "The same as it is for you, of course," he answered. And she then said something to which he had no reply: "And how do you know what the color of the world is for me?"

That night we spoke of the Chamacoco obsession with colors. Emiliano, who remained silent the rest of that day, only commented that Elena's answer had Kantian overtones.

ON CHAMACOCO AESTHETICS

The Chamacoco are obsessed with colors. Colors dye the deepest conceptions of Ishir culture. They illuminate the backdrop of myths and set the Ishir bodies alight during ceremonies; they mark differences and conflicts; they classify, explain, and illustrate; they are signposts to places, hierarchies, states; they invoke the mysteries of geography and climate, of fauna and flora; they name the hues of blood, night, light, and fire. Colors allow for great rhetorical flexibility: they modulate discourse, emphasize figures. This is why they have such a powerful aesthetic mission. When colors place objects onstage, they exhibit and trace its forms, they disturb it and set it aglow. For this reason, too, colors are charged with strong poetic and artistic meaning. By dislodging its primary references, marking its limits, surrounding it with silence, linking it to desire and death, colors force the object to release hidden meanings: meanings that are neither complete nor lasting, to be sure, but that can gesture, ever so obliquely, to truths that remain otherwise concealed.

This virtue of deepening the experience of the real through transgression and the loss of an original innocence links the aesthetic with the mythical-ritual with the numinous. From the perspective of the sacred, the world is not a neutral and opaque exteriority but is populated with meanings, traversed by unseen links that connect things, laden with forces, shadows, and hollows. The sacred presents the world against the light so that its veins and transparencies are briefly revealed; under the slanted illumination of the sacred its textures, breaks, and edges, its shadows spring into view. The sacred names the world from its limits, through the detours of absence, and seeks then to suggest—since it cannot unveil—its shadowy enigmas and secrets. This is why Mircea Eliade says that the sacred is the real, the real saturated with being, the real spilling over (1959, 20). And this is why art has much to accomplish through its labors: it zigzags between the real and the fictitious to awaken the burden of meaning ensconced in the most trivial of happenings.

Like ritual and myth, the labor of aesthetics seeks to interrupt the quotidian, to crawl into its recesses and promote a more penetrating experience, a livelier knowledge of the everyday. For this reason, it erases the clear outlines of events and objects, subtracting our perception of them from the normality of daily experience and cracking them open to the experience of the supernatural. The religious ideas that animate ritual representations and mythical tales must be accentuated through their elaboration of a sensibility and their manipulation of form, that is, through the labor of the aesthetic. The intense images and suggestive colors, the lights, compositions, and disquieting figures enable the world to present a richer, more complex face: inhabited with uncertainty, drawn against the bottomless backdrop of the primal question.

The Ishir women are stunned by the beauty of the gods' colors. To produce such astonishment, to trouble the normal perception of phenomena, the numinous needs to inflame and exasperate forms. To open the sign up to the order of meaning, the sacred must disturb and destabilize it.[1] This is why, in order to move their audience and express meanings that cannot otherwise be communicated, the Chamacoco men plaster their bodies with paint and feathers, exhibiting themselves with the stolen beauty of the gods.

ON CHAMACOCO STYLE

I will not address the question of the relations between the aesthetic and artistic nor discuss whether or not one can speak of indigenous "art." These are problems I have addressed elsewhere (Escobar 1986, 1993). I am, however, interested in repeating some comments on certain specific notes that mark Chamacoco sensibility and characterize their unique style; one that is vigorous and pathetic, and unexpectedly subtle.

It is natural for aesthetic systems to have a dramatic undertone; but Ishir art does this in an open and systematic way—it is programatically expressionist.

In general, Zamuco sensibility (Ayoreo and Chamacoco) distinguishes itself considerably from that of other ethnic families in the Great Chaco. Not only are their temperaments different (loquacious and extroverted, adaptive and combative); so are their cultural histories (marked by independent origins, the Chiquitana influence, and the particular epic of their conflicts with national society) and their geographical conditions (their habitat is composed mainly of wild vegetation similar to the region of Mato Grosso in Brazil and Santa Cruz in Bolivia). Each of these factors conditions the particular makeup of the Zamuco cultures, which nevertheless are still connected with those of other Chaco groups. Not only do these groups constantly traffic in signs, but they also share the common misfortune of discrimination at the hands of Paraguayan society.

The particularity of the symbolic universe of the Zamuco is evident when their expressive patrimony is compared with that of the typical Chaco groups. Zamuco cultures do not include any of the traditional elements identified with the Chaco: the use of wool, beads, wooden earrings, and long necklaces strung with shells. Even the visual and technical principles of featherwork vary among the different Chaco groups. The Zamucos use an exuberant variety of feathers that are scorned by the tribes of the plains (who limit themselves to the sober opposition between white and red). The use of corporal paint is also uneven among the Chaco groups. In contrast to the plains people, the Zamuco never tattoo themselves. Yet the ornamental patterns they paint on their bodies are defined by their expressive complexity, formal flexibility, and figurative breadth. The Ayoreo and, especially, the Chamacoco have developed vehement multicolored systems of facial and bodily painting that contrast with the stylized decorative system of other groups. (I am not referring to the decorative system of the Caduveo, who no longer inhabit the Chaco.) I quote myself to finish: "The Chamacoco image lacks the elegant aesthetics of the typical Chaco indigenous groups but attains a peculiar dramatic expressiveness; they combine colors the other groups never use and mix ornamental systems in profuse disordered images disdained by the others. Yet these images possess a somber, even romantic, vigor that fills the bleak world of these hunter-gatherers, stamping it with original signs that are perhaps the densest expressions of indigenous art in Paraguay" (Escobar 1993, 29).

In addition, it is necessary to mark the differences between the art of the Ayoreo and the Chamacoco and, within this latter group, between the Ebytoso and the Tomáraho. Chamacoco corporal art has figures that are much more varied than those of the Ayoreo, not only because this latter group has proved more vulnerable to the impact of an ethnocidal colonization that virtually destroyed their artistic expression, but also because the complexity of Chamacoco rituals requires a greater diversity in types and characters. The Chamacoco have also shown themselves more flexible in the face of the influence of other Chaco tribes with whom they share similar territories; their expressive models both mobilize the stability of their heritage and enrich it in the challenge of constant adaptation. For the most part, the Ishir are also plains people (this explains their use of ostrich feathers, which the Ayoreo, for example, do not use). With regard to the distinctions between the Ebytoso and Tomáraho, for the moment I want to note only that the first group has developed a greater variety of manifestations linked to what is traditionally called "material culture" (wood carving, basket weaving, fan making); whereas the Tomáraho have specialized in the forms that express the ritual at the heart of their culture. The Tomáraho, in effect, practically lack autonomous forms of crafts. All of their diligence, manual dexterity, and creativity are poured into the ceremony, shamanic practices, and bodily adornments. The body is the essential stage, the privileged site of form.

For this reason, although there are other expressions of Chamacoco art—such as caraguata textiles, wood carving, and basket weaving—this book will focus on corporal art and the ritual that frames it. This chapter will address the use of feathers through three tales that are fundamental to shamanic mythology: the origin of the color of birds, the origin of red feathers, and the origin of feathered ornaments. The next chapter will address corporal painting.

field notes

Potrerito, 11 October 1986

The dwellings of the Ebytoso are separated from those of the Tomáraho by a wide open space reminiscent of a town square. A fence of rusted and sagging barbed wire traverses it, delimiting the territories of these groups whose relationship, according to the Chamacoco system of dualities, is comprised as much by oppositions and tensions as it is by oscillations, complementary links, equilibriums, and controversies. From a distance, the houses, built from the trunk of the carandá palm trees,[2] are indistinguishable from the landscape. One village gravitates toward the river, which is now about fourteen kilometers away; the other is cradled by the fringes of a dense jungle. The villages face each other, watchfully, and Jorge and I trace a path back and forth from one to the other, diligently imitating the wise logic of our hosts. Among the Ebytoso we stay at the house of Clemente López. The Tomáraho, however, have a cabin at the center of the village reserved for warehousing provisions and accommodating guests like us.

Now we are on Tomáraho lands. It is the moment when light falters and the woods and the memory of the river pause in its wake, awaiting some sign that will hasten the first round of shadows. Jorge points to the sky: a flock of storks floats, suspended in the colorless air. Now they circle, tracing for an instant the outlines of a languid choreography that swiftly dissipates, like the unexpected emergence of a group of anábsoro on the ceremonial grounds. The afternoon resumes its course, as if the slight dance had activated some hidden mechanism. A golden glow washes over the sky, turning the birds into glittering points of light that are soon swallowed by the sky. Evening falls. "The briefest flutter of wings is enough for the storks to fasten onto rising thermal currents like birds of prey," says Jorge, "abandoning themselves to the spiral patterns." Perhaps, I say, the movements of the dancers on the ceremonial circle, the dale harra, indirectly allude to the secret of these birds resting in mid-flight. "Perhaps," we agree.

Ishir culture is, after all, consumed with birds. Birds traverse their myths in flocks and inspire their rituals. They provide feathers for ornament, cries and movements for performances, colors for imagination's wakeful vigil and for sleep's depths. Birds constitute the paradigms of beauty: they are the animals whose tones and forms, whose meanings, most lend themselves to an aesthetic apprehension. The birds, like gods, cross the sky freely. Some can dive under water, cleaving the surface. Others can run or wander the Chaco plains, swiftly, tirelessly. They can traverse valleys and hills unerringly at night, anticipate threats, know death. Like birds, the gods are clothed in shining feathers and voice variegated cries. Like birds, the gods have crests and claws, move in flocks. They can be terrible or meek, friend or foe. The shamans also evoke birds in their feathered trappings, effusive colors, and songs. They can even fly like the storks, understand the beds of the great lakes with the wisdom of ducks, and traverse the grasslands with the swiftness and cunning of ostriches. To become gods or shamans, humans dress themselves up as birds.

But they do it as well to differentiate themselves from other humans: borrowing the classification of birds, using their feathers like labels to identify the Ishir from other nations and to distinguish among themselves, even within the groups that separate them.

THE FIRST MYTH: THE ORIGIN OF COLORS

There are times when survival is difficult. There are times of drought when plants and honey are scarce and the number of animals has dwindled. During these times the Chamacoco turn to the fruit of a consistently generous vine called *kapyla*. This is a term they translate as "wild bean." The women play a fundamental role on these thankless occasions: they are the ones responsible for gathering the noble wild beans and then toasting or boiling them, feeding their people as they wait out the bad times and look forward to better ones. This myth takes place during one such painful period. Every day the men would go off into the woods, only to return with a skinny peccary or some scraps of honey that could barely satisfy the needs of the populous village. The season of the carob trees had not yet arrived; the palms and cacti bore meager fruit. One morning, the women set off to search for food. Among them was a young widow who fell behind the group, distracted, or perhaps even amused. She tried to catch up to the other women when she realized she had lost them but could not find their trail. In her disorientation she stumbled upon what was left of a dried-up stream and spied a thick eel (*wäart*) half sleeping in the mud. She placed it in a ceramic pot and took it home to feed her two sons. When the time came, however, she could not bring herself to cook it. She found herself seduced by the eel's shape, which reminded her of the best parts of her dead husband, and decided to return it to the estuary. From then on, every morning when she left with the group of women to search for food, she invented some excuse to fall behind and retrace her steps back to the fish, gazing for hours at its opulence. It seems the fish somehow became aware of her desire and that it coincided with his. In any case, it did not take long for them to become lovers. Thus, while the other women searched for wild beans, she lingered in the pleasure of her furtive encounters with the eel. Every morning she found her way to the termite's nest where her unusual lover hid and tapped on it lightly. At her signal, the eel emerged through a hole and—taking human form or not, depending on the versions—consoled the privations of widowhood.

So that her sons would not become suspicious about the apparent failures of her expeditions, the widow began to feed them eggs provided by the *wäart* that she disguised as wild beans. "Mother," they protested, "these don't taste like the others." She responded that those were the only *kapyla* she could find, that that they were not yet ripe but that, given the times of scarcity, it was not the moment to be finicky. Her arguments, repeated each morning in slightly different tones and variations, did not convince her sons, however, who decided to follow and spy on her. In this manner they discovered the secret of her bestial affairs and the deception of the bitter food they had had to consume every day. The next day they informed their mother they were going out to hunt anteaters. They reached the eel's dwelling before dawn and killed it easily with their *noshikó*.

Luciano's version introduces a twist at this point. The youths discover the intimacies of their mother with the eel (*pöso,* for the Tomáraho) at the urgings of their uncle, the brother of their dead father. The three men plot together and pretend to go off hunting. They return with the dead eel, which they then roast and give to the woman to eat. As soon as she finishes eating, her brother-in-law asks maliciously: "Did you enjoy your lover again?" Crazed (and this is where the two versions coincide again), the twice-widowed woman runs off in search of the eel and when she does not find it and confirms its death, decides to punish her sons severely.

To avoid their mother's rage the youths flee into the woods for days, and for days she pursues them screaming. She has lost her mind and nothing can stop her. One night, the youths discover a huge carandá tree whose uppermost branches seem to touch the stars. "We will hide in the *póorch,* in the sky," says the older brother. When they reach the top they discover that they are still far from the darkened vault (in those times the sky was still low, but not sufficiently low to be touched effortlessly). The youth, who had shamanistic abilities, begs the tree to grow. The carandá shoots up so suddenly it almost knocks them to the ground. It stretches its trunk and branches to the sky but cannot reach it. "Once more," begs the youth. The tree strains as far as it can and finally brushes its highest leaves against the sky's smooth surface. The shaman apprentice begs the sky to open its gates. Graciously the sky agrees and, helped up by his younger brother, the boy climbs into the sky. The second fugitive tries to follow, with the aid of his older brother who now pulls from above, but the crack in the sky is already collapsing (or the tree is already shrinking, according to another account). In any case, he is not able to climb in completely and one of his legs is caught in the crack and hangs there in the sky. (According to other versions the sky, which until then had lingered close to the earth, begins to distance itself due to the pleas of the older son, who wants a greater distance from their mother.)

No one knows if the mother is at this point still driven by a desire for vengeance or by her concern for her sons, but she continues, in any case, to wander through the plains, disturbing the woods with her cries, until at dawn she follows a set of tracks to the foot of the carandá. She is disconcerted. The footsteps lead to the tree but the branches above are now empty. Exhausted, she looks for water to drink and when she bends over a nearby spring she catches the reflection of her son's leg still dangling far above. It seems that at that time humans did not know the power of images: the woman believes that her son's foot is at the bottom of the spring. Desperate, she plunges into the water determined to grasp it and save her son from drowning. When she discovers nothing but mud at the bottom of the pool, she looks up to the tree again and spies, far away, her son's foot kicking in the sky.

The woman knows she cannot reach the foot because by now there is a great distance between the tree and the sky, which has closed forever. At this point in the tale, we discover that she is a character with shamanic powers and has dominion over the birds. She calls on a flock of birds to fly up and free her trapped son. The small birds try to obey her but find themselves incapable of flying as high as the task requires. The woman then orders a succession of other species of birds to complete the mission—each capable of flying farther and higher than the previous kind. After they all fail, the woman has recourse again to the smaller birds until she has finally exhausted the long list of birds that soar the populated airs of the Ishir firmament that now quivers with the wings of the birds sweeping up and down, some vigorous, some languorous, some wide and sweeping, others quick and nervous.

But the woman has one last weapon. She calls upon Chyrpylá, the hawk, whose powers she knows and appreciates: they are supernatural forces, shamanic energies. Once present, the bird—called Híimi by the Tomáraho—

gives her instructions. "You must arrange various different ceramic bowls on the ground because we must not waste a drop of your son's blood. If we lose his blood then you shall never be able to bring him back." She does as the bird tells her and waits beside the bowls, her eyes riveted to the sky above. The hawk takes to the air with great speed and in a single bound reaches the boy. He tries to tear him out of the sky that has trapped the youth, cleaving his sharp beak into the hanging leg and pulling with all his strength. The mother sees a shower of thin drops of blood falling from the sky and, as indicated, she places the vessels under each trickle. But it is not enough and the last bloody thread falls softly on the earth forming the briefest of pools. The mother knows then that she has lost her son. She looks up and sees that he has disappeared into the sky and that the hawk flies back with only his leg in his beak.

Unable to resign herself to having a mere scrap of her son in her possession, she throws the leg aside only to see a huge lake spring up. When she approaches the vessels of blood she is astonished. Each one gives off a different and unknown shine: the colors have appeared. The mother calls Chyrpylá and asks him to gather all the birds that tried to help her so that they will be anointed with the tones of her son's blood, each according to its own choice. She took the soft thick feather of the ostrich, dipped it in black (*wys*) and, using it as a paintbrush, painted the body of the crow, which had been colorless like everything else. The stork asked for white and other birds chose blues and greens. Still others were brave enough to ask for the flaming reds and intense yellows. There were even some who began to ask for a mixture of colors. The last was the hawk, who wanted to be dressed in a dramatic counterpoint of black and white.

The birds were no longer the same. Now there were differences among them. So the woman began to classify them according to their new colors. Then she separated them according to the height they had reached and the effort each of them had put into the task. And finally, she took into consideration their size, where they built their nests, the food they ate, and their song (hoarse croaks or piercing shrieks, dissonant trills, chirps or harmonious warbles). After ordering the birds, a task that took many days, she began to give them precise instructions on how to behave according to their characteristics. Thus she determined the habits and behaviors that govern each ornithological species, their techniques for obtaining food, building better nests, soaring higher, and avoiding the dangers of hunts.

"Now," said Chyrpylá, "she is the Mistress of the Birds." Now she herself is a bird. She is called Póhopó and her face is always turned up toward the sky. Her sharp, accusatory gaze is fixed on the sun when it rises and falls, at the moment the night (her time) begins and ends. She is the *urutaú,* a solitary and nocturnal bird.[3] Her sons stayed in the sky, converted into the benign children of Osasërö. They are birds of the soft rain. The lake that sprouted from the leg of the younger son is called Ymykytä. It is located between the places known today as Kyrkyrbi (Filadelfia) and Nymych-wert (Fortín Bogado), which literally means "red earth," one hundred kilometers west of Puerto Olimpo.

Variations

In different Ebytoso versions of this myth the details shift, some episodes are added, others subtracted. The youths are able to reach the sky because it lowers itself, and not because the tree stretches upwards. The sky opens its doors because it is wounded by the arrows they shoot, or because they strike it with their slingshots. Some Tomáraho versions exhibit more significant differences. One of them coincides with that of the Ebytoso, except that the transgression with the eel and the flight that culminates in the color of the birds is attributed to her husband.

Other Tomáraho versions split the myth into two disconnected tales. According to the first one once the fish is killed, the woman, marked by Chamacoco mourning (the head shaved and the face dirtied with paint and tears), submerges herself in the muddy lake, her lover's homeland, and spawns torrents of eels that soon churn its waters: they are the fruits of their condemned union. Before becoming an eel herself, she classifies her future offspring, which she will forever protect. The second narration refers to a widow who looses all her children in an epidemic. After burying them she wanders in the woods, cursing the entire planet at the top of her lungs. In her uncontrollable pain she loses her mind and kills a child of her own community. He is the son of her brother-in-law, whom she envies for having escaped the ravages of the fatal disease. Turned into a shaman (because of her extreme dementia? for having crossed a threshold in her pain?), she summons all the birds, classifies them, and then paints them with the blood of her victim. The parrots rush to the front of the line and are rewarded with the vigor of the colors that flow first from the innocent body. As the flow of blood wanes its tones also fade and the mad painter zealously tries to hoard her materials, distributing the blood in lines and spots instead of painting the whole birds; but even so the flow of blood comes to an end and loses the power to generate color. This is why white birds exist. Distributed into their ornithological varieties, the woman, driven by an uncontainable classificatory impulse, continues to order the various animal species until she gets to the microbes that transmit diseases. After gathering them together and assigning names and functions, she commands them to spread over the world and infect it with their fatal powers: "Go forth on this planet I have cursed, and fill it with plagues and ills." She is called Pyly Lata, The Mistress of the Epidemics.

Commentaries

Colors

This myth reveals the importance of colors for classification. Their diversity and vigorous presence, and their ability to mark things (emphasizing or deemphasizing them) turn them into privileged taxonomic referents. Colors allow the Ishir to distribute, separate, compare, discriminate, valorize. They establish limits, they delineate. Colors arrive with symbols, with the capacity to distinguish and assign value, with the ability to fear and desire; they arrive with the bodies of the gods who rose up from the ground gleaming with unusual vibrations. But they also sprout from the body of humans. And this opens up another path to access culture (to access the sign, classification, value, beauty).

For the Chamacoco, human experience reaches its culmination both through the sacred and through the shamanic. In one case, a territory opens up beyond human reach; in the other, it is a question of a space founded on the hidden depths of the human condition. There is also a third landscape whose subdivisions are marked chromatically. There, society paints women and men to differentiate them, classifying them according to gender, age, profession, or clan. For this reason—we will return to this shortly—the arts of body painting and featherwork take place in three very different (albeit connected) dimensions: the religious, the shamanic, and the social. And for this reason there is no contradiction between the fact that colors arrived with the anábsoro in the Great Myth and flowed out of human blood in this myth.

The Primitive People

Colors also mark differences between different cultural moments. The informants agree that the narrated events took place during the time of the *ishnanio,* the primitive people, dwellers in the days before the coming of the anábsoro. This was a colorless time in which nature and human beings existed but were misty, as if seen through a veil that dampened the intensity of things and blurred their profiles. It was not a full existence. Men and women hunted, gathered, ate, copulated, and died mechanically, like sleepwalkers: without the flash or shock of meaning, without the force or shadows of color. Cordeu describes this state well. "Without a doubt," he affirms, "the tales do not refer to an *ex nihilo* origin of things and qualities, but, instead, to the emergence of outlines against the backdrop of a reality that until then had proceeded in a kind of intermediate tonality in which everything already existed. Thus death and old age existed, but not forever; space existed but it had not yet displayed its essential articulations. Colors existed, but mixed together into a morass of grey" (Cordeu 1990, 175). Both the anábsoro and shaman mythology presuppose the existence of a primal time that is undifferentiated and neutral. This time slowly acquires meaning not as a result of the action of creationist deities but of civilizing gods or cultural heroes that order, regulate, classify, explain, and name. They establish symbols and, with them, a space to censure shadows and designate colors.

The Colors of the Sky

The changes in the color of the sky also signify cultural changes. Palacio Vera and Luciano, and later Ojeda among the Ebytoso, tell me a tale about the colors of the sky. Originally the sky's tones were neutral (greyish) and hung low over the earth. What we call sky is, in truth, the hard shell at the bottom of the sky. The sky begins farther above and offers a bountiful supply of different kinds of honey. The honey, moreover, is easily accessible: the bees that guard it are tame and it can be extracted from tree trunks with little effort. The cosmic tree, in this case a white quebracho tree,[4] linked these Edenic lands with the earth so that humans could easily climb up to the fertile celestial spheres, gorge themselves, and even stock up and make their way down, laden with abundant riches.

Now the figure of the shamanic widow appears on scene. She had a daughter whom she cared for with excessive zeal. It often happened that when her daughter tried to cross over to the sky to gather honey the other children of the village, perching at the top of the tree, did not allow her to pass and handed her instead bitter, empty honeycombs. This happened so many times that on one occasion the shaman, furious, turned herself into a termite and gnawed at the tree until it fell over. (Here, another Ebytoso tale works with the characteristic figures of the Chamacoco imaginary: the men hid the secret of honey from the women until a female shaman discovers the truth and, in vengeance, knocks down the tree.)

Once the tree that mediated the earth and sky has fallen, the gates of the sky are closed and it distances itself from the earth. It also changes colors. First, it becomes yellow, like the sun. For the Tomáraho this change marks the beginning of a solar phase: once the sky has drifted away Deich (the sun) descends to earth, catalogues things in their order, and classifies people as nations. Next, in the company of his younger brother the moon, he begins a cycle of terrestrial adventures. Without referring to the sun, the Ebytoso also speak of classifications at this point: the widow who knocked down the tree subdivides the population into segments; each community separates and becomes different. She herself leaves with her daughter and founds the community of the Wyrhiasó, another Ishir group. But the greatest separation occurs between the inhabitants of the earth and those who were collecting honey in the sky and remain marooned there. Some of the captives became creatures of rain and storm; they are the birds of Osaserö. Others acquired star-like features: harried by the great darkness that dominated the upper regions, they fabricated candles with beeswax and filled the sky with their small lights. But such small lights were insufficient to orient themselves amidst the darkness and the men/stars, with voices of wind, began to clamor for stronger and more lasting lights and built great bonfires whose smoke filled the firmament with clouds. It was then, some say, that the sky changed colors inside: it was filled with the glow of the fires and became yellow. Every alteration requires compensation: from then on, plagues exist. For this reason, even today, when the sky is yellowish the Ishir must paint themselves with two lines on each cheekbone (the women, one) and one on their forehead to avoid the sickness announced by the skies.

Susnik says that the closing of the sky, its distancing, the transformation of its colors, and even the flood were produced by the death of the eel (1995, 63). The figure of this great "cosmic cataclysm," which founds the yellow strata of the firmament, is projected in the idea of cultural change in the world (provoked on another level by the anábsoro). The stars correspond to the frosty glow of the *pasyparak,* jewels worn by the primitive men (or killers of the eel) who were stranded in the sky and suffered its cold. This stellar dwelling place, where cold flames burn in vain, later becomes the domain of the great shamans of the Pleiades, who have shining eyes and the power to manipulate the brilliant, frigid power of the stars and promote the alliance between the star/men and the terrestrial Ishir (Susnik 1995, 221, 224).

Cordeu has a reference to another myth about the colors of the sky.[5] During a ritual, the men whirled over their heads great bundles of feathers, which constitute the ceremonial trappings of the Ishir: one is red and is called *kadjuwerta;* the other is black (or blue black) and is known as *kadjuwysta.* At one point, they lost control over the caraguata ropes that tethered the feathers and the energetic impulse that the rite prescribes made them fly off and dye the sky, which, from then on, can show itself drenched in either black or red, according to the time of day or the vicissitudes of climate.

According to the explanation given me by Flores Balbuena when I asked him about this tale, the reddish or black tones of the sky were brought on by the primitive people. When they became prisoners of the sky, they had to light great bonfires to ward off the cold and illuminate the somber corners of the sky before the advent of the yellow lights. The splendor of the fires dyed the sunsets and sunrises with red; their billowing smoke formed the dark clouds.

The Colors of Blood

Blood—metaphor of elemental potential; brilliant, obscure cipher of creation and death; intense image in itself—becomes the paradigm of color. It colors the birds and marks them with difference and beauty. The vivifying force of its flow is what bestows color: the parrot, the first bird to rush up to the shaman/widow, obtains the most beautiful shades because it is bathed in the most condensed and radiant energy, that which is most closely linked to the beginning of life. This is why the colors of the parrot reflect the conjunction between the yellow, the nocturnal, and the blue strata of the sky (Susnik 1995, 224). And this is why the presence of parrots announces the fissure between one cycle and the next. According to some versions of the myth, the birds that were painted with the blood that only feebly flowed out of the body are those whose colors are more faded, and so on until they are white (which is, in the context of this tale, a non-color, a color without internal energy, without sap).

For Chamacoco thought, the power of blood (the *woso*) is the organic ground of the human; death happens when its power has dried up. The death of an old person is considered an ordinary event while that of a young man signifies an unfortunate perturbation in the natural order and presupposes the intervention of an adverse power. Wioho, the anábser healer, can bring novices back to life as long as their vital fluids are still fresh; the new generation of women spring up out of the flesh and blood of Arpylá, the doe/woman; Chyrpylá, the hawk, warns the mother that she will not be able to recover her son if his blood is not saved in the vessels. Blood also marks shamanic power: the great Osíwuro of shining eyes, the masters of the Pleiades, mark the neck of a new shaman with a drop of blood, and the *konsaha* who sings until his throat bleeds demonstrates great shamanic ability (Susnik 1995, 224–25).

The Trees

The carandá of the myth of the colored birds, the white quebracho tree of the tale of the change in the sky, and the guayacan in the Arpylá episode are all variations of a characteristic figure that studies on religion call the "cosmic tree," which is related to the motif of the *axis mundi*. The tree is an archetype of nature and its link to other dimensions. The image is enriched by the phallic connotations of a firm trunk that is deeply rooted in the earth, ascends vertically and opens its branches to the sky; it is laden with associations of a natural source that renovates itself cyclically, that produces food and flowers, shade and wood, and that shelters birds and beasts in its leaves. This exemplary model is linked to the concept of the pillar that sustains and retains the sky, the stairway that leads to its heights, and the channel that communicates with subterranean worlds. The *samu'u*,[6] the primal tree from which the fish sprouted, is planted like a brimming metaphor in the middle of the *harra*. The theme of the tree's fall is associated in part with the strong image in Chamacoco culture of the cycle that has been consummated. Susnik writes that the taboo of eating armadillo meat does not obtain for old Ishir because it is assumed that "soon their blood will dry and they will fall like trees" (1995, 62).

The Eel

A variety of serpentine fish are regularly and indiscriminately called "eels." However, according to Susnik, in order to analyze this myth it is necessary to distinguish between a common eel and the fish called *Lepidosiren*, which, however much it may resemble the eel, belongs to a different species entirely. The myth refers specifically to this fish. In a personal communication, Jorge Escobar Argaña explains the difference between the eel (*Cymbranchus marmoratum,* called *mbusú* in Guaraní) and the *Lepidosiren* (*mbusú capitán* in Guaraní). The latter is the only instance of a fish with lungs, rudimentary legs, and a long body. In times of drought it burrows in dry mud and can survive for a long time. According to Susnik the flesh of the common eel is one of the basic daily foods of the Ishir and is not subject to any restrictions (1995, 63). The flesh of the *Lepidosiren*, however, is considered a delicacy and is strictly taboo, especially for women, and can only be eaten by very old widowers. The prohibition has a mythic foundation: the fish corresponds to a metamorphosis of the *pasyparak,* the crown of feathers that distinguishes the adult man and pertains thus to the sexual universe of men. Moreover, the Ishir associate this fish with an erect penis, not only for its form but because any touch excites its genitals, causing a prominent erection. Lastly, the eel is usually linked to the *kapyla* since both are considered an important reserve of food in times of lack (Susnik 1995, 73). Both constitute the masculine and feminine sides of the image of "dependable food." Just as the man who successfully fishes such eels gains a reputation as a hard worker, the woman who is good at gathering and storing the dried *kapyla* beans acquires great prestige in Chamacoco society as a skillful and farsighted woman.

THE SECOND MYTH: THE ORIGIN OF RED FEATHERS

A woman who was menstruating went to gather the caraguata plant to extract the fibers that are used in all the materials woven by the Chamacoco. As she looked for a good specimen she noticed a plant that displayed the reddest of flowers. Seduced by the beauty of its reddish shine she strongly desired to pick it and, stepping on both leaves, she crouched down in order dig it up with her *alybyk,* her digging stick. As she did so she felt the flower penetrate her genitals, which had been left exposed as she crouched. She leaped up but found that the flower remained buried within her. Only its red tips were visible, protruding like pubic hairs. She heard the lightest of murmurs, a dry sound, like the crunching of dried leaves at a distance. Uneasy, she decided not to tell anyone. That night her husband, eager for some intimacy, tried to touch her but she pushed him away brusquely. Perturbed by the event, the woman became withdrawn and solitary. She began to acquire shamanic powers. The next night she received her first revelation: in her dream she spoke with the Master of the Caraguata. She asked him for instructions regarding her strange state, but the apparition of Nekyr Balut was still confused and could not be deciphered: it flickered in and out in brief flashes.

Her husband was a powerful sky shaman. As he noticed his wife's repeated rejections, the strange, faraway look in her eyes and the profound silences that enveloped her, he realized that something serious was happening to her. One afternoon he blew softly on her face and made her sleep deeply. He carefully lifted her caraguata skirt and in place of her genitals saw a red, thorny, and shiny flower opened between her legs. He grabbed his *potytak* (powerful sucking tube) and began to vacuum the tips of this unexpected star that moved lightly as if it were alive. He ripped out some of the silky red plumes but a rustling noise from within the body of his wife prompted him to slide the *potytak* whistle inside her and suction again. He extracted a great quantity of feathers and, amazed by their reddish shades, began crafting various crowns (*pasyparak*) and bracelets, anklets and necklaces. When he finished making the feathered ornaments he tucked them away inside the rolled mat. This bundle is called the *lëbe* and is a powerful shamanic instrument; its interior protects the condensed power of feathers. The man hung it on a hook and left the cabin toward the *tobich* where the ceremony was being prepared.

A strange feeling of silence awoke the woman and even before she checked she knew that the feathers had been ripped from her body. She felt her body and confirmed that her secret had been violated. Furious, she began to search for the stolen, prodigious fruit, the origin of her new powers. She found the *lëbe* and took it. This was a serious transgression: no woman can touch the powerful bundle of feathers. In the *tobich* her husband felt a chill. He asked his nephew, a novice, to go home and bring him the feathers. The man sprang home like a deer, as the *wetern* must when they are given an errand to run during their period of initiation. When he arrived, he found the woman standing in the doorway. She was quiet, her gaze distant, and she hugged the *lëbe* against her body, clearly unprepared to let it go. The nephew pretended to be exhausted by his run. And as soon as he fell to the ground, seemingly fainting, and she released the token to help him, he grabbed it and ran away with the speed of the young hart, as is proper of an initiate.

The woman followed him driven by her rage but when she reached the path to the *tobich* she stopped. Not even in the most extreme of situations is an Ishir woman allowed to cross into the forbidden grounds. She left, trembling with indignation and planning her revenge: she was determined to kill anyone who used the feathers that had sprouted from her womb. She stationed herself among the women and children who surrounded the *harra*. Various anábsoro appeared onstage with their entourages, their cries, their strange movements, and their peculiar similarity to giant birds. When Ashnuwerta, the Great Mistress of Red Radiance, appeared, the woman recognized the red feathers crowning the head of the goddess, circling her wrists and neck, adorning her waist and ankles. Her husband, who was performing as the deity, saw his wife through the peephole in the mask: saw her hatred and feared her vengeance. The woman decided to wait for the moment of the *tsaat* in the ritual, the culmination, which includes nearly all of the participants.

Both took their positions. Converted into *pylik,* the pure impulse to fly, he lifted himself up to the sky (his domain) to seek reinforcements and withstand the onslaught of conjugal fury. It was the moment of the *tsaat* now and the stage was full. Before the third and final round the woman, converted now into pure destructive force, opened her legs and from her innards shot a ray of mortal flames that charred the actors and covered the circle with dark smoke and incandescent whirlwinds. She called her two daughters and instructed them to act as her shamanic assistants. She blew on the oldest (*webiyota*) and turned her into a chaja (*towhä*).[7] She did the same with the younger (*uhurrota*) and turned her into an owl (*tohöta*). Both are sentinel birds: they voice their warning when any enemy is near. Next she submerged herself into a lake near the village and, according to the power given to her in dreams by the Master of the Caraguata, she turned it into a boiling lake of flames capable of striking dead anyone who dared approach the waters.

Her husband, the shaman, turned to the *póorch pëhet* or *pycht,* the first celestial stratum, which is accessible to sky shamans (beyond this region begins the *póorch-iet o wys,* the deepest darkness). Osasërö Balut lives in this region.

Ishir man representing the *anábser* Ho-Ho in a ceremonial scene. He is wearing body paint, a crown of jaguar skin, a mask of vegetable fibers, and a large feather headdress. Potrerito, 1989. (Photo by Ticio Escobar.)

He is the Master of the Birds of Rain and Storm (these beings were originally the men stranded in the sky). The birds of Osasërö are classified into four kinds: the Tenhía are the birds of electric storms, laden with potent rays; the Echyrbo are the birds of light showers; the Botsyrbo command torrential waters; the Kush-kusho command the hurricanes. The Osasërö are divided internally into fractions that oppose each other: the birds of lightning are opposed to those of the showers and the birds of torrential rain are opposed to those of hurricanes. The tensions between these groups, and the various battles that arise between them, disturb the sky and fill the firmament with lightning. On occasion storks can also lend their aid to the Master of the Osasërö, but they are not permanent fixtures among his armies. Generally, they come to defend the birds of rain against the birds of storm. The Ishir know the omens that are brought by the flight of these birds; when the Kush-kusho, a variety of crow, flies in a certain manner it is announcing hurricanes; if it flies north the storm comes from the south, and vice versa. It is likewise with the other birds: through a strange code of cries and movements, they announce the proximity of rains and storms that shamans of certain categories will try to attract or divert with the power of their powerful songs and feathers.

The birds agreed to help the shaman. In the event of an attack the Osasërö act like fearsome warriors; they gallop on celestial horses (*kabíwa*) or captain clouds ("like airplanes," Clemente says), firing fatal blazes ("like machine guns," he explains). On earth, each one of the birds/daughters watched the east and west, vigilantly, since the worst winds always come from the north or south. The shaman advanced rapidly amidst a storm heading northwest. His throng of rainy clouds concealed white swallows (Echyrbo) and black swallows (Botsyrbo). But the chaja and the owl detected the movement and warned their mother with their cries. She sprang from the flaming lake and liquidated her enemies with an onslaught of lightning bolts. The shaman, in the shape of a swallow, returned to the domain of Osasërö and prepared another assault organized around a different strategy.

A furious storm of winged horsemen charged galloping from the west surrounded by dark clouds, flashes, and gales of wind. The birds of hurricanes and lightning that accompanied this army covered the earth in a darkness only broken by shining flashes, thundering howls, ferocious winds. The Osasërö already knew the location of the watchful sentries and the movement of their mother. They dove from the sky, skimming the plains, soaring up abruptly and then, subdivided in four groups, began a crazed game of crisscrossing currents. The birds/daughters screeched and the flaming mother leapt up from her lake but they were disconcerted by the unpredictable whims of the winds, which knocked down trees and houses without nearing the lake, besieging it from symmetrical and opposite sides. While the Kush-kusho inverted their normal movement and furrowed the earth, producing whirlwinds and smoke, the Tenhía flew at a great altitude, covered in thick shrouds of darkness, which concealed their glare. They seemed to be reflected in images of lightning and to repeat themselves in the pure echo of nearby thunder. Then they exchanged positions: the course of their attacks crossed so quickly that it was impossible for the sentinels to clearly track this muddle of comings and goings, refractions and unstable postures. Confused, the mother emerged at an untimely moment and before she had the chance to kill her attackers, a deafening swarm swooped down on her and defeated her in a loud explosion that calmed the lake and extinguished its fires. The Osasërö birds grabbed the lightning that still beat in the charred body and carried it to the skies (inside it, the spirit of the woman still lives). The daughters remained forever in the shape of birds who announce important events. The owl and chaja are powerful birds, and young Ishir cannot eat their omen laden meats. The lake in these events, says Flores Balbuena, is called Lëbyte Ouch ("site of the *lëbbe*") and is located in Madrejoncito, near the border with Bolivia. According to Ojeda and Clemente López the region where these events took place is called Schíchmi.

Commentaries

Times

Unlike the first and third myths I discuss in this chapter, the events of this tale seem to take place not in primitive times but in some moment after the great cultural change produced by the coming of the anábsoro. The incident that involves the performance of the gods in the ceremonial circle is clear in this regard and occupies a central place in the mythic plot. It is true that the temporality of myths obeys the logic proper to them and should be understood rhetorically, rather than analyzed in discursive terms; nonetheless it is important to preserve the post-anábsoro location of these events. This means that the protagonists of this myth are not the Ishnanios ("ignorant of ritual and norm"), nor the Ishir Pórowo ("the first ones") initiated by the gods. They are Ishir men and women who know the interdictions and taboos and the meaning of cult and ceremony.

There is another distinction between mythic planes I would like to emphasize: this tale takes place—as do the other tales in this chapter that refer to plumage—in the dimension of humans and shamans, not of gods as in the Great Myth. The Great Myth referred to the great transformation provoked by the gods and the necessity for a cyclical representation of the time of foundation; its meaning is therefore religious and transcendental. The myth of the colors and feathers, however, takes place on an existential, human level and involves shamanic, terrestrial, and cosmic categories. It is true that the anábsoro make an appearance in the myth of the red feathers, yet they appear not as the gods themselves but as their representations. To emphasize this fact the tale allows for a certain rhetorical license. The husband of the protagonist appears doubled into two roles: as the shaman and as the actor who interprets Ashnuwerta. (The feathers displayed by the goddess figure are feathers of human origin that imitate divine characteristics.)

Shamans

Shamans are the protagonists of these myths: they are the mediators between a phenomenal world and the forces that animate the myths from inside or out; forces that manifest themselves in unusual, disturbing, and beautiful ways. There are two fundamental figures of the shamanic world in this myth: the assistants and the battle between shamans. The shamans rely on the aid of specific instruments: *lëbe*, artifacts made of feathers, staffs, maracas, tubes, and wooden whistles. They rely as well on other beings, generally birds: in this myth the assistants are the chaja, the owl, and the birds of Osasërö. Susnik says that the institution of animal assistants corresponds to the projection of an ideal of human/animal companionship, which lies at the base of the Chamacoco's cosmic vision (1957, 91).

The motif of the battle between adversarial shamans is a common one in Chamacoco narratives and is related to the Ishir concept of a binary opposition resolved through conflict. Basically, the *konsaho* battle during trances, flights of ecstasy, and dreams. The opposing shamans face each other, surrounded by their retinue of animal assistants, and test their terrible powers against each other until one is defeated. The battles, narrated in meticulous details and epic tones, take place through metamorphoses, ambushes, violent assaults, deceits, and betrayals; and insofar as they involve the shamans' corresponding jurisdictions (sky, earth, river, etc.), they unleash apocalyptic commotions of natural forces.

Before fighting, each of the contenders performs a ritual of fasting and song, and lays down to sleep. "Their powers fight above while they sleep and sometimes convulse," says Flores Balbuena. "The loser does not arise: he wants to awaken, and recover the spirit captured by the winner but the winner traps him in his *pamune* (artifact made of ostrich feathers). The loser sees his own body adorned and painted for the ritual of death. He sees his family cry and his widow shear her head, but only after they have buried his corpse will his spirit be returned to him. It is now pure *dykyshybich,* a ghost that wanders silently toward Osypyte, the Land of the Dead."

"The defeated shaman really dies," various listeners assure me. In the case of a confrontation between different communities, their fate is determined by the triumph or defeat of their respective shamans: a village feels itself victorious and free of threat if its shaman prevails over the enemy shaman.

Birds, Skies, and Shamans

Against the backdrop of the essential importance of birds in the Chamacoco imaginary, this myth underscores two of their characteristics: the mediating, prophetic character of birds, and their links with cosmic forces and shamanic dimensions. On the one hand, the birds act as a nexus between the human world and different natural and supernatural dimensions whose dangers they understand. This faculty is expressed in part through the motif of the bird with superhuman ability to foretell or perceive danger and warn the Ishir. Thus Susnik says that the woodpecker and owl sound the alarm when an enemy advances, the hawk communicates deaths in the wood, the owl obliges warriors to change their path, and other birds warn of diseases and other mishaps (1984–1985, 47).

On the other hand, the birds represent important mythic and shamanic figures. The Ishnanios, the primitive Ishir who were marooned in the sky after the fall of the cosmic tree, were split into two groups: one of them turned into the star-men, the other into Osasërö, birds of rains and storms. The link between this latter group and shamans emerges from another myth told to me in different moments by Ojeda Benítez and Clemente López, which I will briefly summarize.

The Master of the Osasërö has a son called Lapishé who, mounted on storm clouds or winds in the form of horses, helps his father command the rains that fall on the earth. In one of these incursions, a ray of lightning he let loose struck a white quebracho tree. As it crashed down the tree fell on Lapishé, pinning him to the ground. Two days passed before a hunter finally came upon him and freed him from the tree. Seeing he was wounded the hunter brought him home, cured his wounds and offered him food, shelter, and familial affection. Lapishé became close to the sons of the hunter and treated them as brothers, so much so that he eventually shared his secret with them: if he lifted his eyebrows or pressed on his stomach he could shoot off lightning and bring down torrential rain. The two boys, however, proved untrustworthy and soon all the village youths began to tease the son of the Master of Osasërö, pulling on his eyebrows and punching him in the stomach to force him to demonstrate his gifts. Irritated, Lapishé placed his adoptive brothers in a tree in order to save them, and summoned a flood that killed all those who had mistreated him. He sent for a horse of clouds or wind and flew off to the kingdom of his father. After a while he regretted his action; he remembered the affection he had developed for mortals and he returned to the earth. He initiated the hunter in the shamanic arts and provided him with techniques to bring drowned men back to life and songs to call down beneficial rains and divert bad winds. He also taught him how to craft shoes out of the hide of the anteater (*láhagua*), which protects hunters from thorns and snakes.

From that moment on, the shamans of the birds of Osasërö exist (they are part of the category of sky shamans). With their songs, these shamans control flocks of birds or the squad of winged riders who, flying or galloping, bring rains and unleash hurricanes. They try to reverse weather, calming torrential furies and deflecting the rage of lightning. Lightning bolts fall on quebrachos, carobs, or palm trees, knocking them down and stealing their powers, which are then offered to the shamans to nurture their own powers. There are shamans who fly in dreams with the birds and try to help their communities and curse those of their rivals. The figure of the *Ndyhypyk áhanak* (literally, "foreign shaman") is one who destroys a village with floods and cyclones and who can only be stopped by another shaman who confronts him. Sometimes enemy shamans take advantage of internal oppositions between the birds of rains and storms and produce terrible aerial battles that disturb the skies. On certain, but infrequent occasions, defeated shamans lose not their life but their sanity. Crazed, they advance with their retinue of birds circling like tops, and spinning off whirlwinds or waterspouts depending on the whims of their maddened fancy. These crazy storms are called *nsyky-námërwa*.

This myth seems to culminate in the defeat of the female shaman, a defeat that is perhaps not definitive and that can later be turned into victory.

During a shamanic battle, the real triumph is determined by the capture of the enemy soul, which wanders lost until it can find its place in the Osypyte, the Land of the Dead. In this case, the shaman's flaming spirit is taken to the sky and to the territory of the Osasërö. She will often return from there, briefly illuminating the rays of the celestial birds, benefiting communities with benign rains or harming them with uncontrolled storms.

Man and Woman: Feathers and Caraguata

Using feathers is a privilege reserved for men. They hunt the birds, pluck the feathers, craft the ornaments, and wear them. Women only contribute by making the supports out of caraguata fibers. Lately I have seen some Tomáraho female shamans briefly displaying the trembling sign of the gods, a prerogative of male shamans and cipher of men: discrete white heron feathers briefly wisp over their ears or timidly adorn their necks. I have even seen them brandish maracas, instruments that are usually off-limits to women. These are, however, recent and rare instances.

In contrast, the use of the caraguata is exclusive to women. Female labor is valorized by its two contributions to Ishir culture and economy: gathering fruits for familial subsistence and manufacturing fabrics with the fibers of the caraguata plant. These fabrics, as we will see, cover a wide spectrum of basic necessities that begin with the quotidian and culminate in the Great Ceremony. The caraguata links women not only with hard and useful manual labor—rewarded by a husband with the best hearts of palm and the sweetest honey—but also with the production of the paradigmatic cloth that envelops, shelters, hides, and sustains the most basic of activities. The work with the caraguata plant leads to other important figures through the metonymic detour of the female *alybyk* (a digging stick in the shape of an oar). Susnik writes that women are idealized, not directly through the caraguata, but through the *alybyk,* which signifies both the activity of gathering as well as the valor of the woman who uses this instrument as a weapon to defend herself on her incursions into the woods. It also symbolizes female camaraderie: the *ágalo,* the institution of Chamacoco companionship is formalized among women with the exchange of the *alybyk* (Susnik 1995, 73). The *alybyk* is a cipher, finally, of relationships between men and women, a complex knot of categorical oppositions, difficult comparisons, and inverted images. The man is charged with carving the *alybyk,* but once he has surrendered it to a woman he cannot even brush against it.

One of the axes on which the myth I am commenting moves is precisely this conflictual relationship between the masculine and feminine worlds. The antagonism is complex: the caraguata, which is taboo for men, is the origin of the feathers, which are in turn taboo for women. Counterpoised, the interdictions reflect each other.

Women cannot use feathers, cannot touch the *lëbe* (the sheath that guards the shaman's feathers), cannot pass the threshold of the *tobich,* cannot know that the red flames on Ashnuwerta's head are mere earthly feathers, cannot interfere with the ritual performance. Men cannot cohabit with a menstruating woman, cannot enter into contact with the caraguata, cannot touch the digging stick. The violation of any of these restrictions produces a serious disturbance and imbalance that must be repaired. This myth registers an extreme case of transgression of these norms: the woman not only handles the shamanic feathers and interferes with the ceremonial representation but kills the actors of the ritual. A transgression of such magnitude compromises the entire social and natural order: from marital harmony to celestial concord.

For this reason, culture busies itself with instituting complicated schemas to maintain equilibrium. And it does so following the previously described parameters of Chamacoco logic. The terms of opposition are either stabilized through compensations or lead into conflicts. They can switch places, mirror each other convexly, or reach an accord. Furthermore, each of these different options can be combined on unequal planes so that the tensions of one level spill onto another and questions that emerge in one arena are resolved in another.

The oppositions between the place of the man and woman follow this logic. The Great Myth of the anábsoro is already one example of how the counterpoints between confronted positions can work themselves out: the use of deception on both sides (a handy way to move pieces to one's advantage) produces a succession of alternating alliances, altercations, and equilibriums.

For this reason it is difficult to determine fixed positions of dominance or loss. On the one hand, the female position appears to suffer damage and often does in various arenas. Women do not participate in the truth of the Great Secret or in the Great Ceremony, which conceals and dramatizes it. Although women can become shamans theirs is a secondary accession. Female shamans are not allowed to possess a secret true name and must be satisfied with nicknames that do not define them intimately. At times, they appear to be considered mere biological procreators, guarantors of the clan's continuity. They seem to play a merely natural role, in contrast with the status of the male as an agent in the reproduction of culture. Every man that is born occupies the place of a dead being; each woman that is born begins anew (Susnik 1995, 112).

On the other hand, however, women assume hegemonic positions in social and cultural spheres and occupy a predominant site in the mythic text and ritual representation. Let us begin with myth: the principal divinities are female. Ashnuwerta, the supreme deity, is female. The great mother goddesses surrounded by their entourage of daughters are obviously female as well. The very material substance of the human being proceeds from the flesh of a woman (the body of Arpylá) in a sense that clearly transcends the natural biological order and moves in a privileged symbolic key.

With regard to the relationship of women with the ritual, it is true that they do not interpret the anábsoro in the ceremonial circle. Yet, in order to appear in the circle, men must appear in drag: they represent the goddesses dressed as women. The ritual pact makes both men and women complicit in the same silence: the men pretend to be gods and goddesses and the women pretend to believe them. It is difficult, then, to determine who owns the secret in this tricky game of masks and reflections, of double deceits and intersecting fictions. In addition, one must consider that although women do not impersonate divine beings, they participate not only as an active public (an essential counterpart: the only gaze for which the drama exists) but as the protagonists of certain symbolic battles against the men/gods. These battles, which will be narrated later, seek to express and compensate for sexual differences through the considerable weight of symbols.

Some positions of privilege occupied by women in the sociocultural realm also restore a certain balance and compensate for the deficit suffered in other arenas. In this matter I yield to Cordeu, who comments on the equality of masculine and feminine rights in familial, economic, and social domains:

> Thus family authority is monopolized by both husbands and wives and the elders. If, in general, the roles of the father and the old men are very respected in the family hierarchy, it should not be forgotten that the matrilocal foundation of this organization and the importance of the maternal figure in the arrangement of the marriages of daughters, lead to a precise matrilocal organization of familial relations. All the old tales assert the broad sexual free-

dom of women. Even today, according to my informants, this freedom is an acceptable means for young women to ensure the correct behavior of men: any misconduct on the part of the men can be punished by withholding favors. The economic roles of men and women are also given relatively equal value. The products of female labor are as important, perhaps even more important, for the daily diet than those of the hunt. Where there is agriculture, it is the patrimony of women. The distribution of food among the members of the family and other relatives is also the task of women. (Cordeu 1989a, 49)

Baldus (1927, 24–27) enthusiastically refers to (and perhaps exaggerates) this point: "The *tchimitchana* (woman) dominates the husband, father, brothers, and sons."[8] He affirms that the very act of matrimony already places women in an advantageous position because "the husband delivers the first tribute to her and her father must please her." He continues, "Women have power over goods while the man must prepare and defend the path, hunt and fight battles, she walks in tranquility. The man must turn to her for counsel even when he is tired, wounded, or hungry. In the domestic economy she is stronger because, in as much as the man depends on the luck of the hunt, she shepherds the domestic animals and guards the food." "The Chamacoco give their women everything they barter with us or whatever they earn." Baldus concludes that women are intellectually, sexually, and morally superior to men in Chamacoco society.

Reds

I have suggested that the complexity of the encounter between men and women is expressed in part through a causal connection established between terms of opposite signs: paradoxically the caraguata, which cannot be touched by men, gives rise to the feathers, which cannot be touched by women. It does so through the woman's genitals, a fact that underscores incompatibility: on the one hand, it projects the image of childbirth; on the other, it elicits the figure of sexual drives. The shaman desires the stolen sex of his wife just as in the first myth the woman desires the virility suggested by the shape of the eel. As I have argued throughout this chapter, the figure of the feather is always associated to dense ciphers of the social imaginary. Blood is a motif that suggests death and revival, loss and passion. But the color red sparks its own connotations. It suggests blood, of course. But it is also associated with the flash of lightning, the burning of water, the incandescent beauty of the caraguata flower, the intensity of pain and pleasure. This is why red is an attribute of Ashnuwerta: the Mistress of the Red Splendor, the Great "Mother" that favors and condemns; the supreme ally and adversary; the goddess who engages in an affair with an earthly lover, who teaches men about the vulnerability of the anábsoro, who punishes with fury, who (converted into Arpylá, a mortal woman) has sex with all Ishir men and offers her blood for the renewal of human blood.

field notes

Puerto Esperanza, 17 August 1986

Alleging different excuses, Ojeda Benítez has been avoiding the tale of the origin of feathers for several days. Today he finally shares it with me, speaking in the Ishir tongue, although his Guaraní is correct and his Spanish self-assured. Bruno is the translator. This morning he seems vaguely distracted and asks for clarifications every so often. Like all Chamacoco narrations this one is told slowly, with an abundance of even the most minute of details, and dramatized with histrionic gestures and loud voices. We are seated inside the cabin of Clemente, our host, because it is still early and cold outside and a damp mist has blurred the outlines of the dense mass of trees in the nearby forest. The old man begins to talk gravely. He stands up, paces, approaches the fire to pour himself a drink of yerba maté,[9] and gestures affectedly (without losing either the sequence of events, or dramatic effects) to drive away Cristián and the other boys who prowl about the house and laughingly spy through the blackened palm trunks that make up the walls. "This is a tale of ancient shamans and there are almost none left," he says in order to increase his importance. "I dare tell it because I heard it many times from them. This myth has a strong charge ('*un woso*,' I recognize him saying) and if a young man—who does not yet possess the wisdom that comes with age and experience—narrates this myth, chaos can ensue." I clarify that Wylky, Luciano, and Flores Balbuena have already shared the myth with me but that I want to hear his version, which they announced as precise. He surreptitiously disqualifies his predecessors in narration: "Wylky and Luciano are Tomáraho," he says, "and they sometimes confuse the tales. Flores Balbuena is a learned man but I don't know if he knows all the episodes of the myth completely." In fact, the four versions are all exhaustive in detail and differ little in essence. I have organized my own account around Ojeda's version, since it strikes me as the most ordered, and will briefly indicate any differences that exist.

THE THIRD MYTH: THE ORIGIN OF FEATHERS

The Cannibals

A father and son were out hunting with little luck. The sun was setting and they had not yet come upon the anteater whose track they had been following since morning. They had not even found any turtles, and there was little chance of finding peccaries or other game in that region. "Let us at least find some honey to bring to your mother," suggested the father, who was called Anérehet (eagle). They found a honeycomb of dark nectar called *os-ap*, and when the father tried to open it he cut himself deeply with his knife. The blood began to flow quickly and dripped on a pile of dead leaves, forming a dark paste that for some reason caught the attention of the young son. He helped his wounded father, binding his hand with a caraguata cloth and told him: "Return home now. I will try to get more honey and catch up with you soon."

As soon as Anérehet had left the youth crept up to the bloodied leaves, picked them up and brought them to his mouth, anxiously licking them, trying to taste the clotted residue of his father's wound. The taste was unbelievably satisfying and filled him, obsessed him with the feverish desire to taste human flesh. He could think of little else as he walked home. The boy soon caught up to his father and they arrived at the village together where his mother awaited them with a roast pig and heart of palm. He could not bring himself to even look at the food, however, and wrapped himself in an inexplicable silence. After two days his fasting and silence worried his parents, who questioned him over and over to little avail.

The next day one of the cyclical nomadic movements of the Chamacoco began, and the village was moved in search of better game and fruits. "I am not going," the youth said. That was too much. Resorting to threats and then to arguments about familial bonds, the father demanded that his son reveal the cause of his strange grief. "I will tell you if you promise not to condemn me." Once Anérehet had vowed to understand and support his son, the boy told him of the brutal desire that perturbed him: he wanted nothing more than to eat a human body. The father assumed that his son was beset by a passing obsession. But the days came and went and the youth wasted away, wanting neither to move nor eat, and Anérehet finally decided to set out and hunt a human quarry. He arrived that night at the outskirts of the recently established settlement and killed an adolescent who was returning late after having bathed in a river. And he was almost happy to see his son eagerly devour him after days of perverse abstinence. The youth thus slowly became an enthusiastic cannibal as his father submissively satisfied his hunger. Shocked both by her son's monstrous practice and the docile complacency of her husband, Anérehet's wife abandoned her house and sought refuge in the village, which she warned of the danger.

Until now the father had limited himself to procuring the victims for his son, without participating in the wretched feast. But, whether because his will bowed to the growing power of the youth or because he himself desired it, he ceded one day to his son's insistences and tasted the prohibited morsel offered to him. From that day on both engaged in anthropophagy. And as the demand for human flesh rose, the population of the neighboring village began to decrease rapidly. Warned of the danger, the people decided to relocate again. And so began a ferocious persecution through wood and over plain with the itinerant village constantly and closely followed by the assassins who occupied the successively abandoned campsites.

As their habits changed, the two killers changed as well. They felt their bodies slowly changing form as wings of brilliant and hard feathers unfurled. One day they were moved by the desire to fly and, after many attempts and failures, lifted themselves up hesitantly into the air. It was not long before they were flying confidently and swiftly. According to the versions of Ojeda and Flores Balbuena (both Ebytoso) the men crafted their own wings. Tired of ceaseless traveling, they had decided to learn to fly and hunt their quarry like birds of prey. Thus, using clay that they had dried in the sun, the son fastened heron and owl feathers to Anérehet's arms. After running about flapping his arms he was pushed by his son and found himself able to jump a few meters, but the clay broke and the man fell to the earth just as he was taking off. Next they tried stork and eagle feathers with beeswax. They had better luck than their Cretan predecessors and could soon rapidly cross the skies without limits, satisfying their lust for the meat, which had driven them to fly. In this way they established a permanent campsite and left each morning to hunt the miserable villagers whose numbers dwindled and fear grew even as they moved farther and farther away.

The Shaman and Her Grandson

On one occasion they flew over a small group of women gathering food, who began to quake in fear as soon as they noticed the cannibals. The son asked his father to kidnap an old woman who was last in line. "You want dry meat to eat?" asked the surprised Anérehet, before swooping down upon her and lifting her effortlessly with his flamboyant talons. The boy answered that he did not want to eat her: they would use her to roast the meat and scare off the crows that hovered about while they went off to hunt. They brought the terrified woman to their campsite and set her down amidst the macabre spectacle of mounds of bones, buzzing flies, and unbearable smells. With horror she saw that she could still identify some of the half-eaten corpses as friends or family members. The cannibals offered to let her live if she cooked the corpses and cared for their campsite. The old woman negotiated "through words." She insisted that she would do as they asked only if they agreed to feed her what real humans should eat: animal flesh, honey, and fruit. After they agreed to her conditions, the woman silently mourned her dead, swore to avenge them, and began her ill-fated task.

One morning the son awoke with the urge to taste the tender flesh of a newborn child. Obedient to his fancy as always, his father brought him a pregnant woman. The old woman had to make a huge effort to control her indignant disgust as she saw them cut up her countrywoman. They gave her the child they tore from the womb so she could roast it. She, however, felt the small body still throbbing with life and, in order to distract Anérehet and his son, pretended to be fainting with hunger. "I will cook for you was soon as you bring me my food, I haven't eaten since yesterday." (It seems that while in real life—let's call it that—attaining the rank of a shaman requires resolute study, well-earned revelations, and copious practice, in the myths the effervescent intensification of human experience makes such a process unnecessary, and anyone who overcomes a limit situation, who crosses an essential threshold and attains higher wisdom, can become a shaman.)

The woman, who had become therefore a powerful shaman, lifted the child and with a skillful slice of her fingernail cut the dripping umbilical cord, which she cauterized with black ash. Then she brought him close to her and blew strongly in his ears to bring him back to life and imbue him with powers. "You will be my grandson," she said to him in a low voice and, after bundling him in a *pypyk* (caraguata cloth), she hid him outside the cabin and once back, began to cook the placenta in a clay pot. "The meat was so tender that I could not roast it and had to make a soup," she explained to the cannibals who, unsatisfied with such a puny meal, demanded a second course with the body parts of the unfortunate mother.

The Initiation

As the steady exodus of the villagers distanced them from their executioners, the expeditions for human flesh took more and more time. This situation favored the plans of the old woman. As soon as Anérehet and his son leapt to the air she ran to the hiding place where she concealed the child and, blowing on him always, stretched his limbs to precociously hurry his growth. On many occasions (and Chamacoco tales linger with pleasure on this kind of episode) the cannibals suspected that the old woman had something up her sleeve. But her shrewdness disarmed the suspicions of her dark masters. She explained the imprints left by the crawling infant by saying that a strong back pain had forced her to get down on her hands and knees. The inevitable sounds and smells produced by the nearby child were attributed to birds, rabbits, or armadillos.

Meanwhile the child grew, blessed by the powerful air blown from the mouth of his grandmother. His understanding (*eiwo*) increased through her wise words. When the adoptive grandson was fourteen (either because fourteen years had past or because his growth was accelerated through her powers), the shaman, taking advantage of the absence of her fearsome winged masters, had a long conversation with him. She disclosed to him the damage being visited by the cannibals on his people, the assassination of his own mother, and the danger in which they found themselves. "We must kill them," she said. Convinced of the justice of the cause, her grandson began to eagerly receive the initiatory teachings.

The Weapons

The fateful day agreed upon by the conspirators finally arrived. The grandmother told the cannibals that the well that provided the campsite with water had dried up, and that it was necessary to dig another. The cannibals decided that the father would go hunting alone while the son stayed behind to dig the well. The old woman, a self-proclaimed expert in such matters, promised the youth she would instruct him. She led him to a site where the ground was extremely hard and told him that this was the only place in leagues that possessed water and that he needed to break up the earth with great patience because the water was buried deep underground.

While the youth struggled with the stony ground, the grandmother and grandson took the opportunity for a swift lesson in martial arts. The shaman said that given the immense power the cannibals had acquired they could only be eliminated by special instruments. And so she invented weapons. Her powers were at least as strong as her adversaries' and she instructed her grandson to practice against her. He had to attack her with each weapon she built. If she should be felled by one of the weapons, the child would then blow and bring her back to life, as she taught him, and use that weapon to confront the winged creatures. The woman first crafted five sharp, sturdy spears. She then built weighty staffs from the heart of the black carandá, used in the game *kymychyló* and designed to knock down anyone. She fabricated slingshots (*ahlakaro*), and bows, arrows, and projectiles from the sharp wood of the *wáharo*, weapons that are eager to tear through even the hardest flesh and embed themselves deep within their victims. She elaborated powerful maces in the form of spatulas that could be thrown to slice the neck of even the most robust of opponents. None of these weapons, however, could kill the powerful shaman. The blows shook her briefly or knocked her down for a short while but she was soon again on her feet conjuring up new forms of attack.

Meanwhile, tired of his fruitless digging, the young cannibal asked how much longer he had to keep trying. "Don't be lazy," the old woman encouraged him, "only a few meters more and the water will spring up from the ground." There was not much time left. Then the shaman decided to invent nothing more, nothing less than the rifle. She took a sturdy reed of the *ahäporo* (wild banana)[10] and made a barrel; she prepared a mixture of pulverized coal from the quebracho tree, mud, and powder of *pórkärro*,[11] blew upon it forcefully and filled the recently fabricated tube with the mixture. This time the weapon had the desired effect and killed the old woman. After her grandson brought her back to life with his breath, the woman gave him new instructions. He had to bring her to the village where she would recruit the people and return to confront the cannibals. With the invention of the efficient weapon and the virtue of the young child's powers, victory was now in sight.

She approached the edge of the pit. "Keep digging, you worthless boy," she yelled down to the unhappy youth who struggled with exhaustion. Then she told her grandson to follow her through the dense undergrowth of the woods. There she spoke to a tree called *wopalo,* to the guayacan, and to the *wáhar-ro.*[12] "Don't worry," she told the boy, "these trees will open a path for you and hide your escape if necessary. Return to the campsite and do what you must."

When the old woman reached the village, the people were practicing the ritual ball game the Ishir call *póhorro.* She addressed them loudly, telling them what was happening and encouraging them to prepare the victory ritual, the *tináh,* to weaken their enemy, strengthen her grandson, and celebrate their coming triumph. Most of the people followed her lead in the dances and songs, but one man mocked her. "This crazy old woman comes here and interrupts our game with her stories," he said, incredulous, ridiculing her. She turned to him and cursed him with a phrase that no one understood at that time: *kedu du kë* ("let it be hard for you to pluck").

The Battle and the Feathers

While the shaman cursed the man, her grandson peered into the pit where the duped youth still dug in vain. He threw down a piece of cactus to catch his attention. When the cannibal lifted his head and saw the stranger he began to shout for his father. *"Dió, dióoooo,"* he called from the bottom of the barren well. The winds carried his clamoring cries to his father over the hills, waters, and sand, but though he sped back swiftly, Anérehet arrived too late to help his son. The claustrophobic hole and the yells and stones that his enemy showered down upon him forced him to leave the pit. The opening was so narrow that he had difficulty flying but he was finally able to lift himself out. He launched himself, beaks and claws, onto the aggressive stranger with his powerful weapon—and the young cannibal fell to the ground slain. Later he turned into ïhïa-kayr (the bird called jacana).[13]

Anérehet arrived. The child was stricken with fear. The cannibal's strange powers had made him grow unusually large and he looked like a giant winged monster, his body covered in feathers, the nails on his claws sticking out. The air echoed with his cries and screeches. Instead of firing his weapon the boy fled. As he ran, he felt—as his grandmother had promised—the trees and plants yield to him and close off the path of the cannibal whose wings caught in the thick vines and thorny branches. It was not easy to kill the monster, even with the aid of the trees that detained him, and the boy had to fire many shots before he could slay him. Once he had done so, the terror inspired by the appearance of his enemy turned to wonder at the sight of the feathers that covered the dead body. He tore off some red feathers and crowned himself. Not satisfied, he festooned his wrists and ankles, neck and waist with the different colored feathers and down. Decked out, he presented himself before the villagers—still gathered around the game—who praised him and proclaimed him chief. The old woman, recognized as a great shaman, introduced the use of weapons and caesarean childbirth. (According to Flores, she was soon after kidnapped by the Ayoreo, and then by the whites. This is why white men learned the use of firearms before that knowledge spread among the Ishir.)

The Origin of Feathers, Part Two

The people were astounded by the feathers adorning the body of the flamboyant new chief. The men and women celebrated not only the end of the cannibal nightmare, but also the grandmother's promise that they would each have their own feathers. She beckoned them to follow her and after a long walk they arrived, mid-afternoon, at the site of the battle where the giant feathered creature still lay. The grandmother gave them instructions on how to pluck the feathers from his enormous body. Anxiously they did so, using the

Detail of a man ceremonially adorned with a bracelet, belt, and double skirt of feathers. Puerto Esperanza, 1986. (Photo by Guillermo Sequera.)

feathers to craft diadems in various shades of red (*nymagarak*), wide anklets of brown and green (*omeikarbo*), thin bracelets in red, yellow, and black (*oikakarn*), necklaces of green feathers (*naselá*), and chokers of thick pink, black, or white feathers (*chipió*). They also made great black helmets with nape-guards of a metallic sheen (*lepper wolo*), skirted belts of grey feathers (*pamune*), elegant feathered poles in either white, green, or red (*báteta* and *shak-tern*), and the many other headdresses and adornments they began to use from that day forward.

The man who was cursed by the old woman, however, could not obtain any feathers. He was able to push his way through the greedy mass that fought to rip out the best feathers, and lodge himself in a good position near the wings, but all his efforts—and he was a vigorous man—were in vain. He could not pull off a single feather. The curse of the old woman was thus fulfilled, and ended up having serious consequences for all.

The man's loss made him very resentful, and for good reason: a Chamacoco without marks of identity is a being that is socially unmoored. For this reason, when the group busied itself with preparations to migrate to a new site he told his wife, "I won't go." Under the weight of a strong sense of inferiority he had decided that if he could not find his own feathers, he would leave the community permanently. For this reason, when the villagers began their march the next morning he did not accompany them: he moved away to a river bank and lay on his back in the sand with his legs and arms spread open. He hoped the carrion birds would think him dead and perch on him, at which point he would capture them and grab the desired feathers. He was approached by birds of many different kinds who were, however, driven by curiosity instead of hunger. They were disconcerted because the apparent corpse did not smell like one. The birds called on Nentó (the buzzard) and Dyshyker (the carancha), but they could not explain the strange behavior of the man who appeared to be dead but did not exhibit what to carrion birds are the essential signs of death. Dyshyker decided to seek the advice of an expert, Ïisa the *quirincho,* who dwells in the highest skies. Ïisa approached the body suspiciously, smelled it, and noticed the man's effort to hold in his breath. Quickly, he ripped off the man's nipple and flew away. The poor man howled, confirming the suspicions of the *quirincho,* and jumped up and grabbed two birds who were closely watching the unusual scene. He pinned them against his body, holding them captive despite his pain and their riotous commotion of screeches, flapping wings, and pecks.

He was lucky. The birds were *Iñakar-ro* (the Tomáraho call them *Chipakar-ro*). Luciano describes the bird to Jorge Escobar, an ornithologist, so he can identify it: "It is a beautiful bird. Its breast, shoulders, and beak are yellow and its back is sea-blue. It is not carnivorous," he says, and adds other technical facts. Jorge identifies it rapidly: "According to the description it is a blue and yellow parrot (*Ara ararauna*)." Luciano (Tomáraho) and Ojeda (Ebytoso) both affirm that the birds captured by the man are highly esteemed among the Ishir: the first details their name, the second simply says that the birds are ones of great rank and radiant color. The other informants speak generically of the birds, and do not mention their rank or attribute particular value to them.

The carancha returned, prepared to negotiate the liberation of the captured birds. The man proclaimed that he would only let them go in return for his nipple. A bird known for its speed and capacity for height—the Tomáraho call it Hárteta, the Ebytoso, Pysty—was sent to the *quirincho*. The emissary returned quickly, bringing the stolen token, which was put back into place thanks to the shamanic powers of either the hawk or the carancha, depending on the version. Once the confrontation was solved, the birds asked for answers to his enigmatic behavior. What was he doing, pretending to lie dead on the sand? The man told the story of his frustration and expressed his desire with such vehemence that he moved the birds, each of which—beginning with Bubö (the black swan)—gave him a handful of feathers. Only the carancha was left. "My feathers are not beautiful," he said, "I will give you another gift." And he gave him a pipe (*monyak*) filled with tobacco and dog excrement.

After two days of intense marching the man reached his people as they were settling into a new village. He burst into the center carrying on his back his bundle stuffed with feathers. Perhaps out of desire to compensate for past humiliations, he began to divide them among the people since there was enough for him and everyone else. He also carried the pipe in the bottom of his caraguata bag, but did not mention this gift to anyone because—according to the instructions of Dyshyker—the *monyak* had to be used in secret and with great caution. It was a tool imbued with the most intense charge of *woso*, filled with essential power: depending on its use it could either attract greater providence or disaster. "You must only smoke the pipe after midnight and expel the smoke in the direction of the four corners of the village. This will cover it with blessings. No one must see you smoking and no one can smoke with you. If you do not obey these rules, death will strike down your village." Thus the bird had spoken to him. Although the menace did not seem so great to the man, he decided to strictly follow the bird's orders.

It did not seem so serious to him, my informants explain, because at that time death was not definitive. When someone died, he or she was buried and abandoned by the community, which moved to another place. After a time, the man or woman returned to life and went back to the village under a different appearance, or moved to another village, or wandered for a long time in the wide open spaces of the hunting grounds. It is true that the resuscitated person was not exactly the same and that sometimes Dyshyker himself (guardian of graves), cleaved his lance in the door of the tomb and kidnapped the spirit of the recently deceased who was then lost—more than dead. But in any case, death did not have a sense of absolute end and was not endowed therefore with an essential meaning. As everything else that happened in the primal world, it was only a half-death.

In any case, as was said, the man decided to strictly follow the bird's directives. To stay awake during his nightly vigils he rested during the day. Every midnight, and with increasing delight, he blew out the fragrant puffs that blessed the four corners of the village. These nights of insomnia brought about a time of peace and plenty in his village. Men, women, and children were healthy and their bodies satiated since harvests were fertile and hunts successful. There was neither disease nor war. All in all, the village lived a calm and peaceful Edenic existence. Too calm and peaceful. One night an old man followed the smoker. The man's change in habits seemed suspicious to him and he was intent on revealing the mystery of these sleepless nights. He caught the smoker as he slowly expelled the auspicious smoke (which would soon cease to be auspicious) from his mouth. "Share it with me," the old man said, appearing suddenly. The man refused, citing the reasons given to him by the carancha. But finally, under the pressure of the respectable old man and considering that, if he had already discovered his secret there was little use in keeping it from him, he allowed him to join him in his solitary ritual. They smoked a long while together until the pipe's owner decided to take advantage of his replacement and go to sleep. He covered himself with his rush mat and instantly died. The old man continued to smoke enthusiastically, until right before dawn when the people began to waken. Attracted to the delicious smell and strangeness of the smoke, an old man who had risen early approached the smoker, pleading for a chance to try the pipe. He resisted a while but after warning him, without much conviction, of the pipe's powers he passed it to him and died soon after.

Thus was a fateful chain formed, which lengthened with each passing night. The potent instrument was passed from hand to hand by men and women who begged to smoke it, leaving a trail of deaths in its wake. Terrified by so many deaths, the villagers buried the corpses and kept moving. When the community realized with alarm that the losses had become too frequent, that the generation of elders was on the verge of extermination and that none of the deceased had returned, they decided to treat the issue seriously. A group of men was charged with keeping watch over the nocturnal grandparents. They saw the remaining old men smoke the bewitching gift of the carancha in secret and die off, one by one. Finally, the last of these, who had been informed of Dyshyker's instructions, explained what was happening. Then the men went to the cemetery where the carancha sat in the form of a human (according to Flores Balbuena). With lance in hand the carancha awaited the dead, extracting their souls with a whistle and shepherding them to Osypyte. Osypyte had been the land of those who died forever, but was now the place of all who died. The men asked the sinister sentinel why he had instituted the eternity of death among their people (among all humans). Dyshyker explained what had happened and concluded: "It was the Ishir themselves that chose the path of shadows." He took on his bird form and flew away. Based on his story, a shaman taught men the correct use of the pipe. Everyone has their own pipe; some are made of wood, others of clay. The pipe is carried in the hunter's pouch and no one is ever invited to share its smoke.

Variations

Oedipus's Gaze

As noted above, four main versions were used to construct the myth of Anérehet. The greatest difference lies in the story of the cannibals as told by the Tomáraho, Palacio Vera. According to Vera, the myth begins in a season of intense rains during which no one could leave their cabins, not even to search for sustenance. Bored, the youth lay on the floor listening to the falling water and lazily staring at the roof when he saw his mother's genitals through her half-opened skirt as she walked by him. The disquiet produced by this vision functions like the anxiety to taste the father's flesh that appears in the other versions. The youth is restless and agitated until he forces himself one day (or night) on his mother. At this point he goes mad, turns into a monster, and drives his father into the perversion of anthropophagy. The rest of the myth is identical to the others. There is another myth that begins with the same incident of the incestuous gaze—told in like fashion—which leads to the apparition of the jaguars. Undoubtedly, as oral myths travel in time, many episodes are loosened like modules from certain tales and embedded in other bodies, other tales. The hinges and articulations that hold myths together are sufficiently flexible to allow for this process of decoupling, grafting, and metamorphosis.

This Pipe Is Not a Pipe

According to Luciano (Tomáraho) the pipe is not given to the Ishir by Dyshyker the carancha, but Nentó (or Wopúu) the crow. When it takes human form, this bird is a woman, a widow, and powerful shaman called Emuntah. Each night, after midnight and in secret, she would bless the people with the powerful smoke of her pipe. One night she is discovered by a shaman apprentice who begs her to teach him the uses of that magical tool. Wielding it, she says, requires a long learning process. Diligence is needed to master the songs that summon an abundance of fruits and game, ward off pests and keep disgrace at bay. Only after assiduous training will the youth be ready to use the pipe for the good of his people. And this is what happens: he takes great pains to learn shamanic lore and only when he is mature enough to exercise its powers does the old woman give him the pipe. As soon as she does so she becomes a crow again and flies away. And so begins the time of his village's good fortune, health, prosperity, and peace.

The germ of real death begins to incubate at the same time. Either because his gloomy ministry compels him, or because he wants to enjoy the benefits he has seen the shaman bequeath on his people, Dyshyker plots to steal the pipe. When the young shaman lies down to rest at dawn, the carancha rummages through his pouch and exchanges the pipe for a pipe whose appearance is identical to the original, but which produces the opposite effects. From that moment on, the false pipe not only fails to bring grace and providence upon the people—it curses the village with the anguish of finitude, the pain of loss, and mourning. Death slowly becomes irrevocable. Frightened by the consequences of his well-intentioned ritual, the shaman dies of grief. A group of wise men, known since by the clan name Dyshykymser (plural of Dyshyker), take it upon themselves to destroy the nefarious pipe and attempt to recover the benefits of the first pipe by fabricating new ones. But from then on Osypyte, the Land of the Dead, never again returned the souls that cross into it.

Commentaries

This tale of the origin of feathered ornaments—like the preceding ones concerning the emergence of colors and the origin of red feathers—clearly expresses the dramatic tone, and even the tragic air that envelops the color of feathers and featherwork itself among the Chamacoco. All of these arise in liminal situations of the human condition. Stained with blood, color is tied to sex and death, the essential enigma and the first anguish, somber sociocultural transgressions and guilt (crime, madness, incest, anthropophagy). This happens because the myths on the color of feathers are fed by figures that lie at the center of personal experience and history: eros, vengeance, familial and social organization, food, the thirst for knowledge, and beauty. Beauty takes on a terrible dimension in these myths: the *splendor formae* emerge in tight intensity, before the threshold of nothingness. Poetry fills the wide horizon of the plains with lightning and brusque silence. It renews language's disquiet.

Like the other two myths in this chapter, the myth of feathered ornaments involves a bloody event (the tale begins with the father's hemorrhage) and a serious disturbance that unsettles the limits of human existence. Once these limits are crossed, two paths open up: the paths of monstrosity (the option of those who violate the basic ethical codes) or shamanism (the option of those who break the natural order to accede to its silent powers). Yet another option, religion, is not mentioned on the level of these myths. There is another path: that of death. Featherwork emerges at this terrible crossroad. It materializes from the shattered remnants of the human, reaches out to buried powers, and takes shape against the backdrop of death. According to Ishir logic, it is reasonable that the greatest intensity of human experience be opposed to the most radical finitude. Only such a categorical antagonism is capable of generating the maximum tension required by form to release its different truths. The Ishir accede to beauty but pay for it with death. Art cannot exist without the memory of time.

The question is, therefore, an ethical one. And it points to ritual, which is capable of restoring the violated order and conciliating beauty and death, at least for an instant. The first act unfolds during the *póhorro* competition: an intense ritual that delights in playfulness and simultaneously contests and reflects (symmetrically inverted) the ceremony that the dead celebrate under the earth. Cordeu says that the younger brother in the first myth, the young protagonist of the second myth, and Anérehet in the third myth represent "the properly human contribution to the physical, moral, and religious order of the universe. The first gives the colors of his blood, the second gives his plumage, and the third imposes the use of feathers in ritual celebrations . . . thus, as these myths emphasize, ritual is an essentially human creation but in order to perform it men had to trespass the frontier of the sacred" (Cordeu 1990, 205).

The figure of human limits, attained only through a methodical and painstaking process, leads us to the theme of shamanism. The grandmother's wisdom matures precociously under the weight of extreme situations. The truncated time of myth does not simply shorten the long path of shamanic formation, it condenses it. The grandson is instructed by the old woman and, in his learning process, recapitulates the ideals of Chamacoco initiation: the plenitude of *eiwo* (reason) and mastery of the powers of the real (beginning with dominion over one's body and ending with dominion over the forces that power the cosmos). It also presupposes a difficult process of physical and affective privation, concentration, passion, courage, and the patient study of the words transmitted by teachers. The grandson's triumph is the end product of a task to which he dedicated all his effort and desire to accomplish. As in every tragedy, this plot is moved by intentions that escape human will. But, through their actions, the Ishir men and women gain the possibility of affirming a place, conquering a power, and venturing into a possible path of meaning in this strange place they have been destined to live. I suppose that if it is possible to speak of a general "function" of culture it would consist, to a greater or lesser extent, in fulfilling this task.

Other Chamacoco ethical values play a part in this myth: the weight given to words, for example. Words are double-edged and can favor or harm according to how they are used. Words can empower the dialogue of negotiation, promote the growth of *eiwo,* permit the profits of deception, and instate norms whose transgression must be punished. Thus, through "strong words" (a characteristic Chamacoco feature), the old woman makes the pact with her captors, foments the intellectual development of the grandson, plots the ruses to ensnare and defeat the cannibals, and gives instructions to her people. The man who does not follow them is punished and deprived of feathers. In the second part of the myth, it is Dyshyker who imposes the precepts through words. When his orders are not followed, punishment falls again upon the transgressor and his community. Or it is Emuntah, the crow/woman, who is charged with teaching the arduous path of initiation into shamanism and promulgating the essential value of the canonical word.

ON FEATHERWORK

Featherwork, one of the central moments of the Ishir system of aesthetics, makes multiple appearances in these myths in scenarios that barely graze each other. On the one hand, the feathers originate in the context of the divine: to supplant the gods they have eliminated, men must imitate their feathered appearance. On the other hand, the Ishir use feathers in a space that only concerns what is properly human. The myths on the origins of the colors of feathers and featherwork do not even mention the gods—they speak of desperate women and men, they speak of shamans. These figures are prototypes of existential experience and of the most quotidian of actions taken to radical extremes. The shamans have less to do with the sacred than with the limits of the human: they work the secret links that unite men to each other and to different aspects of their environment. Such links are expressed in powers that must be conquered. In this context, men do not dress themselves up in feathers to resemble gods or to remember primordial times, but in order to wield their powers more effectively and distinguish among themselves according to clan, age, social function, and personal taste. They also adorn themselves because feathers exemplify the Chamacoco ideal of a beauty that is alternately turbulent and intense, dark and ferocious, and at times even delicate.

In this way we can say that the Ishir cover themselves in feathers for three reasons, all of which depend on the realm of the aesthetic. First, they do so for theatrical/cultural/religious reasons. They seek to represent their gods, the distant anábsoro, and to do so need a repertoire of forms, textures, and colors as diverse as the varied aspects of all the members of the Chamacoco pantheon. Each kind of bird, each feather, and each way it is used corresponds to a sacred model, and any mistake is severely sanctioned.

Bruno Sánchez Vera adorned with a crown of feathers. Asunción, 2004. (Photo by José Escobar Argaña.)

Second, they use feathered ornaments for shamanic reasons. These reasons correspond to four modalities: (1) the therapeutic, to prevent and cure diseases; (2) the magical/propitious, to manipulate natural forces and bring food, provoke or thwart droughts and floods, control human behavior, avert misfortune and evil deeds; (3) the ceremonial, for shamanic rites or the blessing of the stage of great collective rituals; (4) the ecstatic, for flights undertaken to augment wisdom, receive oneiric revelations, and battle other shamans. Shamans use feathers as insignias of their ministry (ornaments used as part of their dress) and as professional instruments (the same pieces are employed to sweep away sickness and capture an enemy soul, for example).

Three youths recently initiated. María Elena, 2001. (Photo by Nicolás Richard.)

Third, feathers mark social status. The feather is a sign of ethnic identification: it identifies a Chamacoco, then a clan. A person will wear duck or parrot
feathers to indicate, for example, their place within the Tahorn or Kytymáraha
lineage. But it is also an individual emblem. The tiny silhouette of a heron
feather or the trembling red feather fastened to his quill will distinguish Wylky
from Luciano. Feathers also transmit a variety of information, which used to
be infinite and now is reduced to the bare essentials. For example, the messengers who brought news to and from different villages used yellow feathers to
announce favorable news. To indicate that their suit was accepted, suitors inverted their feathered earrings so that the feathers pointed skyward. Rejecting
a bracelet of feathers was enough to transform an *ágalo* (friend) into an *ymasha*
(enemy). The color of red feathers indicated (and still indicates today, at least
formally) the end of the period of initiation, and so on. Thus adverse or favorable predispositions, moments of civil status, ritual phases or gradations that
mark status can all be communicated through the vehement colors and languid bodies of feathers and their varied placement on the signed body.

The Forms of Feathers

The aesthetic of featherwork constitutes one of the aspects of indigenous culture most damaged by overpowering colonial and neocolonial expansion. On the one hand, ethnocide transforms the logotype of difference into a stigma, and ritual into a barbarous excess. On the other hand, day by day ecocide restricts the habitats of chosen birds, turning many of them into nostalgic examples of extinct species. Both processes undermine the premises of ethnic continuity and provoke the deterioration of featherwork and other forms of indigenous expression. Yet the Chamacoco, especially the Tomáraho, stubbornly preserve an important repertoire of feathered forms, undoubtedly the biggest and most complex repertoire in Paraguay today.

Tomáraho featherwork is richer and more complex than that of their Ebytoso kin because it has developed through the group's cultural experience, preserved almost at the cost of their extinction. The aggressive assault of an intolerant missionary front succeeded in forcing the Ebytoso to abandon the *debylyby,* the Great Ceremony, in the 1950s. Since then, the Ebytoso have maintained feathered expressions linked only to shamanic practices, reduced by the semiclandestine space in which they have had to be performed for a long time, and impoverished by the tourist spectacle to which they have often had to resort. The return of the Tomáraho to traditional Chamacoco territories has led to various phenomena (which are still taking place) related to the recuperation of ritual.

These different historical experiences must be placed side by side with the particularities of their sensibilities and variety of habitats: the forest of the Tomáraho boasts a greater variety of colored birds than do the riverbanks of the Ebytoso. The situations produced by this complex of factors produce a notable difference between the visual inventories of feathers in each group. The feathered ornaments of the Ebytoso privilege dark colors and neutral shades, based primarily on grey ostrich feathers; the Tomáraho wield a wider chromatic spectrum and favor a scale that includes intense and contrasting colors, as well as a greater variety of ornamentation. The former elaborate more violent and uniform textures, choose rough textures, and produce rigorous designs. The latter oscillate between coarse and delicate aesthetic effects: from the somber density of the black feathers of Nemur, to the spectacular feathered jewels that shake the flamboyant headdress worn by Ashnuwerta;

from the barbarous mane of Wákaka, to the refined bracelets and elegant necklaces that tame the brutal appearance of other anábsoro.

Despite these opposing tendencies, it is possible to speak of a common culture of featherworking among the Chamacoco. Their style is vigorous, baroque, generous; its force is sufficient to name finitude and ward off fear, to convert mortals into gods and push human potential to the very limits of a long-lost meaning.

On Ishir Featherwork

Among the indigenous groups of Paraguay the Chamacoco use the greatest spectrum of birds for crafting their artifacts. Despite the above-mentioned differences between the Tomáraho and Ebytoso, both groups use the same set of birds. The basic list (and there are many other birds) includes the stork, white or red heron, spoonbill, ostrich, duck (*pato bragado*), *cotorra* (Monk Parakeet), woodpecker, owl, *chopís, charata* (Chaco Chachalaca), chaja (Southern Screamer), *karau* (Limpkin), magpie, toucan, and even macaws captured in neighboring Brazilian forests. The feathers of birds of prey—because their duller tones are less appropriate for finery as well as, perhaps, for calling forth the appropriate power—are used much less, and only appear in small bundles.

The codes that determine the use of a specific color or feather are tangled and varied. It is impossible to try to decipher the meaning of a specific artifact. Not only do I not believe there to be a fundamental truth that can be revealed, but I am sure that the rays of meaning opened by each feathered ornament are provisional, pertain to different semiotic levels, overlap, change and refract, renovate and elude themselves. The meanings of each piece depend on the colors and shapes of its feathers, and the bird from which they derive; from its relation with another piece, and possible insertion into yet another; and from the occasion on which it is used (religious, shamanic, or civil). Then, for each of these occasions, the value of each unity also depends on the role assumed by the actor who bears it, the category and social function of the shaman using it, and the place it is carried on the body. In addition, each variable operates according to the frame of various oppositions, associations, and figurations in which it is inscribed. Red acts as the opposite of black in certain registers; as the association with blood in another (and in this case can imply either a vital force or death); as linked with the fruits of the cactus, the shades of sunset, or with fire in a third register; and so on. The birds are esteemed according to flight, appearance, alimentary habits, relations with sky and trees, aggressiveness, or vital cycles.

If one considers that, in turn, many of these frameworks overlap to comprise an intricate network of signs, one will conclude that it is impossible to isolate the final meaning of a feathered ornament. As in any other cultural system, every form is, in Lyotard's words, the herald of an impossible message. The energy of so much expression produces flashes of lightning, crashes and echoes, points to a horizon of meanings, and resists capture by a single figure or naming by a single concept. These expressions deny commitment to one truth, one path.

Feliciano Rodríguez ready to enter the ceremonial scene to play the role of guardian of the *anábser* Honta Abich. His back is painted black and covered with white handprints. He wears a skirt of ostrich feathers, a bandoleer of beads, and a sash of caraguata fiber, from which a cowbell dangles. Potrerito, 1989. (Photo by Ticio Escobar.)

CORPORAL PAINTING

THE maximum expression of Chamacoco art takes place on the body. Feathered ornaments and corporal painting imbue the image with the weight of unlimited social content, driving it to the limits of its expressive capacity. That is to say, these arts order colors; compose, balance, and dislocate figures; act on appearances and sensible effects: they manipulate form. And they do so to signal and hide culture's most pressing truth, the body of its first enigmas.

The confused activity we call art consists in the effort to work forms so as to produce the most intense signification, adulterate the normal appearance of phenomena, perturb the order of the ordinary to reveal the most radical of absences and renew those essential, unanswerable questions: this is what the Ishir do through feathers and through shining, somber, bloody paints. Drenched in feathers and paint, the body becomes the cipher of dark, indispensable dimensions that can only be glimpsed—never attained—through the perverse detours of beauty.

The Ishir man paints his body the way an artist, sitting in front of an easel, paints the body he or she represents. That is: he invents and recreates it, draws it again, correcting the error that confuses it with nature. He redesigns its contours and colors to adapt them to forms and tones required by the usurpation of the place of the gods; alters its features with the stain of guilt or flash of pleasure; adds the necessary motifs to invoke the riches of the woods and river, launch the flight of dreams, and steal the soul of the enemy shaman. He inscribes the signs of difference on skin. Difference: this is a key issue. Through corporal painting, the Ishir address the thorny question that troubles and drives the course of culture: that which confronts the self/same and the other, that which tries to define the frontier of identity and separate the alien. The Ishir color their skin to differentiate themselves from (but also identify with) animals and gods, to mark the distinction (and link) between natural time and the timelessness of ritual, to emphasize oppositions and analogies in social status, gender, age, and profession. The painting of bodies, says Mauss, is the social skin. Yes, but it is also the ritual skin, the mythical skin: the skin before the skin.

field notes

Potrerito, 11 August 1989

Under the pressure of confused forms that originate elsewhere, the tightly woven dream begins to unravel and voices and vague clarities start to slip through the dream's filter. I am finally awakened by a shove and the indecipherable voice of Daniel (son of the chief, Emilio Aquino). The light from his lantern parts the dark room in two. Now I make out the word *tobich*. Yes, something will happen or is happening in the men's ceremonial grounds. Túkule told me last night that today they would celebrate a ritual but he did not know, or did not want to tell me, the exact hour of the event. It is five in the morning and outside the temperature is four degrees Celsius, Mito announces sleepily from inside various superimposed layers of ponchos (how he has obtained such alarming facts is a mystery to me). It is still dark out but I feel that it is late.

The women have begun their early morning tasks and the men are already absent. Mito, Cristián, and I trot after Daniel, without time to wash or eat breakfast, complaining once more of our hosts' terrible habit of not warning us of events we have been eagerly awaiting. We have missed more than one ritual for this reason.

When we arrive at the *tobich*—sleepy, panting, and numbed with cold—nothing seems to have happened. And nothing happens except that light slowly spreads through the sky as the light from the bonfire languishes and the trees, custodians of the ritual clearing, slowly announce their indecisive silhouettes. The men talk among themselves unhurriedly. They drink maté, clear their throats, spit, briefly chuckle. Now they fall silent. The birds seem to awaken suddenly in the mist-laden woods interrupted by the *tobich* and the trees seethe with squawks and shrieks. Is this racket an omen? Are these strident flocks a signal? Of course not, says Clemente. But the shamanic song that immediately wafts up in the morning air seems to belie his words. Stationed on the edge of the clearing the shamans face out, shaking their maracas with increasing force, stirring the frozen air with their dry rhythm. Now the omen seems to be mere silence. For a moment the shamans cease their noise and a group of men moves toward the heat of the fire, shrugging their shirts off their tense torsos. An old man approaches. He sinks his finger in the warm paste of coal that has recently been prepared and traces a thick black line over Wylky's shivering chest. It is followed by another line and another until he has completed a meticulous calligraphy of lines. Around us other scribes repeat the task on other cold-stiffened torsos and with other colors until together, the group of men resemble a text comprised of a sequence of black, white, or red lines.

The sun has now passed the compact line of trees, and its fleeting rays illuminate the scene, piercing the straggling mists of dawn. The shamans sing and the tiger-striped men are silent. Something is happening. The stage is set. "Soon," explains Cristián who prepares his camera, "soon they will begin to cover themselves in masks, feathers, and yells. And the path that leads to the *harra* will tremble beneath their musical steps. And the silence of frightened gazes will resound." A hawk (a hawk?) screeches and is answered by an unknown cry, or perhaps an echo. It is a sign. "Something will happen," I think or say. What happens, however, is the antithesis of the event we await. The tense solemnity of the moment is broken by prosaic voices and banal comments. The men quickly dress in sheepskins and walk away, with neither a tumult of voices nor the rattle of animal hoofs. The stage is emptied, crossed only by the lazy buzz of lost bees, occupied only by our frustrated presence.

The explanations given later by our different informants as to why the magic of the ritual had been broken and the performance cancelled are so confused as to not merit being put to paper. Hopupora's announcement, Palacio explains, exasperated. Hopupora is one of the manifestations of Ashnuwerta: a manifestation of sound that takes place when it is still night. Does this mean that the goddess gave some sign that cut the ceremony short? (I am obsessed by announcements because the Ishir horizon is filled with them and what are imperceptible for us—especially the calls of birds—are, for the Ishir, clear portents.)

Yesterday I noticed another strange event. Cristián pointed out that night that the men still bore the painted stripes underneath their clothes. They had not therefore washed them off, as they normally do after a ritual: the novices carry great basins filled with water and the participants strip down right there in the *tobich* (even if the day is as cold as it was today), wipe off the signs stolen from the gods and recover their mortal skin and human features.

This morning I remained in Ebytoso territory with the intention of unearthing some myth concerning corporal painting. Until now I have not been able to amass any such references except for a few brief expositions collected at different moments. (Two tales by Flores Balbuena on Ostyrbe, the personification of red paint; and two more by Balbuena and Enrique Ozuna, respectively, on the oneiric origin of certain shamanic paintings.)

Today I recorded some important narrations (a new version on the fall of the cosmic tree, various shamanic sagas, a short myth on the origin of honey) but none related to painting, though I stubbornly pursue references to it. When a Chamacoco narrator begins to speak, no one can interrupt him during the lengthy exposition of each epic or fable, anecdote or drama. The tale is often dramatized, always accompanied by gestures, by expressive sound effects and vibrant silences. If the monologue is translated, the translator superimposes his own dramatization and commentaries. Thus, the tale, augmented with glosses and acting, often turns into a dialogue—or even a debate—and its doubled libretto can last for hours.

This particularity of Chamacoco narrative style makes it difficult to amass myths. When a narrator has begun to tell the wrong (if we can call it that) story, it would be discourteous, if it were even possible, to rein in his dramatic impetus. Furthermore, the store of registered myths is rendered fuller, more complex. Each version adds not only changes in the plot and new content, but rhetorical richness: inflections, tonalities, particular emphases that, to my understanding, are as important as the naked scheme that obsesses Lévi-Strauss (the buried essential structure that unites the barbarous logos with enlightened reason).

Thus, today's work enriches already collected tales but adds little to my search for a mythic foundation for corporal painting; in other words, to my search for myths that speak to the shamanic and social use of such paintings, since its religious use is already articulated in the Great Myth (men paint their bodies to mimic the brilliant skins of the gods).

I think that the highest expression of Chamacoco art is found on the body, through feathers, which correct the outlines of the body and through painting, which disturbs its bronze tones. For this reason I find it strange that, given the existence of such important myths on feathers, the allusions to body paints are so scarce. The references I obtained from my informants are meager and even the profuse compilations of Susnik and Cordeu, who have archived the most exhaustive ethnographic corpus on the Chamacoco, did not hold more information. In order to argue for corporal painting through narration I will therefore refer to the Great Myth and the aforementioned four short tales by Flores Balbuena and Ozuna.

Asunción, 10 July 1994

Members of the Tomáraho group of Potrerito (Peishiota) are in Asunción. With Bruno—the Ebytoso chief who is an expert in the languages, ways, and schemes of whites—they have come to buy their land or obtain the necessary documentation for their land. They demand that a significant portion of Puerto Esperanza be registered in the name of the community or, as an alternative, that the INDI (official entity charged with indigenous affairs) or ACIP (an NGO working with indigenous issues) intervene and help them acquire the adjacent lands. Basically they want the security of their own territory. They know that the title of landownership for which they bargain with the whites constitutes a symbol of formal guarantee. This is why they desire it.

Present are Wylky, Emilio, Marcelo, Crescencio, Peíto, Clemente, and Bruno. We analyze different alternatives. Sooner or later fault lines will trouble the precarious cohabitation of the Ebytoso and Tomáraho. Both groups need to settle into distinct and distant territories. We eat at a bar on Hernandarias street, close to the INDI. The main issues have been addressed and the formality of the conversation (conversations) dissolves into spontaneous exchanges in parallel languages. The indigenous people argue their rights in Guaraní or Spanish. They laugh, make plans, talk, fall silent, and worry in Chamacoco. Sometimes Bruno translates a phrase or two that he considers relevant. Sometimes they themselves repeat what has been said in *jopará*,[1] adding new inflections to their rough voices. Suddenly—I don't know why—we are speaking about the ritual of Hopupora; and suddenly I unravel the mystery of the painted bodies that frozen morning that ended without the ceremony those stripes of color seemed to announce.

That confused moment marks one of the starting points of the *debylyby*, the Great Ritual, when a new time begins to incubate (the greening of leaves, the fragrant laziness of the air, celebrations, games, and excesses) within the dry winds of the depths of winter. This new time is heralded by certain signals of Hopupora, the most patent and the most invisible manifestation of Ashnuwerta. Associated to a nocturnal bird that bears her name, Hopupora never shows herself: she appears only through the piercing voices in the shadows that announce the coming season. Her first cry is heard any night at the end of August or beginning of September, after the long shamanic songs that invoke the divine signal. It is on the dawn of the following day that the men gather at the *tobich* to be painted. The ritual is called *Hopupora mä* ("the fingers of Hopupora," in other words, the prints left by her fingers) and means that the men have been marked by the goddess, their bodies notified of the renewing proximity of that other moment. In one way, these corporal paintings foreshadow those that will come later; in another, they protect the Chamacoco from the power of the cry of the nocturnal deity. ("They are like vaccines," says Clemente, who likes intercultural equivalences.) For this reason the rite is also called *Otar woso:* it serves to neutralize the noxious effects of the *woso,* the numinous powers. And for this reason the men do not wash off the red, black, white lines that cover their torsos, the dark and shining ciphers of death and resurrection written on the body. Hopupora cries out on two other occasions and, hearing her, the Ishir know whether or not the awaited ceremony is to begin.

"Did you understand?" asks Wylky, mediated through Bruno's words. We laugh: after having expressed himself in Spanish, Bruno had translated him into Guaraní. *"Antendé porä,"* I, mediator, answer in *jopará.*

OSTYRBE

First Tale by Flores Balbuena

Ostyrta is a creature that resembles the stingray but is larger and more powerful. Its contours are even more uncertain than the stingray's: it cannot be fished because it devours hooks without suffering any damage; it cannot be caught because it dissolves into blood as soon as it is touched; it cannot be slain by an arrow or spear because its body does not offer enough resistance to be pierced by them. It lives on the bottom of the large burrows dug by armadillos, breathes soft small breaths, shoots sinister glances through its tiny eyes, and bleeds continuously, leaving pools of bloody mud around its body. But this amorphous being—almost incorporeal, almost liquid—has a small dense core that beats inside it like a seed (if seeds could beat) at the center of a fruit teeming with juices. And this red heart of stone, called *ostyrbe,* can sometimes be abandoned by the ungrateful Ostyrta who slides, or pours itself somewhere else, incubating another crystallized piece of entrails in its flaccid body.

When an Ishir discovers a piece of *ostyrbe* he or she must take it immediately to a shaman or anábser for it to be purified and its harmful powers reversed. Once this is accomplished, it can be used in corporal painting as a source of good fortune. If the *ostyrbe* is not dealt with appropriately disgrace ensues. Upon contact with it, women die of menstrual hemorrhages and men bleed to death from trivial wounds inflicted during the hunt. Thanks to the power granted by Ostyrta to certain shamans, they can spit blood on the *kadjuwerta* to increase its favorable powers and inflame its hues.

Second Tale by Flores Balbuena

"I am Posháraha like the anábser Kaimo because my first ancestor killed the leader of the Kaimo and usurped his clan," explains Flores Balbuena. For this reason, the Posháraha represent the Kaimo in the ceremonial circle. Doing so requires great industry and work because the skin of the Kaimo feature intricate images and complex colors. The beauty of Kaimo determined the destiny of the Chamacoco. It was because she was enthralled with this god's appearance that one woman neglected her maternal duties and, in her clumsiness, let slip the secret of the existence of the men. The corporal ornaments of Kaimo link him to *ostyrbe,* whose red sap dyes his presence, and to snakes, whose tangled designs are echoed in his skin. There is more: Kaimo feeds on the body of Ostyrta ("the mother of the *ostyrbe,*" says my informant) as well as on certain snakes (like coral snakes, whose scales display intense, alternating combinations of beautiful colors). Kaimo's staffs, used during the ritual in the battles with the Posháraha, are painted with the *ostyrbe* and buried by the novices at the feet of certain trees that outline the initiatory grounds. Later, these staffs become snakes of beauty and power (seductive, dangerous power). The Ishir hunt them and exchange them with the Kaimo for honey and animals eaten by humans. The Ostyrta are captured directly by the anábsoro, because the Ishir cannot trap their ambiguous, threatening bodies. Kaimo swallows the fluid mass of the organism, drinks its blood and viscous parts, and sometimes spits out the hard nucleus lodged in the body. The Ishir take the red nut, which in this case has been purged of dangerous forces by the divine body, and paint their browned skins with it. Now the bloody tint acquires a beneficial power. In the ceremonial circle Kaimo and the anábsoro in his retinue take the children brought to them by their mothers and rub them against their bodies so that the red patches can protect them from evil and make them grow up strong.

Commentary

Featherwork and corporal painting—the privileged forms of Chamacoco aesthetic expression—are both directly connected to intense figures and dramatic experiences. Blood is a metaphor of vital forces and primal materials. The *os-*

tyrbe's paint (secret nodule, heart of a bleeding monster) connotes the buried force that beautifies bodies. It suggests the ambivalent nature of beauty, which always watches death out of the corner of its eye and keeps company with the darkest and most terrible aspects of existence. The snake is a sign of attraction and danger, just as the *ostyrbe* is a cipher of splendor and calamity.

The complicated serpentine movements of Ishir rhetoric: Kaimo, paradigm of the beauty of paintings, is metaphorically related to snakes for the patterns on their skins, and to blood (*ostyrbe*) for the force of its color. But the similarity is not enough: Kaimo feeds both on serpents and on the *ostyrbe*, and his alchemical body transforms the negative power of poison into a source of good fortune. Now the figure is pushed to the limits of metonymy: the god rubs the children against the patterns and colors of his body, hoping to imbue them with its benefits. The relationship between design and color is consummated in the figure of the god's staffs, which turn into serpents once painted (only to be devoured later and converted into a new principle of beauty and power).

The situations and objects that are attributed with heavy symbolic weight have a great capacity for mediation and linkage. They irradiate beams; they cast thick webs that connect unrelated things. (Art underlines these links: it sometimes discovers or at least imagines them.) The *ostyrbe,* the hard nucleus saturated with various meanings, points to an extensive semantic field and establishes varied relations. Buried in the center of a gelatinous, bleeding mass, this strange figure occupies a preferential position of signification: a quadrivial seed that opens to the mineral and animal kingdoms and to divine and human dimensions. On the one hand, the *ostyrbe* is the heart of a threatening creature: a beast that can certainly be classified among zoological species inasmuch as it resembles a fish. On the other hand, the petrified, oxidized center of that tremulous monster is a mineral: it is pure red hematite. This rare entity involves the human dimension: it adorns the skins of men during celebrations and provokes the bloody vomit of shamans. If handled correctly it promotes the growth of children; if used incorrectly, unsuspecting hunters and menstruating women hemorrhage fatally. But it also comprises sacred spaces: it is, as we saw, Kaimo's food. It enables him to transform his divine scepters into serpents (yet another source of nourishment for him). It awakens the intense hues of divine skin. It is related to *kadjuwerta,* the principle that concentrates supreme powers, saturating it with the colors of the goddess of red splendor.

THE ORIGINS OF SHAMANIC CORPORAL PAINTING

Part 1

The borders between sky and earth are rainy ones: night and day water falls in the form of drizzles or showers, or even the occasional deluge. In these wet limits, the dreaming shamans link up with animals. The *konsaho* who belong to the category of subterranean shamans (*nymych ut oso*) sink into the shady depths of the soil. The *konsaho póorch oso* (the sky shamans) wander in the desolate landscapes of the firmament. The first group of shamans transform into subterranean creatures; the others become the birds of Osasërö and as such take on the forms of storms and rain. When they awaken, both groups must mark their bodies with paints and feathers according to the characteristic of the animals they dreamt. They must sing, accompanied by their maracas, to invoke the power of the dreamt creatures. This way they gain access to their corresponding powers (*woso*).

The water shamans (*konsaho niot ut oso*) dive into the rivers, lagoons, and streams, sliding into fish forms. Elisa was the name of one such Ebytoso shaman (her Ishir name was Yrry Ne'ër). She lived in Puerto Diana and died when Flores Balbuena was being initiated in the *tobich*. During her oneiric underwater expeditions Elisa became a *surubí*.[2] As soon as she immersed herself in the deep waters of the Paraguay River, a shoal of fish appeared and led her to Shyr-ohüta, a tranquil pool where she began to sing and communicate with the fish. They played with her, tangling themselves in her hair and sliding up against her legs and arms, which became increasingly viscous, taking on the texture of a *surubí*. Ndoshío Mbalota, the Master of the Fishes, would proudly say: "She is my daughter." And he watched her turn into a fish. When she awoke, Elisa had to repeat the song learned in dreams, and to paint herself like the fish to wield their power.

Part 2

About twenty kilometers from the place currently known as Puerto Olimpo was a paradisiacal place called Emyk-taa (known to Paraguayans today as Ymákata Ranch). Its soil was fertile; the trees were laden with fruit, the woods abounded in prey, the water of the rivers brimmed with fish, and honey was plentiful. Also abundant were snails and poisonous pests. For this reason when some anábsoro fled from men during the massacre they sought refuge in these lands, where they had previously hunted for the spiders, snails, snakes, and scorpions they relished. The host of men pursuing the gods reached this hidden Eden and, impressed by its bounty and opulence, decided to settle there. Feeling besieged by the camps and villages that were soon erected by men, the anábsoro turned into eels and tunneled deep into the earth, leaving behind empty spaces and passageways. When they scream, their voices echo through the hollowed subsoil and emerge far away through one of the openings of these multifarious canals.

In those times, the humans had not divided into different nations. Emyktaa was settled by a single integrated population composed of Ishir, Krymyro (Ayoreo), Wyriaso (Nivaklé), Ketiu (Caduveo, Mbayá), and many other ethnic groups. They lived thus, undifferentiated, sharing the bounty of this strange land.

It was a strange land indeed: not only were its gifts plentiful, but it was also generous in its cares. It was not long before the new inhabitants realized that its birds had the ability to foretell danger and the inclination to announce it. In this way, they discovered that there were some birds specialized in heralding accidents, sudden assaults, fires, undesirable presences, and even prosperity and good fortune. The most observant Ishir devoted themselves to learning these precious skills and transmitting them to others: "These birds that cry at night are called *waká;* they warn us that a man will soon die, that we will have a new widow. Those screeches presage the proximity of an enemy: when we hear them we must ready our bows and arrows," they said. "We must never eat these birds who proclaim important messages with their voices," they taught.

These studious Ishir became specialists in the lore of birds; they could not eat them, but used their feathers as a compass when they wielded their powers. With time, such men became shamans. One of the most important birds is the *chuko,* the parrot. It has beauty and power and can guide sky shamans (the *konsaho póorch oso*) to the celestial spaces. These parrots are also the best prototypes for the shaman's body paintings. The blazing colors and abstract designs of their plumage are inexhaustible models. ("This is true for the sky shamans; the other shamans seek inspiration in subterranean or aquatic animals," my informant clarifies.)

The myths are compendia of deep knowledge about the human condition. They assume that idyllic situations are not eternal. In this tale, conflict breaks out when the inhabitants begin to fight over space. As fertile as the lands of Emyk-taa were, its reserves dwindled, exploited by too many people. Encouraged by propitious conditions, the inhabitants had multiplied excessively; they had also received many newcomers who, attracted by news of the magnanimity of those soils, had migrated there and erected new villages. Confronted by the scarcity of resources, the people began to fight for the best sites, for access to the best hunting grounds and the most bountiful waters. Thus they split up into conflicting groups and factions, consumed by constant arguments and frictions, skirmishes and even battles. Finally, by common accord, they decided to divide into different nations, abandon the shrunken paradise and set off in different directions. Each group was accompanied by shamans, experts on the powers of different animals. It seems that the shamans who went with the Chamacoco were those who had studied best the secrets of the parrots. This is why they know how to paint their bodies better than any other indigenous group.

Commentary

Travels

The shamans move on levels that are not the same as the spheres on which the actions of the gods are staged. Often both dimensions loom close to each other, and sometimes (but rarely) they will intercept and cross over one another; they can also collide or reflect each other inversely. The spaces are, however, always differentiated. For both the Ebytoso and the Tomáraho, shamans and anábsoro never coincide in the terrains of myth, and only meet in the ritual circle when the shamans watch over the acts of those who impersonate the gods. Even in such cases they continue to move in different fields. The divine cycle takes place on the level of representation while the time of the shamans does not. The shamans never use masks or act. In a certain sense, they intervene by protecting and blessing the men from outside the scene of drama.[3] For this reason, the mechanisms of corporal painting obey specific drives in each case. The shamans imprint their bodies with motifs taken from animals; the actors steal the patterns of the gods. Both spill over the contours of a human order, opening it to contiguous spaces (the kingdom of nature and the divine strata). Through corporal painting the Ishir graze their limits, facing, for an instant, the tense plenitude of their human condition: one that unfolds against the backdrop of the organic and before the horizon of the absolute.

The shamans move back and forth across the thresholds that separate the sky and earth and across those that keep the human and animal universes apart. They do so through the non-time of dreams, the canceled space of night. They do so through the transgression of another frontier: that which divides the oneiric from the real. Or better: that which distinguishes the banality of everyday experience from profound knowledge. Thus, in order to bring the Ishir relief from the burdens of their many liminal positions, the shamans come and go, trespassing limits. From one shore to the other, they relay different truths that can end up intermingling or exchanging appearances. In order for the Ishir to approach the edge—in order for them to explore the margins of their vulnerable conditions, and better control the different powers that inhabit the infinite extension of the Chaco—the shamans paint themselves like fish according to the designs they find at the bottom of dreamt rivers. They are human, birds, or fish: they are *konsaho,* shamans. They acquire the power of animals through the power of form. (Through the power of beauty: for without it neither theater nor magic can function.)

Tales

These four brief tales correspond to a genre the Ishir know as *mónene.* They are minor mythic narratives that parallel and sometimes intersect the serious march of the great myths (religious and shamanic). While they are narrations of a secondary order, intended fundamentally for the entertainment of a wider audience, they divulge fundamental principles of Ishir thought and sensibility and are capable, therefore, of obliquely offering fundamental clues.

Models

All of these tales mention the origin of shamanic corporal painting. If the purpose of this painting is basically auspicious / magical, its sources are in essence the motifs of the natural world: the skins, hides, or feathers of animals (or, as we will see, their tracks), the images of plants, or the figures suggested by pure phenomenal energy. In dreams the *konsaho* cross the frontier separating the land and sky, underground, or watery depths, according to their particular categories, and identify with the animal, the vegetable, or the forces that populate these regions.

What is the ground of the *cet,* this principle that identifies the shamans with the elements surrounding them? The shamans are great manipulators of the forces that condition the human world. To wield them they must, according to Chamacoco thought, neutralize or reverse adverse powers and appropriate favorable ones. This requires that the *konsaho* acquire in dreams the properties of the elements that contain *woso.* That is, it requires that they occupy the position of such elements and assume their appearance, or at least certain aspects of it. The first tale synthesizes the essential characteristics of the shamanic world: metamorphosis, song, maraca, feather, painting, and dream. Elisa turns into a fish, acquiring their physical appearance and certain powers associated with the aquatic world. She communicates through the maraca and song: through both, she enters into contact with the essential powers of fish and meets with other shamanic souls who, like her, plough the murky depths. This metamorphosis is possible through dream, in whose sheltering shadows the shaman can double herself, detach herself from her body, and dive into the river waters.

From the depths of his or her dream, the shaman returns with the strength of revealed knowledge. This revelation is not the free gift of a superior principle but the product of a resolute conquest: the hidden face of the real is grasped through a difficult process, a constant struggle, a great effort that is not always successful. Through the dream or ecstatic flight, the prodigious proceedings of *externization*—or however we want to call this shadowy act and scarcely nameable process through which the shaman cleaves off his or her own sleeping body and confronts the physical and supernatural powers that condition human survival and projects—the shaman, the wise man or woman, the magician, attains knowledge and can then wield it.

In a certain sense, and on certain occasions, the shaman knows the archetypes, a concept that we can, without forcing it too much, understand in Platonic terms (they are similar to those used by the Guaraní to refer to celestial models): the exemplary forms of the real. In the first tale, the feathers and colors of *chuko,* the parrot, constitute an original standard that must be imitated. This mention is especially interesting, not only because it refers to the application of transcendental guidelines obtained in dreams, but because it links the origin of the feathers with that of corporal paintings. It is the only tale I know that makes such a link.

field notes

Today we had no opportunity to return to the village to eat because the agenda of rituals was especially packed, for reasons I do not know. We prepared some food in a clearing near the *tobich*. The Ishir ate dried meat and peccary salad; we ate bread, cheese, canned tuna, and apples. We shared a delicious local dessert made from honey and roasted hearts of palm. It has been some time since I stopped feeling guilty for our gastronomic differences. On my first trips I tried to eat what they ate and to convince myself, as well as them, that I derived great pleasure from these strange tastes. But I ended up with a greasy mouth, hunger, or indisposition—and guilt, of course. On a certain occasion Bruno, Clemente, and I met in Asunción and were invited to dinner by Luke Holland, a representative of Survival International. Bruno is a professional chief, a stoic *gentleman:* he ate the pasta and creamy sauce with cosmopolitan unflappability. Clemente however pushed aside the plate and asked for a piece of grilled meat. "How can you eat such things?" he asked, frankly curious. When the Chamacoco began to come to the capital for business or pleasure and visit me at home, Tere made a great effort to produce spectacular meals. But her prestigious honeyed ham and olive pies were considered inedible and rejected by our laughing guests. After such experiences, it seemed that my resigned acceptance of food I did not like was paternalistic, and even damaging. "The relations," I explained to Cristián, biting into my imported fruit, "need to be symmetrical. To respect the difference of the other, I need to affirm the right to my own difference."

After our separate lunches, a session of corporal painting began in the center of the *tobich*. I was disconcerted by the appearance of a group of youth gleaming with red tones: the *ostyrbe* is rare in these new regions and, used sparingly and carefully, it produces sparse and faded images. How had these initiates achieved such bright colors? "From a warehouse in Bahía Negra," responds Daniel. Bahía Negra? They sell *ostyrbe* in commercial establishments in Bahía Negra? The boys and men laugh. No, they sell lipstick there; the youth paint their bodies with female beauty products. Will there be one day a myth about lipstick? Obviously I do not venture this question out loud.

THE MASTERS OF COLOR

Who paint their bodies? When? Why? The Ishir paint their bodies on such different occasions and for reasons that are so varied that it is not practical to enumerate answers to these questions. Are these signs that brighten or darken the rough skin of the Chamacoco figurative? Do they refer to recognizable objects? And if they do, is it in the hopes of summoning the presence or favor of such objects? Do they intend to interpellate something by pronouncing its name or imitating its image? Many signs must be interpreted as rigorously abstract: although they present themselves as imitations of the patterns gracing the skins of the gods, there was no prior referent for these patterns. Yet the Ishir themselves sometimes recognize a referential intent in the forms of corporal painting. "These spots are the skin of the ocelot," they affirm. "They *are*," they emphasize—not "they seem to be," or "they look like." For this reason, their figures constitute metaphors: they do not compare, they *identify*. In the ceremonial circle, the men *are* gods. They metamorphize into the gods, occupy their places, and assume their appearances. The copula of the metaphor acts in oscillation: it neither annuls the connected entities nor produces a synthesis between the terms in constant tension.

Sometimes metaphors are denotative. They take on the physical features of the linked subjects (colors, contours, textures, etc.) as the basis for similarity; as when the Ishir say, "such forms come from the spots on that bird," or "they are the tracks of the anteater," or "they are the spots of a peccary." And yet at other times they are also connotative: they refer to the images suggested by the crazy gait of the ostrich, the undulations of the snake, or the dark fear brought on by jaguars. Sometimes the suggestions of the rhythmic cries of certain birds can be converted into laconic pentagrams that mark the skin with a counterpoint of notes and pauses. Obviously, the complex rhetorical mechanisms of corporal painting (as well as featherwork) do not only recur to metaphor, but also put into play a wide spectrum of tropes, symbols, indices, and allegories. There is even room for individual associations. And these figures are often blended into hybrid figures and intricate semiotic chains. It is consequently impossible to identify a referent. The processes of signification do not close or linger on a final meaning. Signs slide into each other, forming unstable clusters and fluid constellations that bleed into the backdrop of primal questions; and they return, saturated with meaning, onto the now sweaty bodies, to renew the questions that urge the vigil of culture. (And which keep it watchful, alive, and restless.)

The connections between the paintings and certain objects or phenomena of the natural world are, therefore, so complex and variable that it is best to simply mention them without attempting to follow their tortuous and misleading path. The question is further complicated when we consider that the references—when there are references—can obey intentions as varied as sociopolitical information (signs of status, rank, and profession), mythical/pedagogical purposes, or magical/propitiatory ones (such as warding off disasters and attracting good fortune). But they can also serve merely aesthetic objectives: the Ishir adorn themselves with the spotted beauty of the jaguars and drape themselves in the fiery shades of the spoonbills.

For this and other reasons, we need to give up our pretensions to deciphering the meanings of corporal painting (or any other form of art). Its designs and colors display signs that are slippery, and open to many meanings; signs that are unstable and beyond our grasp. Instead of exhausting a list of the occasions on which the Ishir paint themselves, I will limit myself to commenting on certain specific instantiations of painting in order to suggest the plethoric and unstable fields of meaning to which these open themselves up.

Novices

The initiation of young men into socioceremonial life is one of the central nodes of Ishir culture. The youth gain access to the many obligations and rights of adults through a complex ritual attached to the *debylyby*, the Great Ceremony. This ritual is a rigid and efficient symbolic filter that orders, unifies, separates, and regulates the central issues in the Ishir horizon. During initiation sexuality, death, personal growth, community conflict and cohesion, power, leisure, subsistence, and transcendence become intense figures proposed as essential ciphers, questions, or enigmas that must be confronted (not resolved) through an arduous process that engages the development of the individual and legitimacy of the group. The apprentice (*wetern*) dies and lives again, suffers, intuits the plenitude and risk of commitment, accedes to the dangerous, essential word: the secret, the buried lodestone that sustains the complicated cultural architecture of his people.

During the period of seclusion, which is part of the initiation process, the novice's body is covered with small ash-white dots that he reapplies every day after the obligatory morning ablutions. The dots are organized in ordered lines. On his face, a line of dots traces the bridge of his nose while sets of five, three, and two dots follow the contours of his face and punctuate his chin. After seclusion—after the tests and words of the essential, existential, sacred apprenticeship—the youths present themselves in the *harra*, their naked bodies entirely covered in red paint. No one can talk to them and the women cannot even look at them (even though they may want to see the irreversible signs of the ultimate secret on the transformed bodies of their sons). The youths are not only naked; they have also shorn themselves of all body hair, even eyebrows and eyelashes. They are radically naked. Only the intense power of pure red shields and covers them.

During the second appearance, which generally takes place the following day, the youths ("the recruits," Daniel translates) present themselves again, but now only their faces are painted in red. Their bodies display the ornaments of those who have fulfilled their training and are now participants in the words of Ashnuwerta: *nymagarak*, headdresses of red feathers, which identify "one who knows the secret," crown their foreheads; sashes strung with alternating *byrbyre* seeds and shells, called *oso-uhúna*, are slung around their necks and across their chests; *oikakarn*, bracelets of yellow or red feathers, adorn their wrists; and a belt of caraguata called *yrak*, from which hang parrot feathers and deer hooves, circle their waists. The latter piece is typologically identical to the belt called *yrrote*, from which feathers also dangle; the difference lies in the bird species whose feathers are used to make the two ornaments. The initiates' pieces use only green parrot feathers, while common ornaments display the white or dark feathers of other birds, especially the *piririta*, hawk, or *charata*.[4] Finally, below the belt they use a loincloth of caraguata called *otyrpe*.

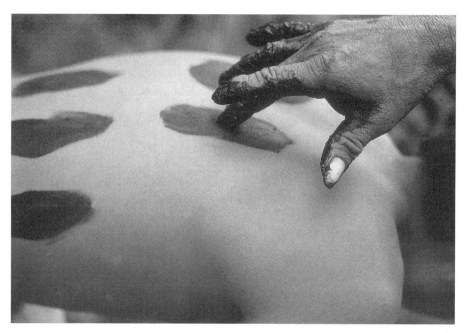

Detail from a scene of body painting. A man applies lines of black paint on the back of a young officiant. Puerto Esperanza, 1986. (Photo by Ticio Escobar.)

During the following months, and until the next collective ritual, the apprentices repaint their faces red every day. "When we did not have a mirror in the *tobich*," says Daniel, who was initiated in San Carlos in 1982, "we used a tortoise shell, cleaned with caraguata and polished with the pelt of an anteater. The apprentices couldn't distinguish features on this surface, but they could identify the oval contours of the face and make out the mass that had to be painted." They shave their heads twice. During a period of approximately two weeks—which begins after their second appearance and ends when Hopupora's second cry announces the start of a new *debylyby*—the recently initiated replace the *nymagarak,* red headdress, with the *manänha hijá* (literally, "duck belly"), a crown crafted with the black feathers of the *bragado* duck. This ornament is formally very similar to the *manon wolo* (or *lepper wolo*), but is smaller and lacks the piece that hangs down over the back of the neck like a cape.

Susnik and Cordeu both relate the painting of dots on the novices to the figure of Arpylá. While their interpretations are implicit in what I have just de-

An example of the impression of hands on the back of an officiant at the initiation grounds. San Carlos, 1986. (Photo by Ticio Escobar.)

scribed, I will transcribe them partially now. Susnik says that before the instruction of the sacred words, the initiate learns to detect the whistle of the anábsoro (1957, 65). From this moment on he has the right to change color. Instead of painting his body like a deer (with greyish dots) he begins to use the red that men use in festivals. The descendent of Arpylá, the woman/doe, begins to participate symbolically in the dimension of the anábsoro. Once the secret is revealed, the beginner receives a bracelet of red feathers related to Ashnuwerta, as well as the long necklace of seeds of the same fruit used in ceremonial sound making. The initiate's right to this ornament indicates his acceptance into the community of the *tobich*. In the past, the apprentice received a bone labret to pierce his bottom lip; such a practice coincided with the *pasyparak* (or *nymagarak*) ornament that was granted once the period of testing had concluded. The end of the rituals of initiation coincides with the last appearance of the anábsoro in the ceremonial circle.

Cordeu writes that the youthful initiates entered the *tobich* painted with a greyish smattering of spots, and that the initiation culminated with their return to the village covered in red. The *wetern* is called *Arpylá abo*. This name means "son of Arpylá"—"and connotes the idea of meta-temporality that links the Ishir in a common regime of blood symbolized by the deer" (Cordeu 1991b, 184–85)—but also refers to the figure of the "small deer." Moreover, the red adopted by the youth at the end of the rite also refers, by analogy, to the color of adult deer. The chromatic change, which imitates that of the deer, symbolically represents the process of maturation that takes place in the initiatory trance: "red testifies to the efficacy of a biological process which, on another plane of reality, is analogous to the social and religious maturation of the individuals in the secret society" (Cordeu 1991b, 184–85).

But the itinerary of the paintings' significations is inexhaustible, and the fact that it is the novices themselves who apply the paints on the bodies of those who will represent the gods is charged with meaning. Emilio Aquino, the Tomáraho leader, says that the *wetern* paint certain anábsoro so as to "expand their *eiwo*, understanding."

Players

During the ritual games, corporal painting has a double function. On the one hand, it stresses the ceremony's special moment and elicits a variety of auspicious connotations promoted and endorsed by corporal painting. On the other hand, painting marks the difference between the players: it graphically demarcates the confrontation between groups, a confrontation that also mobilizes and balances the becoming of Ishir society. In this second case, corporal painting acts as a principle of distinction, much like the uniforms of different sports teams.

During the game called *kymychyló*, the Tomáraho paint themselves around the mouth. The members of one group paint themselves red, the others brown. The Ebytoso mark each group differently when playing this same game: the *onota oso* (team of the riverbank) apply white dots on their skin with their fingers; the *yrmych oso* (team of the woods) color one half of their bodies red and the other half black. In the game called *katishé*, one of the rival teams paints their bodies black, the other team plays with their bodies unpainted. During the competition of the *póhorro,* one group covers their bodies in white handprints over a black background; the other group paints their bodies in white and then stamps them with black handprints. This is the Tomáraho schema. The Ebytoso use other markers: the riverbank teammates have red bodies and faces lined in white stripes; their rivals have red bodies with white handprints and faces striped in white and red.

Although the *senne* is basically a female game, on some occasions men play it too. While it is not based on opposing teams, all Tomáraho participants use the same black and white colors and facial designs: a vertical line emphasizes the line of the nose and another divides the chin, while three horizontal stripes cross the cheekbones. To participate in this game, the Ebytoso men and women paint their faces black and furrow it with white stripes.

Gods

As indicated, their attempt to identify with the gods is one of the fundamental reasons the Ishir paint themselves. The basic tones of the anábsoro (red, black, and white) are combined in an infinite number of compositions to imitate the designs on the skins of the gods they killed and whose place they usurped, and can refer to a plethora of collective meanings. Given this variety of forms, colors, and functions, I will offer simply some illustrative cases as examples.

Among the Tomáraho, the Tiribo plaster their bodies with the black and white handprints of the recently initiated young men. The same painting, which is in this case considered to favor the gathering of honey, is reproduced on the trunk of the *palo borracho* tree[5] planted in the center of the ritual circle, and becomes an emblem of the ceremony. The Ebytoso Tiribo (called Byteta) also paint this pole, but with different colors and designs: they apply stripes of white, brown, black, blue, and red with the edge of the hand. Striped in this fashion and crowned with feathered ornaments crafted by the Posháraha clan, the *debylyby icha*—the trunk-sign of the celebration—is erected, filled with auspicious energies, and purged of threatening ones.

On some occasions, the paint on the bodies irradiates beneficial powers that can be transmitted to whoever enters into contact with them. Thus, for example, it is common for women to bring their children to Wioho, Wiao, Kaimo, and Wákaka: they wait for these characters to touch their children

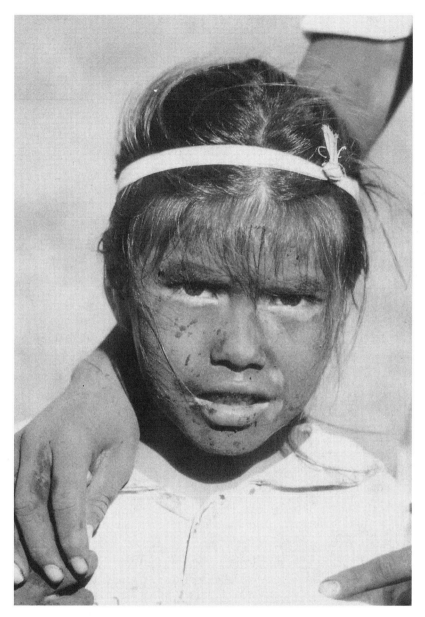

A young girl with facial paint, held close to the *anábser* Wo by her mother so that the god can imbue her with auspicious gifts. María Elena, 2001. (Photo by Nicolás Richard.)

with their painted hands, wrists, arms, or torsos so they can benefit from the virtues of colors and grow up healthy and lucky. The Tomáraho Wákaka present themselves onstage with white bodies crossed with black stripes. The Ebytoso have two variations of Wákaka: the Wákaka with black stripes are beneficent, those with red stripes have negatives powers. But power, even when virtuous, always includes a destructive principle. This is why the women who approach the Wákaka Wys (the black ones), seeking to rub the sick parts of their bodies against the painted arms, must be blindfolded to avoid being damaged by the power (*woso*) they exude in excess. The women who gain access to the ceremonial circle to fight ritually with a character called Honta Abich paint their faces red and carry staffs that mimic the patterns of corporal painting used by the entourage of Holé (to which Honta Abich belongs). These paintings ward off madness, melancholy, delirium, convulsions, and disturbances of the spirit in general. If the guardian of Honta Abich does not paint himself with the god's colors he is exposed to a gamut of diseases, from diarrhea to blindness.

The different anábsoro present themselves with specific patterns, which refer both to their own appearances and to certain natural elements they can secretly name or summon. The rhetorical links that tie those paintings to their natural referents are intricate and inexhaustible and, rather than untangle them, it is best to simply point them out silently and from afar. It is like observing a ritual whose inner logic remains foreign to the observer. The same effervescence of signs that confronts the outsider with Otherness represents, for the Chamacoco, the place where the cardinal points of meaning intersect. I will enumerate some illustrative cases.

Among the Ebytoso, the Holé Mother has her body painted in red and black on her opposite sides. The black zone is connected with red arms and legs; the red zone with black arms and legs. The black part of the body is covered in white painted circles, and the red zone in black circles. "These colors," explains the shaman Faustino Rojas, "come from the water (?). The small black and white circles are called *ko ehi*, shells of *ko*, wild peanuts. Their purpose is to summon these peanuts." The paintings of the seventeen Okala anábsoro are related to fish. For this reason, each one bears a different combination of colors (red, black, and white) and motifs (circles, lines, and dots) applied on the arms and torsos. When seen together, these anábsoro resemble a quivering, multicolored school of fish.

Mä has black arms covered with white circles; his chest is painted in black, white, and red. Among the Ebytoso he is called Mä-Mä and his appearance is more complex: half his body is red, the other half black, and both colors are covered in white dots; the right leg is painted in red from the knee up, and the rest is black; the left leg bears the inverse pattern; the left arm is red from the wrist to the elbow, and black up to the shoulder; while the right is black below, red above. "This signifies," says Enrique Ozuna, "the color of the frog." "It is a call for rain," he says, complicating the figure even further.

Referring to Wákaka, Ozuna says that he uses the colors of *isör* (an underground insect) to recall the deity's subterranean origin. The corporal paintings of Wichau are based on the reiteration of three brief parallel lines of alternating colors (black, white, red), which invade legs and arms and end up crowding the torso. The Ebytoso insist that such a design reveals the watery origin of these anábsoro. Ho-Ho and his followers are dyed entirely in red and then dressed with light black stains applied with rhythmic pressure with the side of the hand. "They resemble tigers," say the Ebytoso, "because they are good hunters. Ho-Ho was one of the anábsoro who taught the men to track and shoot down their prey and overcome even the fiercest beasts." In order to bring about the abundance of fruits, Wä-Wä must be painted with small grayish circles over a black background. "Those circles are fruits," Flores Balbuena assures me with conviction.

I want to end by pointing out some especially notable paintings that characterize certain gods. The Tomáraho Kaimo appears divided in symmetrical halves: one is black, the other is white, and each is the base for a series of black and white motifs that create a counterpoint of oppositions and function as an interplay of positives and negatives. Arms and legs are drenched in contrasting colors and inverted designs, which complicate the duality and extend it into an unending zigzag. Among the Ebytoso, the opposition takes the form of a red/black axis that divides the body in counterpoised, alternate halves. (As mentioned above, both the color of blood and the designs on snake skins are fundamental for identifying Kaimo.)

Among the Tomáraho, the Mother, central figure of the Holé retinue, appears painted in white. The bodies of the Holé Abo (the daughters) are covered in black and their legs are furrowed with red lines, like delicate wounds that have opened up in a black and brilliant skin. Both Honta Abich, the husband, and his guardian are presented with back and extremities colored in black; their chests are covered by a great vertical band, flanked with white dots. The same motif is repeated by Wahö, Ñana, and Wo. Shínimit is red with white spots. The Tomáraho Kaiporta is colored with watery ash, while the Ebytoso Kaiporta has black feet and red extremities striped with dark bands.

According to the Ishir preference for doubled and inverted images and for the interplay of relieves and hollows, the body of Pahö appears divided in two halves: one is black furrowed with white lines, the other is white crossed with black rays. The whitish skin of Okío appears populated with the dark imprints of opened hands; the black skin of Katibyshé is flooded with the same hands in milky white.

Warriors

The Ishir no longer engage in bellicose corporal painting and it has been impossible for me to gather information on these practices. The various war sagas recounted with relish by the Ishir simply mention the "black paints" without going into further detail. According to Susnik (1995, 21–24), whose information I will follow here, the impression of black handprints on the bodies of soldiers in the vanguard guaranteed success in the battle. While the men fought, the subsistence of the village was the responsibility of the women, who assumed male functions and were denominated "the gatherers of eels." During this time of masculine absence, the women could agitate the ceremonial maracas, invoke the Woman / Doe (considered a powerful shaman in metamorphosis), and listen to the rousing speeches of a "great orator" (normally an old widow). On such occasions, the woman painted themselves with *nantyk* (blue-black) in the hollows of the eyes, nose, and chin. When the soldiers returned, bringing back captives and terrible stories of deaths, victories, or defeats, the women prepared the *otarn nykymyrta,* the war celebration. Women also danced in the circle of the rite while on the side combatants recounted their deeds and goaded each another with interclan word games to bring forth new tales.

In another of her works, Susnik writes that the soldiers also painted themselves in red. In this case the use of hematite was obligatory (the combatants could not paint themselves with vegetable dye from the *urucú* plant[6]). As leader of the army, the chief (*pylota*) painted his body in black and covered it with white stripes. In his role as a great hunter, the chief added yellow stripes "obeying the principle of identification with the master of the woods, Xoxit" (Susnik 1957, 121–22). The night patrols painted themselves with *wys*, the somber color of the third celestial stratum.

Hunters

Hunters use corporal painting for magical ends. They seek to attract good prey or obtain the good graces of the Master of the Animals who can choose to facilitate their efforts in subsistence. Although I will refer in more detail to the "propitiatory magic" of certain indigenous cultural forms, I want to anticipate that many cases of so-called "magic by mimesis" should be understood rhetorically. The indigenous man identifies himself metaphorically with the animal he wants to hunt and represents it metonymically through certain markers of the animal, or elaborates his ambivalent relationship with it through strictly symbolic resources. The "call" to the animal through paint or feathers should therefore never be understood literally but as part of a dense set of operations that culturalize the material act of hunting, mediating it by wrapping it in obscure languages and codes, norms, and prescriptions, in the useless and indispensable arguments of poetry.

Nature does not present itself as a smooth exterior that must be occupied, but as a multidimensional and mysterious territory filled with secrets, keys, false bottoms, threats, shortcuts, echoes, and hiding places. In general, the Ishir stalk the principles and track down the relations and forces acting behind the factical immediacy of all living beings. Every phenomenon is understood through the schema of oppositions/alliances/identifications that comprise Ishir logic. Humans can enter into alliance with these phenomena or confront them, and while they are sometimes victorious and sometimes defeated, in the long run it is always a draw.

The question is even more complicated in the case of hunting. The hunter has an ambivalent and conflictive relationship with the animal, one that is burdened with guilt, fear, and uncertain desires. On the one hand, the beast is his adversary; on the other hand, the beast is his means of sustenance. Humans recognize an inverted reflection of themselves in their prey: both depend on nature to live and share a common fate as survivors in a world traversed by the same trails and waters and threatened by the same supernatural powers, unknown hybrid beings and angry gods, greedy white men, droughts and storms, fires, floods, and cosmic disturbances. For this reason, such a complex relation cannot be dealt with in the prosaic terms of tracking, catching, and eating. They need to be mediated by subtle rites and arcane words, enveloped with the colors of the light, night, and blood, signed with the illegible figures that mark animal hides or are left behind by hurried tracks.

When men track a band of peccaries, their cheeks and the hollows of their eyes are painted in black and white to avoid being run over by the animals (Susnik 1995, 55). During certain collective hunts they paint themselves yellow, the color of the mythical benefactor of hunters Xoxit, the invincible grandfather (Susnik 1978, 212). After the obligatory morning bath, the initiates paint their bodies in imitation of the tracks of the wild boar or anteater to facilitate the capture of these animals (Cordeu 1991b, 186).

As will be seen further on, in the ceremonial circle, the Chamacoco paint themselves with different motifs and colors to promote the successful hunt or fishing expedition according to the anábser they incarnate.

Shamans

The shamans, as said, are intermediaries between the Ishir and the world of phenomena with whose friendly or hostile forces they must negotiate. To do so—to cure diseases, bring back lost spirits, ward off ills or bring them upon the heads of their enemies—the konsaho borrow their paintings from the excursions of their dreams or flights of ecstasy.

Civilians

Corporal painting is also used in certain aspects of private life (which is never very far from—and often confused with—the public sphere) to signal distinct states. When they are in mourning, widows and widowers paint their faces black: the furrows etched out by the path of their tears on this black surface signal their pain. To communicate their commitment to each other, a betrothed man uses reddish tones and the woman yellowish tones from the oré

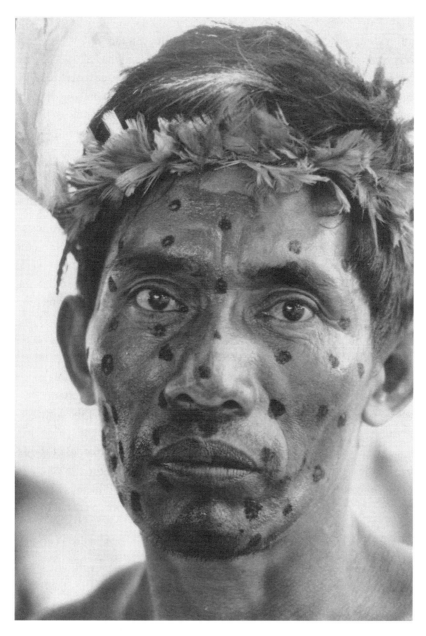

Portrait of Luciano Martínez, Tomáraho sky shaman, with facial painting and a crown of feathers. Puerto 14 de Mayo, 1989. (Photo by Luke Holland.)

fruit (Susnik 1995, 164). When a man wants to express his desire for reconciliation with his wife after a serious quarrel, he paints his face red. If his plea is accepted, after one or two days of cautious distance the wife will appear with the same colors and "peace is reestablished" (Baldus 1927, 28). According to Boggiani, resentment and pain are expressed by "singing, dancing or, curiously, by painting one's face and body with black, red, white or yellow, or adorning oneself with brightly colored feathers that are gracefully interwoven" (in Baldus 1927, 53). If someone dies, his/her closest family dress him/her up with their best ornaments and paint his/her face, hands, and feet red (Boggiani 1900, 80).

When a youth dies during the tests in the *tobich,* his body is painted in red from the waist down and his torso and arms are colored black. According to Cordeu (1991b, 182), the body paint of the novice whose father has died is the inverse of this schema: the upper part of his body is red, and the lower black. The Tomáraho informed me that when a baby (less than one year old) is anguished by the absence of the father (who is secluded in the *tobich* to instruct the beginners) the mother can ask a member of the Kytymáraha clan to bring him to the initiation grounds so the father can calm him. But in order to enter the *tobich* the infant must have his forehead, the bridge of the nose, and the skin around his mouth painted in red. This exception is beneficial only to the *osir-härk* (children that do not yet speak). (The word installs a distance that must be safeguarded until language becomes the incarnation of the word that reveals the secret and renews the essential enigmas.)

The paintings that mark clan differences derive from the codes of the *debylyby:* the different segments identify themselves according to the paintings that distinguish the gods killed by their predecessors. It is difficult, therefore, to speak of clan painting independently; I will refer to it when I detail the different characters of the Chamacoco pantheon.

THE FORMS OF COLOR

Designs

The motifs used in corporal painting are very elemental. The complexity of the final image and the intensity of its expression are based on combinations of forms and colors and on the characteristics of the painted surface: the body intervenes dramatically in the configuration of visual effects. The body that sweats and trembles, the muscle that contracts, and the resolute signs of human flesh add variable and potent forces. A black circle painted on an inert surface is not the same as a circle applied to the tense torso of a god/man or magician of "shining eyes." One must in addition consider that the colors and forms of the paintings interact with feathers, and each completes and enhances the other.

The basic motifs of corporal painting are as follows:

Bands or straight lines that can be wide or thin, short or long: these can alternate with dots or be constituted by dots. Sometimes, as in certain Ebytoso representations of the anábser Wákaka, the alternating threads of colors begin on the neck and end at the ankles. On certain occasions, the lines curve or branch out.

Dots, specks, spots, or rings: in general these motifs are applied in white over a red or black background or in black and red over a white background, or simply over the skin's natural color. It is common for them to alternate in contiguous zones.

A spattered effect produced by throwing a fistful of paint on the face: it produces a strong and expressive effect, similar to that of the *dripping* of North American abstract painters.

Planes of colors: the smooth distribution of one color is usually the base for the application of other motifs and covers specific parts of the body in combination with other zones of color. For example, it is common to alternate red, black, or white planes, which simultaneously cover different areas of the body.

The imprints of open hands fall on the torso, arms, and legs: on skin that either retains its natural tone or is drenched in bright colors. Susnik associates this motif to certain cave paintings from Patagonia and links it to the Chamacoco cultural complex "blood, gaze, and hand," three intense figures that animate the world of the shamans and engage the dimension of the gods (1995, 222–24).

Spirals: this motif, possibly of Caduveo origin, is rarely used. I have heard of its use in the representation of the Kuahé, a little-known anábser whose representation I have never seen.

Techniques

The most common tool used in painting is the hand: one's own hand or some-one else's hand. Men paint each other as well as themselves. Lines are drawn with fingers that slide over the skin or that tap rhythmically, leaving bright-ened, somber, luminous trails. Spots are produced through rhythmic impres-sions of part of the palm or the side of the hand. Spatterings are achieved, as suggested, by throwing fistfuls of white ash on the face. Handprints are liter-ally produced by the pressure of open hands on the back or chest, legs, or arms. In this case, it is rare to use one's own hand: not only for practical reasons but for symbolic ones as well, for the signs of a foreign power are at stake.

It is not uncommon to find objects employed as stamps. Cut in large or small pieces (according to the effect desired) the stalks of the caraguata plant serve to imprint rings. The skin of a fruit called *ko* by the Ishir (translated by them as "wild peanuts") is also used in a similar fashion. After the fruit is cooked and eaten with great appreciation, the Ishir bore a hole in the center of each of the halves into which its hard shell split, and slide thin sticks in both sides to serve as two handles. This way, each fruit produces two seals that imprint oblong forms (generally white). On certain occasions I have seen the shaman Wylky use the teeth of a comb to stamp lines of dots on his legs, which were already painted black.

Colors and Materials

The basic colors of Chamacoco corporal painting are black, white, and red; in the past yellow and, more rarely, brown were also used. These are the colors linked to strong expressions of existence and the cosmos. They are the colors of celestial regions and strata that intensify during storms to announce diverse messages and warn of the advent of calamities. "Four colors rise on the horizon to announce a storm: black, white, yellow, and red. One must know how to ob-serve them in order to be well prepared," says Emilio Aquino, a Tomáraho who knows such things.

Black—a thick, bright color—is produced by diluting burnt palm leaves in water. Métraux also mentions the juice of the genip fruit[7] as a colorant that produces black (1996, 133). White is obtained from the ashes of a reedlike plant

An Ishir man painting his legs black before he enters the ceremonial circle. Potrerito, 1989. (Photo by Ticio Escobar.)

called the *totorra*. Red is derived from hematite and also, in some occasions, from *urucú* and even by lipstick, as we have seen. According to Métraux, *urucú* was frequently used among the Chamacoco who traded it with tribes in the south in the form of natural seeds or loaves: these are prepared by diluting the pigment in water and later boiling the liquid until only a thick paste is left, to which honey is added (1996, 132). Yellow was produced by the ashes of the burnt *pirizal* (a family of papyrus-like plants) and, according to Susnik, from a fruit called *oré* (1995, 64). Brown was extracted from *katishé:* the liquid in which the bark of this tree is boiled is then mixed with ashes to produce a paste, which acts as the base for this color. The Ebytoso also mention the flowers of a tree called *ha-lä,* whose chewed petals let off a juice that can be used as an ink for brown. The flowers of another tree, the *oskála,* when chewed produce a blue paint, which the Ebytoso use to paint the *samu'u* during the rituals of Tiribo. According to Flores Balbuena, some shamans use a product obtained from a tree known as *py-lë* whose leaves, when ground in a wooden mortar and diluted in water from the caraguata plant, produce a distinctive green color.

Like the forms of feathers and painting, the meaning of colors is slippery and relative. Cordeu, a rigorous analyst of Chamacoco culture, maintains that red and black, the principle colors, are opposed semantically. Both, he says, have connotations that are the opposite of those in common experience: black is linked with light and clarity; red is linked with darkness, and even blindness. These references determine that black denotes the positive sacred aspects of the supernatural *woso* (power) whereas red refers to this power's negative moments (the "numinous terrible"). For this reason, depending on whether anábsoro present themselves in predominantly red or black, they can be *om* or *sherwó*: "peaceful and good or ferocious and malignant" (Cordeu 1990, 136). While it is true that red sometimes connotes the ferocity of the numen and black its benevolent aspects, if we assume that the red/black opposition does not express a semantic antagonism but a formal confrontation it allows for a broader range of interpretations. That is, basically, the red/black opposition stages opposition itself since the semantic values of the colors fluctuate and depend on the scene or place they occupy in a schema of logical relations.

To illustrate what I have just said, I would like to refer briefly to some cases of opposing pairs:

Nemur and Pfaujata: both anábsoro appear together on the ritual scene. They oppose one another over a backdrop of shared notes. He is black, she is red. And while both are fearsome and even dangerous, both can present beneficent faces. For the Ishir, power has two sides. Red refers both to the principle of vitality and spilled blood, to the creative flame and the devastating fire. Black suggests shadows and storms, mysterious threats and unknown forces, as well as the profound stillness that shelters dreams, the dark refuge of first truths.

Ashnuwerta (Red Mother) and Ashnuwysta (Black Mother): the first synthesizes the adverse and favorable aspects of power; the second emphasizes its darker side, linked to epidemics and storms, but also open to the operations of counterpowers and negotiations that certain wise Chamacoco know how to use to their advantage.

Pohejuvo the Red and Pohejuvo the Black: the presence of the counterpoised shades of paintings and costumes used by these anábsoro expresses nothing but the relationship between the self/same and the other, the old paradox of difference. This is so to such an extent that the current Chamacoco call them Pohejuvo Colorado and Pohejuvo Liberal, referring to the traditional opposition between the two most established political parties in Paraguay.[8]

Kadjuwerta and *kadjuwysta*: names of the two great mallets of feathers used in different moments of the Great Ceremony, to condense the powers unleashed by the ceremony (*kadjuwerta*) and to overcome the drought that frequently lashes the Chaco (*kadjuwysta*). The chromatic opposition indicates the gradation in the power of the colors. *Kadjuwerta* ("the red power") is superior in positive and adverse forces to *kadjuwysta* ("the black power"). Clemente explains it thus: some colors are more efficacious than others. For example, if one fishes with a white hook, the *pacú*[9] can slip off and escape into the water, whereas if one uses a black hook the fish will remain hooked. In this case the issue is not benevolent versus harmful colors, but colors that are more or less powerful.

Holé, called Honta upon entering the circle of ceremonies: one of the most complex dramatizations in the Great Ceremony belongs to this goddess. At some moment in the representation, Honta Abich ("the husband of Honta") symbolically confronts a young woman from the Tomáraho clan who is painted and dressed in bold crimson. Why is the woman who attacks and defends herself from the godly consort colored in red? So that Honta Abich does not steal her strength, says Wylky. Honta Abich, for his part, takes a child from the arms of its mother every so often and rubs it against the parts of his body painted in black: in that context black has properties that promote healthy growth.

Wioho, the healer: prototype of the benevolent anábser. The bearer of curative powers, he can dexterously reverse the adverse powers of things and promote peace. He represents the god that tried to resuscitate Jolué, the son of Syr who was devoured by the insatiable mythic cannibals. The color of Wioho's skin, as well as that of his entourage, is red. In this case, red takes on a protective, beneficial, and even healing power.

Female ritual of mourning: a group of mourners burst on the scene during the beginning of the Great Ceremony. In the foreground Eligia Ramírez, Tomáraho shaman, presents herself with a bare chest in a sign of grief. Puerto Esperanza, 1986. (Photo by Ticio Escobar.)

THE RITE

FOR Rousseau the festival begins when there are no actors and society becomes its own spectacle (Duvignaud 1980, 207). The rite is, in effect, the representation of the social. Re-presentation: as it is placed onstage, costumed and masked, presented under lights and effects according to the vicissitudes of plot, society suspends its norms and divulges other aspects of itself than those conveyed daily. This transition between the time of the everyday and the "effervescent" time—to use Durkheim's term—the time of the stage and its excess, of simulacrum and poetry, is an essential part of the ritual.

While it depends on the play of forms and is linked to an assortment of aesthetic and rhetorical artifices, ritual nonetheless obeys its own logic. It should not, therefore, be understood simply as the literal dramatization of mythic plots. Myth and ritual both operate in their own manner and through their own rhetorical resources: one with words and the other with images. And each brings its own presuppositions. Ritual does not pretend to interpret episodes of myth or incarnate its characters according to the logic of narration. For example, the anábsoro that appear in the circle of the ceremony do not represent any particular episode in the cycle of the apparition of the gods and their violent deaths: the ceremony is driven by other plots, ones that are more hermetic (if the term can be used) than the storylines of myth. Perhaps because they originate in a variety of arenas (visual, musical, choreographic, theatrical, literary) the metaphors of rite are even more obscure than the knotted figures of the mythic tales.

The recalcitrance of form also prevents it from adapting itself meekly to the requirements of society. Therefore, when the socially integrating and legitimating function of myth is mentioned, it is necessary to avoid falling into reductions that make such a function absolute. Certainly rite is a principle of "total cohesion" as Mauss affirms, but its elusive, fleeting forms exceed the necessities of collective institutions and can even unsettle them. By dramatizing and re-presenting social order, rites render visible the architecture concealed by such an order so as to maintain its equilibrium. Rites, therefore, are also a destabilizing social factor: by exposing the darker side of institutions, by abruptly signaling buried desires and fears, by naming the enigma without revealing it, rites perturb the foundations of society, disrupt its regular course, and open up the social contract for discussion. Rites, says Duvignaud, are "useless sacrifices," pure excesses which burst social bounds and "brutally" assault the tranquilizing duration imposed by the reproduction or conservation of societies (1980, 208).

Why does Duvignaud refer to rites as "useless"? In doing so he leans close to Kant who declared the uselessness of aesthetic forms. Although rite, like any other cultural text, simultaneously upholds and questions the social order, it does not do so directly: it does not have immediate practical effects on the relations that weave that order. The transsocial properties of ritual forms—that is, the fact that they unfold beyond the arena organized by social structures—means that these forces are, in great part, pure dramatization, unproductive in terms of social benefits, and as useless as art, whose forms they share. Based on the example of Balinese cockfights (and citing an elegy to Yeats which states that "poetry makes nothing happen"), Geertz maintains that like any art form—"for that, finally, is what we are dealing with"—rite does not "alter the hierarchical relations among people." By vigorously articulating profound meanings of collective experience, however, rite allows these relations to be perceived more intensely. "What it does is what, for other peoples with other temperaments and other conventions, *Lear* and *Crime and Punishment* do; it catches up those themes—death, masculinity, rage, pride, loss, beneficence, change—and, ordering them into an encompassing structure, presents them in such a way as to throw into relief a particular view of their essential nature. It puts a construction on them, makes them . . . meaningful—visible, tangible, graspable." The function of ritual "is neither to assuage social passions nor to heighten them (though, in its playing-with-fire way it does a bit of both), but in a medium of feathers, blood, crowds, and money, to display them" (Geertz 1973, 443–44).

By laying out the metaphors of their most obscure desires and fears in the *harra*—those that are disturbing and dangerous enough that society wants to forget them—the Ishir peer into the disquieting depths of what they can neither explain nor analyze. Of what they can only imagine, interpret in poetic registers, and sometimes perceive through the key of spectacle, game, orgy, and tragedy. If ritual is useless because it does not intervene directly in the social dynamic, it nonetheless plays a necessary role through the detours of its strange figures. Through the convulsive, flashing exhibition of ultimate limits—of what cannot be deciphered, of the radical violence that must be muted—ritual permanently agitates social forces and prevents them from resting in a paralyzing equilibrium. Through the traffic of furtive meanings, by stirring up tensions that norms keep silenced, ritual maintains the social body in shape and enlivens its various cycles.

Ritual can also be considered useless in another way. I am referring to the rites of auspicious magic, a set of practices that summon fruit and prey, avert disease, and keep at bay the forces of dissolution that surround a community. All Ishir culture, like indigenous culture in general, is full of gestures, words, and images that summon fish, honey, or wild boar; that revert the direction of the *woso* like a boomerang, bring or avert rain; that incite love, thwart snakebites, and dispel anguish, malign gazes, and infections. But these rites cannot be considered performative in any strict sense: that is, they do not seek to act directly upon the world, but rather to have effects through complicated rhetorical mediations. And although, in the end, they help to produce practical effects, they do so by activating the sensibility and efficiency bequeathed by the symbol, by the mobilization of who knows what real energy incited by the power of the stage.

Since the *debylyby* is linked throughout with the fundamental rites of Chamacoco culture (and often even includes them in its representations), this chapter will focus exclusively on the analysis of that Great Ceremony and refer only tangentially to other rituals (games, initiation, shamanic rites, etc.) which are mentioned and commented on in passing in other chapters.

THEMES OF THE GREAT CEREMONY

The *debylyby*, the Great Ceremony of the Chamacoco, encompasses numerous rituals which overlap or link up at various points and around different axes. It is, for this reason, an immense array of symbolic formations, an extremely complicated knot which points in multiple directions and involves endless levels of signification. What follows is not a systematic and closed list of functions, motifs, or meanings of the Great Ceremony, but notes on some of the themes which shape it.

Natural Rhythms

The *debylyby* is the condensation of the Ishir experience of the natural world. The Ishir are extraordinary observers: they can catalogue every movement and color, every form and design in their environment and denote the astonishment, awe, and fear produced by the presence of a space populated with secrets, mercies, and threats. All these images are elaborated through a powerful nucleus that bequeaths to the community the forms through which they can venture a possible path through such density and vastness, such confusion and risk.

The *debylyby* works the link between man and nature through the figure of the regularity of its cycles and the periodic restoration of forces. The new year, which coincides with the start of spring, indicates a notable inflection in cosmic time: the world concludes a moment, begins another, and restores its ·rhythms and vital reserves. This cycle is the source of intense metaphors and doorway to other, no less powerful, motifs.

Gods, Norm, and Knowledge

The idea of a cyclic reiteration mobilizes the figure of the repetition of a primal time that is (as Eliade remarks) not only primary in the sense of being first or anterior, but in the sense of founding values, cosmovision, and knowledge. Exemplary time is recoverable through the Great Celebration which evokes it every year and allows men to submerge themselves in a parallel dimension, occupy the place of the gods, and return to their places revitalized and full. The search for this plenitude presupposes a real "nostalgia for being," an "ontological obsession" with regaining an intact and total reality, if only fleetingly (Eliade 1959, 77–95).

This *imitatio dei*—the annual identification of mortals with gods—implies a weighty human responsibility that gives the Ishir cultural horizon its dramatic and often anguish-ridden hue, and that brings it closer to Christian theology than to magical beliefs, according to Cordeu (2003, 528). The human representation of deities not only stages complicated processes of identity and opposition, it also ratifies the norm: the secret must be safeguarded, liturgical codes followed, and the complicated order of social instances, taboos, and architecture of the clans preserved. The first obligation of the Ishir is to observe the words of Ashnuwerta, the great corpus of prescriptions which organizes their vision of the world, powers their life, and challenges them with an ineluctable desire for transcendence.

The Vicissitudes of the Social Pact

The *debylyby* is an important reserve of arguments through which Ishir society legitimates itself, presents itself whole, and ensures the continuity of the pacts which constitute it. On the one hand, the Great Ceremony is a factor of social integration: it reaffirms the artifices of collective identity and gathers dispersed groups. On the other hand, the conflicts, ruptures, and breaches of society are tacitly assumed through the complicated ritual practices that stage, cloak, or mask the oppositions between gender, age, and social segments, and either repair or alleviate their dissociating effects. I have already argued against a functionalist reading of rituals: the elaboration of meaning presupposes mechanisms that dodge all models of social control; once unbound, figures can no longer be forced in a single direction. While it is evident that the Great Ceremony weaves an enormous symbolic tapestry capable of protecting, if not explaining, almost all communal experience, it does so in a figurative register: abruptly, obscurely. And it never shuts down the errant flux of signs.

The figure of cyclic renovation works through the theme of the restoration of collective good spirits. Cordeu affirms that the sequence of the *debylyby* corresponds to "the scheme of a purifying practice" that leads progressively to the "reintegration of the scene and its actors to a new condition of purity" (1984, 262). This is why the end of the ceremony produces a sensation of communal relief, expressed in the metaphor of an invigorating breeze which sweeps away pain and sadness. When society faces its losses cyclically, it must turn to potent figures in order to recover its spirits, accept absence, and console grief; the *debylyby* offers forms that enable the collective work of mourning.

The social body is also renovated through the incorporation of new adult members. Like the natural environment, the young men have reached maturation and are ready to take on communal duties and participate in the severe responsibility of sharing the laws. Then they are called on (they are, in fact, compelled) to take an active role in Ishir destiny. For this reason, one of the driving forces of the *debylyby* is the necessity to formalize the incursion of the youth into a life governed by words—intricate, difficult words.

Practical Uses

As indicated, the performative level of the rite should not be taken literally; that is, the Ishir cannot hope that their invocations mechanically produce the desired effects. The results are manifested in ambiguous figural detours. The *debylyby* is filled with acts that aim to lead to a good hunt or collection, incite health and success in love and war. It also brims with representations that seek to promote the development of understanding and strength of character, as well as dexterity in the use of a variety of techniques. The array is so broad that it involves almost all possible cultural experiences. The staging of desire is a powerful procedure: it ratifies convictions, precipitates actions, and mobilizes forces that would be incomprehensible in the horizon of a different culture.

field notes

Though during the day our skin informs us that soon the north winds will blow, bringing mist and the first heat, we still feel the cold tonight. The cold is even more brutal here in this provisional encampment of tents, which are open to the winds, and elemental shacks that barely shelter the eighty-seven Tomáraho while they work as day laborers and await better times. While they wait for land to be cultivated beyond hunger and fear—for their own land—far from these woodlands the Compañía San Carlos has rendered alien. But in this temporary village they also await another time: one that will cancel a season of dry cold and hasten in a season of fruits, buds, and tender green; one that will bring them closer to the warm smells of a new season.

Last night the shamans sang; today the festival begins, Clemente whispered to us during the first round of maté in the predawn darkness. Yet, throughout the day, we have been unable to perceive any preparations that announce the movement of forms and lights. This is not strange; there is a murky moment before the rite, something like a curtain that conceals its preparations. Experts in the artifices of simulacrum, the Ishir erect a wall of discretion around the preludes to the ceremony so that it would seem rude, or at least inopportune, to ask when such or such an act will begin. And if we dared to commit this indelicacy, we would be met by a brief exchange of glances, sly (not always friendly) smiles, and strict silences.

How do they, then, coordinate their efforts? When do they discuss and organize the complicated flow of phases, choreography, and parts? It is known that a member of a specific clan is in charge of pronouncing this precise word or solemnly tracing that gesture; it is known (they must know) who will incarnate one divine character, who will represent another, but the outsider never knows when the parts are distributed. "Do they practice?" I ask Mito. "How do they project this enormous edifice of plumes and paints, of dances, leaps, gestures, and pantomimes, of sweat and dust, crazy shadows, and flickering fires? How do they orchestrate this concert of howls, voices, and sounds?"

Suddenly the circle is closed, the fullness of the stage unfolds, and all happens exactly as if scriptwriters and makeup artists, stage directors, choreographers, actors, and audience (which must exist under so many other names) had agreed upon the most trivial details with diligence and time. And everything happens so suddenly that one always arrives late to the performance to find that some important act has already begun. This pact of silence ("Aren't we perhaps slightly paranoid?" I reflect with my companions) is especially striking if one considers the small space and population of the village, and the fact that all its members participate in the rite no matter what their relationship to the stage, whether they act as god or shaman, astonished audience or excited novice. I do not remember a similar setup among other indigenous groups. I have seen the Chiriguano prepare the *chicha* and masks and ready the instruments in the preliminary phase of the *atiku,* their festival on the occasion of the apparition of the Pleiades. Among the Chiripá the miracle of the stage is produced suddenly, but the performative event is preceded by whispering circles of secret meetings, and their acting is so essential—so reduced to a strict, geometric expression of the archetype—that they do not seem to need complicated preparations.

A cry. That is all. The ritual announced by Clemente and for which we have waited a long time (our cameras, tape recorders, and notebooks are ready, our breathing eager) consists in a brief cry, piercing and potent, that leaps from the bushes near the *tobich* and shatters the quiet of the night which is still cold. Is it a man? Yes—who else would scream like that? Isn't it a bird? Yes—in a certain sense it is a bird. An anábser? Yes—of course—it is an anábser. It is Hopupora who announces the advent of a new time. The cluster of houses is quiet and watchful.

Potrerito, 6 October 1989

Songs begin to rise from different corners of the village. At first they confront one another. They then complement each other and end up in tune, blend into a single, vibrant, sonorous line—another nocturnal contour superimposed on the soundscape of millions of frogs, insects, birds, and who knows what force—carve a path through the rough soil and pierce the mineral air of tense heights. The shamans are singing, someone answers me: they invoke (answer?) Hopupora.

How do they agree upon the instant Hopupora enters the stage? At some moment the excitement of the village is noticed. Whispering, the men creep away in small groups to the darkness of the *tobich,* which then flickers with the light of small fires; small nervous laughs are heard among the women, mixed in with the frightened cries of children. The sounds are abruptly silenced by an essential pause: a ferocious stillness cloven or violently torn by a cry that condenses all the voices and songs, all the sounds that stretch over the bleak extensions and compact heights of the Chaco.

What strange force sets the machinery of this conspiracy of silences, whispers, and cries in motion? What imperceptible inflection takes place so that they all know the moment has arrived, so that they simultaneously smell the exact cadence in the air, the signal, which tells them to occupy their assigned places without a prearranged accord, without speaking a word?

Preliminary Comments

After having been present at so many rituals, listening patiently to a great variety of baroque narrations and diligently reading different texts, I have finally understood (or intuited, at least) that the preparation of the ritual is itself another rite that is at least as complex as the one that is staged. I have nonetheless wanted to preserve these two texts, written in different places and times in my field notes (and touched up only when necessary). I transcribe them because they serve to illustrate the impression one has from the outside that the ritual arrives like the assault of a sudden storm: with no warning other than the cry of a prophetic bird. This impression serves to emphasize that ritual spectacle takes place in a different dimension; like any work of art, it always stages a scene.

THE BEGINNING

I will try to follow the preliminary steps of the *debylyby ahamich,* the Great Ceremony. I insist on this moment (it will be impossible to go into all of its stages in detail) for motives similar to those who seek to produce a dramatic effect: the aperture of the drama marks the atmosphere of the representation, it introduces the climate of the stage. To catch a glimpse of what takes place before the spectacle and on the other side of the stage, I will attempt to start from the wings and move out toward the audience (always full, always predisposed).

When does the ceremony begin? The signs of spring unfold through intense and perfumed omens. At a certain moment the fields begin to flower, the breezes sweep in laden with moisture, and the woods begin to promise hearts of palm, wild beans, and carobs. Both fields and woods begin to recover their sap, color, and barks; gentle sprouts and fresh buds burgeon everywhere. They are sweet, warm ciphers that indicate the end of the cycle of dry lands (*nymych lulyt*) and the start of the cycle of abundance (*nymych kysyryt*). The climate is literally propitious, and the entire community prepares to celebrate the renovation of the new year. Through the festival it readies itself to reestablish the energy of its drives and the convictions of its desires, rendered threadbare with the routine of consummated time.

Who decides, organizes, directs the concert? I asked myself this several times. Later I received at least a partial answer. When the Dyshykymser—the men who belong to the clan of the carancha bird, and are responsible for the most secret and closed aspects of the ceremony—detect certain signs wafting in the air or present in the intense looks of the villagers, they ask authorization from members of the Kytymáraha clan to initiate the complicated and silent ritual apparatus. If after deliberation they agree, the Kytymáraha, who wear crowns of jaguar skin, give them permission laconically and confidently, as is proper to the calm wisdom that distinguishes them.

This consultation is strictly secret and takes place at night, its confidentiality protected by the closure of the *tobich*. (Obviously I was never able to attend such an assembly. I have with difficulty reconstructed fragments of this enigmatic protocol on the basis of elusive bits of information.) This is the occasion on which the Ishir discuss at length hierarchy, acting, positions, and choruses. In general, the part played by each clan during the representation, the organization of the anábsoro's appearance, and the dynamic of the competitions and different rituals are rigidly determined by traditional ceremonial etiquette; but there is still a wide margin of variations whose causes I have never been able to decipher (I admit that I never even tried to do so). Often the circumstances require adjustments, changes, and even improvisations. It is evident that the difficult present conditions of the indigenous groups, the decline in population, and the religious persecution to which they are submitted are responsible for important alterations and innovations;

but at other times unknown reasons prompt the shifts in choreography, acting, and text.

At this secret conclave it is decided who will play the part of the divine herald, Hopupora (which can be one or sometimes two people). And it is after this enigmatic council that the cry of Hopupora, induced finally by shamanic songs and the rattling of maracas and anklets, notifies the village that the special time is near. But the cry is not definitive yet; it is only the sign of a possibility, the beginning of an expectation. The next morning is when the ritual I have already described takes place: *Hopupora mä, "*the imprints of the fingers of Hopupora." The men go to the *tobich* and paint each other's bodies with vertical red, white, or black stripes. They have been blessed, touched by the goddess, and cannot wash themselves until the next day so as not to erase the marks of grace. But, according to Palacio Vera, this rite also expresses the pedagogical qualities of the goddess: when Ashnuwerta taught the men to represent the anábsoro she showed them how to paint themselves and how to cry. The rite of *Hopupora mä* describes the apprenticeship of the men and is a dress rehearsal of paints before the ceremony begins; much as the rite of the *dysyker labo,* which I will later describe, is a rehearsal of cries. The men prepare themselves by practicing forms that will later burst out.

I do not know if it is valid to call Hopupora—this mediator which refers always to another—a "goddess." The nature, unity, and gender of this messenger are essentially ambiguous. On the one hand, Hopupora is sent by Ashnuwerta (or is it Ashnuwerta herself in one of her phases?). On the other hand, it is a figure that is obscurely linked to the bird with which it shares a name and cry.[1] This bird's cries announce the advent of a fertile time, so that in a certain way the character of Hopupora is constructed by the transference of a natural fact into the arena of ritual; this operation requires, as one may suppose, complex rhetorical maneuvers and is never simply a mechanical transplant. Finally, although Hopupora acts as a singular figure, it is also split into characters which, like the Christian Trinity, do not conform to a single entity. Sometimes she/he/it appears converted into the dark face of Ashnuwerta—Hopupora Wysta or Ashnuwysta—and signifies, then, one of the incarnations of Arpylá the Doe/Woman.

This figure displays another characteristic which complicates it even further: Hopupora is a strictly sound-based being and the ritual that accompanies her is a pure symphony of noise, songs, rumbles, and silences celebrated in the heart of darkness. When she manifests herself, says Emilio, she is no longer Hopupora, but Ashnuwysta, because she has colors and feathers (she has an image). Visually, Hopupora only appears through her traces: through her lack of figure (the imprints she leaves behind on the bodies of men).

Hopupora screams a second time. She/he/it does so the following night or week of the first announcement. This signal is not definitive either. Only the third signal is definitive, the one that determines finally if the *debylyby* will or will not take place. As one can suppose, this last scream is different: it is even more vigorous than the preceding ones, and is emitted in intermittent hoots, sometimes duplicated in echoes and counterpoints (which requires a second character). According to Enrique Ozuna (Ebytoso), the Kytymáraha submit the person selected to proffer these primordial sounds to strict tests. The sounds must resemble the sinister laughter of the demented Kánasy or the terrible guffaw of Totila the insane one. This cry of crazy laughter and deep tremors crosses the breach that separates the *tobich* from the houses and settles itself in the village, shaking the barely contained silence. The chorus of voices of the shamans and recent widows fills the air. Maracas are shaken, barks, cries, and vague screams are heard: the howling of uncertain beings that erupt from the houses or escape from the woods, sounds without names, residues of the night or of memory. And then silence. This silence is broken by the rustle of movements in the wakeful village. This silence is threatened, overcome, by the frenetic noise of the *polasho* shaken by Hopupora through her invisible circling of the *tobich*. The *polasho* are anklet rattles traditionally crafted from deer hooves: their quivering buzzes and creaks give them a special protagonism in this darkened stage erected through sound. In this scene of sleights of hand, the anklets are taken off by someone at some point and hidden in the village. Hopupora must seek out the anklets in the darkness, or Ashnuwysta—the goddess draped in black, the visible face of Hopupora—must find them.

According to the decisions made in the wings, these announcements can mark different moments of the ritual or can accelerate the entire ritual, the *debylyby ahamich*. Sometimes the signals simply stir up the village's overly relaxed rhythms; Hopupora sings some night to remind them that the depths of silence are filled with the beating of strong words, or with even denser silences. At other times, the cry unleashes the mechanisms that help to dissolve mourning or other no less heavy griefs, and to reaffirm the desire to constitute the collectivity. Still other cries announce the competitive games. On a certain occasion the heralding cries veer away from their conventional path and culminate in a laconic protocol through which the youth exchange their first crowns of dark duck feathers for the red headdresses called *pasyparak*.

When the Kytymáraha decide that the conditions are adequate, the cries of Hopupora lead to the complete ceremony (that includes, as said, rites of mourning, games, auspicious actions, celebrations of the new year, and the dense ritual corpus of masculine initiation). In this case, the third cry warns the community that the "long celebration" will take place. This moment is called *sorahá* and cancels the time of wait. In the complicated flow of codes and resounding signals that weave the beginnings of the rite, the *sorahá* is usually communicated in the following manner: after Hopupora's last cry and the deathly silence it ushers in the Kytymáraha, ceremonial masters of this stage, break this severe silence; from the shadows they frighten a dog, provoke a child's cries, the laughter of a young boy, the stumble and exclamation of an unsuspecting man. Any one of these small sounds confirms the awaited moment. The clamor of relief bursts out. Soon it will be dawning.

Immediately the preparations for the circuit of ceremonial sites begin: the grounds and perimeters of the *harra*, the *tobich,* and the *depich* must be meticulously clean. The stage (*harra*) consists of a cleared terrain located in the vicinity of the village which is circular in form and whose diameter ranges from twelve to twenty meters in length. In its center lies a compact pile of sticks called *harra ahärn:* according to some the sticks signify the forest, according to others they mark the center. Carved out from the undergrowth of a nearby forest or located in a natural clearing among palm trees, the form and dimensions of the *tobich* are similar to those of the *harra.* The *depich* is the narrow path, generally opened through thickets for half a kilometer or less, which communicates both circles. Small mounds of dirt called *nepyte* are placed on both extremes (the *harra ebich* and the *tobich ebich*). These mounds represent both the ancient springs the anábsoro used to magically leap from the *tobich* to the *harra,* as well as the site from which they emerged from the ground. Filled with energy, "these sites beat like hearts." "They are the traces the anábsoro left of the place from which they sprung forth," says Flores Balbuena. Wylky says, "These places are reminders of the original holes from which the anábsoro appeared; when the women see them they are convinced that the subterranean gods still leap up from the ground."

At this moment begin the arrangements to summon the enthusiasm required by the great effort of collective renovation implied by the festival. First the pain installed by death must be extracted. The old men sent by Ashnuwerta approach a group of weeping women and spill pure water in front of them to wash away their sorrow. Or two bands of youths painted in red, adorned with bells and crowned with flowers fix a *kashy* or *kashta*—the sticks of the ceremonial game, the signs of a time of distraction and contentment—in front of every cabin in mourning. Among the Ebytoso, the youths approach the mourners like shadows in the middle of the darkness of the Hopupora's nocturnal scene and seek out the soles of their feet, armpits, or stomachs and tickle them until they wrench out their laughter, adding sounds of pleasure to the blind chorus raised by the goddess. After, or before—according to the requirements of unknown events—the blessing of the masters of ceremony takes place (*Kytymáraho Tíhemich*): plumed and painted, the men of this clan approach the community auguring grace and the bounty of a new land, health for the officiants, and discipline and concord in the village.

There are other dramatic mechanisms which galvanize desire and revive the contours of collective identity. The Ebytoso use the name *ochukuna-hárro* to refer to the ritual expedition of hunting and gathering and the happy procession that follows it. Men and women return from the woods bringing meat and fruits, flowers and honey, and make the rounds of the village inciting its lagging members to join the jubilant march which proclaims the festival.

One afternoon, usually after the *sorahá*, Hopupora presents herself. It is actually no longer Hopupora, Tybygyd (called Luciano by the mestizos) tries to explain: she is now Ashnuwerta. But not Ashnuwerta proper, Mistress of the Red Splendor, but Ashnuwysta of the Dark Power, the nocturnal deity who reminds them of storms and pests, both of which are sanctions for any lapse in the sacred precepts. They are different phases of the same goddess, the Supreme Giver of the Word who, as pure sound (as voice which announces) has no image. As image, she can present herself in black or red, depending on which aspects will manifest themselves in the circle of ceremonies. Now she appears in black. The black goddess always appears first, someone says. And she presents herself, like all the goddesses, surrounded by a court of daughters: all feathered and masked like her and, like her, covered in cloths of caraguata, their calves and arms painted black. Ashnuwysta and the four Ashnuwysta Ebe are represented by men of the Tahorn clan: the mother appears with a closed fist of *henemich,* a coarse grass that symbolizes the bounty of the forest; each of the daughters bears a *pyk,* or mallet, made from wood of the carob tree. These heavy instruments are used to frighten animals from the path and symbolize the aperture of the sacred passageway. Escorted by four shamans, Ashnuwysta and her retinue advance along the path that leads from the *tobich* (space of closure) to the *harra* (stage). The goddess faces west and proffers, one last time, her characteristic cry in chorus with her daughters. The voice has revealed itself, has been transformed into figure, into something else. This revelation marks another moment of the preliminaries of the *debylyby.*

THE PLACE OF GAMES

Hopupora not only opens the scene of the Great Ceremony; she inaugurates other scenes as well. In the rituals of the end of mourning or the exaltation of collective spirit, her cries indicate another space that parallels yet is intensely connected to the *debylyby.* This is the space of the ritual games whose content and distraction oppose the gripping drama of the Great Ceremony and compensate for the primordial gravity required by sacred time. Celebrated simultaneous to and alongside the Great Ceremony, the ritual games privilege ludic and agonistic arguments; they emphasize chance, entertainment, joy, and euphoria over the solemn ceremonial representations, calming its rigors.

There are two kinds of games. One kind is ceremonial in character and has a defined mythic backdrop: these games move in the orbit of the gods and present the great cultural themes in the register of competition and luck (like the *póhorro,* the ceremonial ball game, and the *kymychyló,* a club-throwing competition). The other kind is minor in tone and serves as mere distraction for the groups present at the ceremony. Various dispersed bands are brought together during the *debylyby* and this proximity requires a channel through which differences are worked out, spirits relaxed, and the cohesion of the new groups reinforced so that collective enthusiasm is kept alive and boredom averted. These games are more banal than the others; they are played during the course of the ceremonial cycle and are based on riddles, contests, bets, races, competitions of manual dexterity and physical prowess, and tournaments of words which fill the nights of *harra* with laughter and jokes.

Here I will refer solely to ceremonial games, that is, to those which not only accompany the ceremony from the outside, but which also mobilize ritual themes.

The Gravity of Games

The ceremonial games work through the same themes as the *debylyby* but do so from an independent site that includes chance, recreation, and competition. The contentment the games elicit expresses the jubilance of the time of fruition and new shoots and closes the stage of mourning, countering the call of death. The games are also auspicious: mythically, the *póhorro* is associated with luck in hunting and the *kymychyló* with the emergence of fish. Lastly, they are efficient social regulators: the teams that participate in the competitive games are called *onota oso* and *nymych oso;* "the aquatics" are always rivals of "the foresters" in a confrontation that brings together the counterpoint of clans and mobilizes the refined Ishir machinery of oppositions, alliances, and intersecting compensations. Susnik says that the ceremonial games, active metaphors of social positions, ratify the clan system: in the ball game the youth expresses his clan belonging and his Ishir identity (1995, 140–41). This link with the regime of clans has consequences that cross the threshold of death: the Dyshykymser are guardians of the *tobich,* the ritual, and the domain of the dead (Osypyte). This is why they do not participate in the game and this is why, once dead, they do not enter Osypyte, where the spirits also play: they remain stationed, lance in hand, at the entrance of Hades, guarding the access to its somber lands.

Like all rites, perhaps, the game refers rhetorically to the figure of death. On the one hand, its staging requires a state of general well-being and special frame of mind: for this reason two bands of young players, painted and feathered, crowned with flowers and covered in bells, approach mourners and either offer up or plant the *kashta* (sticks of the ceremonial game) in front of their houses to invoke the calm that follows the time of grief. On the other hand, the community's high spirits, reinforced by the game, allow them to resist the calls of death. Located in the direction of the setting sun, beneath a place near Bahía Negra, Osypyte is in a certain sense a pale and even inverse reflection of earthly life. Faded, ethereal, and zombie-like, its floating inhabitants wander the great underground cavern which is traversed by a river of dark and frozen waters, the Ishir Styx. The great prototype of the *samu'u* grows in its foggy center. Driven by nostalgia for their loved ones or envy of those who are still alive—or by the boredom inspired by such a colorless place, or even by the vocation awakened by their fate—the spirits that inhabit the Tartar plains of the Chamacoco want the living to hurry there. They call them with tempting, disquieting sounds they produce by hitting the trunk of the *samu'u* while they dance or entertain themselves with the same games that mortals play. Every year the dead celebrate the *Osypyte ahamich,* the Ishir Avernus, a lugubrious version of the *debylyby ahamich* timed to coincide with great ritual of the living.

The same sounds that call the living also guide the spirits that have detached themselves from their bodies, pointing out the unavoidable path. Sometimes the Ishir hear unknown rumbles that are not thunder because the sky is clear. "The dead are calling us," they say, frightened. The ceremonial games are one means to resist this dangerous invitation of the dead: dangerous because it is inscribed in a human being's most radical possibility and does not imply a twisting of the path but the hastening of a necessary end. Faced with these fatal siren calls—these disturbing echoes that emerge from underground— humans erect the vital happiness of the competition and the exhilaration of risk, the irresponsible euphoria of pleasure. And when the innocence of the game is not enough to conjure away the designs of death the Ishir resort to orgy, that irrefutable argument of uncontrollable jouissance.

The Lost Game

The Ishir ritual games seem to be disappearing. They threaten to disappear even among the Tomáraho, who continue to eagerly celebrate the Great Ceremony. They play games but shorten them and space out the occasions on which they are played, forgetting essential codes and emphasizing the aspects of entertainment over their serious ritual implications. They list with pride the name of the best players of *póhorro* and *kymychyló* as well as the women who are most skillful at *senne,* but year after year their enthusiasm dwindles. The Ebytoso are forgetting the game, Daniel says, almost without nostalgia. Abbreviated, sterilized, purged of their original meanings, in Puerto Diana the games are played halfheartedly at Christmas and New Year according to the impositions of the missionaries. Clemente López has tried to reintroduce the *póhorro* in Puerto Esperanza but has failed, according to him, for lack of *técnicos* (coaches). It has been many years since the ritual orgies have taken place, the Chamacoco say. But it is a delicate subject: both Ishir groups know it is subject to controversial readings and avoid speaking of it.

Although it is not difficult to venture reasons for the deterioration of so many moments of an indigenous culture which has evolved against the grain of neocolonial models, accounting for the gap between the celebration of the Great Ceremony and the slow abandonment of ritual games which configure that drama's counterweight exceeds the intentions and possibilities of this book. Perhaps the pressure of adverse times obliges them to make recourse to other systems to compensate for the gravity of the primal representation. Or perhaps the community needs other arguments to mobilize a thwarted desire and unlock the space of pleasure and rapture: the buried place serves as the foundation of the stage and as the trench of vital pulses.

LOSSES

The game is not all that wanes or recedes, its outlines fading. Rushed by the barbarous rhythm of foreign cycles, disrupted by so many amputated forests, so many lost people, and confused by an imposed forgetfulness, many preliminary stages of the rite have been shortened and others erased. Many colors, forms, and sounds have been left by the wayside. Before, they all say, there were more paintings, more feathers, and more men whose different cries rendered the villagers speechless. Before, the informants comment, the festival lasted for months and the succession of acts and intermissions, chapters and episodes, numbers and games was governed by obscure omens deciphered by the Dyshykymser and legitimated by the Kytymáraha. Now the ritual lasts as long as is allowed by their occasional jobs and landowners' orders; as long as it can escape missionary control; as long as the concentration of the encampments lasts. In Puerto Diana and other places, the Ebytoso ceremony was prohibited by the New Tribe Missionaries. In San Carlos the representations of the Tomáraho *debylyby* take place on Saturdays; in Potrerito and

Puerto Esperanza they are organized according to the necessities of the new farming and old hunting practices, the availability of paints and feathers, the number of men in each clan, and the visits of Ebytoso groups whose shamans and people enrich the Tomáraho cast.

Before, the old men tell me, after Hopupora's last cry the entire village moved to commence the adventures of a new phase on intact grounds. Now this is almost impossible: nomadism is conditioned more by the needs of the new landowners than by the strict orders of form or the whims of spring. Before, Susnik writes (1995, 214–15), during the nocturnal clamor that followed in the wake of Hopupora's last cry the men carried a shell labret, and after the tumult of voices the *tobich* became the grounds for a great ceremonial banquet of armadillo meat, symbol of the collective communion between adult Ishir men. Age marks the degree of participation in the sociotribal secret, so the oldest men cut up the flesh and distributed it among those present in an act that symbolized ritual transgression: under normal circumstances the meat of this animal is taboo for men because the Mother of the Armadillo is linked to the mythical ancestors of the Ishir. Armadillo food has its counterpoint and reflection in a great feast of anteater whose flesh, strictly prohibited to women, reinforces masculine socioceremonial companionship.

field notes

Potrerito, 1 October 1989

10:00
I arrive at the *tobich:* the hermetic place where the ritual is organized, the backstage or backdrop, the other scene. Snooping out furtive signs and interpreting brief commentaries by Bruno and Luciano, I have realized that today a condensed ceremonial succession will take place, beginning with the event called *Ahanak Teichu* (literally, "song of the shamans"). Through this ritual, the *konsaho* or *ahanak* bless the village so as to close the preliminaries of the Great Ceremony and clear the stage for the apparition of the gods. Last night the *sorahá* took place—the confirmation that there would be a "long celebration"—and this morning the young men meticulously weeded and swept the *tobich,*

the *harra,* and the shady path that communicates them. Both the *sorahá* and the cleansing of the essential grounds are signs that the representations will take place soon. I am thus alert, attentive to all movements, stationed in the clearing of this cavity opened up in the woods which is still off-limits to the villagers.

10:45
The first to arrive is Wylky, who occupies his place at one end of the *tobich.* He faces the trees, shakes his maraca vigorously and begins to sing with the broken voice of a shaman who has spilled blood by the sheer force of his screams. Other Tomáraho shamans arrive next: Aligio and Palacio Vera, then Isabelino and Luciano, Máximo Martínez, Juan Torres, and Sánchez Vera. Led by Clemente López, three Ebytoso shamans also arrive from a neighboring village. As they arrive, each of them repeats Wylky's motions so that after a while a powerful chorus of songs and rattles fills the air. When the number of shamans that will participate in the celebration is complete, they all stop abruptly (who gave the order?) and the men approach the center of the *tobich,* clearing their tired throats. It seems that the old *tobich* consisted of a great hut where the youth and their instructors secluded themselves during the entire period of initiation. Today the space is a clearing in the nearby forest, open to the elements. Current conditions make it impossible for a large contingency of men to leave the vicinity of the village; they must work even in sacred times. Therefore they do not distance themselves very much and although they remain in seclusion, disciples and teachers alternate long periods of training, instruction, and revelation with prosaic tasks necessary for their sustenance. Only the teaching of the "words" takes place in the center of the *tobich;* other teachings are proffered in the woods or even in the farms, between temporary jobs and different routine labors.

12:30
Once the act of the songs is over, a long session of corporal painting and feather decoration begins. When the men disguise themselves as gods, the novices bring the feathers, masks, and caraguata costumes that will be used in the representations. The boys arrive, running as novices must always run, and deposit a great bundle of soft feathers and coarse cloth in the center: from this abundant collective stockpile the officiants will select the diadems or neck-

laces, bracelets or masks required by each part. But when the shamans dress for the ritual, they use the trappings they carry in their *lëbe* specifically for their personal use. Clemente, who enjoys intercultural equivalences, says the shaman's *lëbe* corresponds to the bag in which the doctor carries his professional equipment and instruments. Aided by the young apprentices the men paint each other's bodies and their own faces. Sometimes they use small mirrors purchased in Bahía Negra (or bartered for iguanas); the well-worn glass replaces the polished tortoise shells used not long ago. Sometimes the shamans need to replace a piece: I see Palacio Vera hard at work at a new earring that will be added to his wardrobe. He is sitting on the recently swept floor; he picks up small, dark ostrich feathers and after sharpening their milky white quills with his knife, bends the points and strings them on a long rope of caraguata whose other end is tied to his big toe.

14:00
While the shamans adorn themselves at their leisure, a group of men who belong to the Tahorn clan go two or three kilometers into the woods, cut the tree trunk of a *palo borracho* that is approximately four meters high and lay it beside the path that unites the *tobich* and *harra,* next to a place called the *nepyte:* a remote place that indicates the spot where the anábsoro appeared and the site of the original springs. The trunk, which has a fundamental function, is converted for now into one of the many ciphers that indicate the start of the *debylyby* and which strictly delineate the consecrated space: women cannot cross over the limit it establishes. If they do, when they become pregnant they will abort their child; if they dare to cross the threshold of the *tobich,* an act that is almost unthinkable, they will be fulminated by the fury of the anábsoro.

17:15
The sun sinks lower on the horizon. The shamans have finished adorning themselves and, returning to their songs and rattles, they move in a single file toward the *harra* where a large, silent audience awaits them. (The shamanic rituals are the only occasions that assemble a mixed audience in the context of the *debylyby.* This is because the representation of the anábsoro requires the participation of all the men as actors and all the women as spectators.) The eight shamans walk onstage, radiant in polychromatic feathers. Two women leave the audience and approach the shamans. They are Ramona and

Nyerke, two prestigious shamans. Both are marked with plain red spots on their faces and, behind their ears, a flutter of white feathers: these are sparse signs of their shamanic status (in principle, only the men have the right to colors and feathers). The shamans, male and female, circle the *harra* counterclockwise in single file. There is an increase in song and the crazed clatter of anklets and maracas; the movement of the parade quickens; now the line is broken and all move in different directions with great leaps or lively steps. Then the shamans come together at a spot at the entrance of the ceremonial circle and each reverts to the rattle of instruments and the discourse of song.

17:45
The shadows of the shamans begin to blur together and spill off the stage to mix with the shadows projected by the audience. When they are indistinguishable from the shadows of the trees in the dusk, the shamans withdraw, followed by the spectators. Nyerke walks away enveloped in a sadness that turns into a sob and then another, in crescendo, until it culminates in a convulsive fit of cries; she still has sorrow to wash away. She was widowed this year, comments an Ebytoso woman called Chonga Marecos. Only the eight male shamans are left; they raise their voices and shake their rattles more loudly, as if they still wanted to be heard by the villagers who walk home along the darkened path.

20:00
The Tahorn return to the *harra* and, over the ceaseless background of shamanic songs, bring the trunk of the *palo borracho* tree that was lying alongside the path to the *tobich* and lift it up on the stage, slightly off center. The men surround the post that rises as if a naked tree had suddenly, erroneously, sprouted up. They surround it with a wall of cries, whistles, and flutes which immediately parts to give way to a shaman, Aligio, who approaches shaking his maraca with conviction and his song with pride. Led by him, the men form a circle that rotates around the post, raising their voices deformed by winds and distances, by echoes, and by the sounds of nocturnal beasts that answer the din. The procession stops, the clamor ceases: one by one, the men climb the mast and crown its ragged top with dark ostrich feathers, white feathered sticks, and wands that sprout the light down of herons. After being thus honored, the great pole suffers the punishment of dry blows as the men hit it with sticks. In the village, the women and children know that the sounds of these blows are thun-

dering signs of the divine steps: the anábsoro are coming. But the men also strike the *samu'u* tree trunk to wrest its powers: to oblige it to release its negative *woso* to the wind and its positive powers for the benefit of the village. In the silence that follows the ceaseless ringing of shamanic songs is again heard. The men move away; only the shamans remain, agitating the night with their tired maracas.

While this rite takes place, another group of men erect a large semicircular fence to safeguard the *harra* from the glances of women in the village; although it is night, imprudent wakefulness is always a possibility. This fence, called *eiwa,* is provisionally constructed with palm trunks, branches, mats and cloths made of caraguata fibers, rough sackcloth, and when available plastic, sheets, visitors' tents, or any other flat object. The fence is meant to conceal whatever happens on the stage because, even in the darkness of nightfall, the fires and moon can briefly light up a profile, an angle, a glance which gives away the secret.

22:00

Once the curtain has been closed another ritual based solely on sounds begins backstage and is repeated each night before a performance. It is called *dysyker labo* and constitutes yet another announcement of the ceremony: a resounding, thundering condensation of what will be represented. But this obscure ceremony has other functions as well: on the one hand it is a sound rehearsal aimed at checking the memory and tone of voice of each actor; on the other hand it is the verification of the presence of each character, a roll call of the anábsoro. *Dysyker labo* literally means "roll call of offspring," and according to the Ishir this term designates the control exerted every night by Hopupora to determine if each man is occupying his place and preparing his cry. Lastly, the *dysyker labo* seeks to provoke the impression of the thundering power of the gods in the nearby village. The powerful, divine howls (*tihá*) echo through the expanses of the Chaco and knock over men, birds, and beasts that—struck down by the power of the scream—fall to the ground with no visible wound. In groups that incarnate each anábser and his or her retinue, the men circle the trunk erected on the enclosed stage, emitting loud yells that are the voices of simulated characters. They do not need masks or costumes because the darkness and fence prevent the revelation of anything beyond the essential din and, in the pauses, the obstinate singing of the shamans which has not relented all night long and which will connect with the rites the following morning. After this representation of sounds, the men sit on the bare floor of the *harra:* returning to the soil any negative powers they may have absorbed during the representation.

The darkness is filled with a concert of howls and roars, whistles and snores, which is sometimes unbearable and always disquieting. A group of anábsoro produces a low, gruff murmur which increases threateningly and spreads in quick waves only to concentrate in a single shriek, split into clamors and voices, and finally burst in a resounding explosion that fills the air with small, dispersed echoes. Another group begins a thundering and confused racket that is cut short by a stentorian silence and then is reborn in distant sounds: in a rattling that raises intermittent horizons and topples invisible birds. It is as if each small woodland noise, each whisper and sigh of the village; each bellow, grunt, and croak of the beasts that tread the Chaco; each creak of the constellations and vibration of the earth were amplified to the limit and exploded into cries that orchestrate all the noises of the world in the terrible music that men invent to orient themselves.

Potrerito, 2 October 1989

Following the array of preliminary announcements, expectations, and play of tension and relief, the Tiribo appear at dawn to establish a positive atmosphere in the stage that now begins to open. If they enter the *harra* so early, it is certain that they readied themselves in predawn darkness; I have seen preparations begin at two in the morning by the restless light of small fires, in almost utter darkness. Unlike other anábsoro who appear alone, or surrounded by a court of daughters that bear their name, the Tiribo are divided into various masculine characters subdivided into two categories of equal rank, each represented by a man of the Tahorn clan. All appear masked, painted in black, stamped with white handprints, and festooned in stork and heron plumes. The first apparition is so quick that it passes before one realizes what is happening. Three anábsoro called Tiribo Webo come running from the path that leads to the *tobich;* they circle the *harra* rapidly and then, still running, leave the same way they came. It is yet another announcement of the many that constitute the complex script of the drama. A second group advances. One can feel them coming before they appear due to their shrill squeaks that sound like a maddened flock of birds. They are four, crowned only with the insignia of the hunter—the luxurious cap of jaguar skin—and carrying canes or clubs made of carob wood (called *pyk* or *noshikó*) which are decorated with peccary and deer hooves. They use these tools to keep away animals that might have crossed the path, especially dogs (their natural enemies), and to strike the tree trunk on the stage at a given moment.

With the first light of dawn, the men repeat last night's sequence in reverse order. After striking the trunk with their carob sticks, each of the four Tiribo climbs to its top, tears off a stick or strand of feathers that crowned it during the night, and throws it to the ground forcefully, replacing it with an equivalent piece that is knotted around his neck or tied around his temple. This complicated operation is intended not only to convert the negative *woso* into an ally but also to call forth an abundance of wild honey. The climb to the top of the tree is a metaphor for the strenuous high path presupposed in the wielding of superior forces, but it also symbolizes the extraction of honey: to gather it the men must skillfully climb trees. *Tiribo ihitsime* is the name of the thrashing of the pole. The blows must be exact: if they are excessive, the men will become insatiable and violent; if they are too light, they will become lazy and indecisive. Only if the correct amount of strength is applied will they become sober without losing the valor required by the hard work of being Chamacoco.

The representation of the Tiribo requires the participation of two clans: the Tahorn, who act; and the Posháraha, who direct the hands of the young apprentices over the body of the actors and ready the soft, plumed ornaments and abrasive disguises that will be used onstage. They are also charged with taking care of the ceremonial post. Among the Ebytoso (who often call the Tiribo "Byteta") this post is painted in profuse colors which are either impressed by handprints or dense traced lines. According to Flores Balbuena, the *palo borracho* is swathed in red (from the *ostyrbe*), white (from ashes or lime), brown (from the flower of the tree called *ha-lä*), black (from diluted vegetable coal), and blue (from the flower of the tree called *oskala*).

"Why is the post painted? Why is it struck and crowned with feathers? Why do they dance and sing around it?" Because, the Tomáraho now say, the *cháarro* (*samu'u* or *palo borracho*) is a special tree. It communicates the earth with the places where the anábsoro originated: the sky, the waters, and the depths of the earth. Hopupora planted It as a landmark of sacred space; before it is erected the *harra* does not exist, its space is only a sandy clearing. Once thrust in the ground, the post is called *debylybyta icha* (literally, "the insignia of the ceremony"). When the representation of the Tiribo concludes, the post is taken out of the ground and deposited alongside the path where it lay before to signal the limit women must not cross. It has to rot on its own: no one can touch it. (Now I remember having seen three trunks of *palo borracho* lying beside the wooded path that unites the *tobich* and the *harra*. This indicates that between February 1988—the date when the Tomáraho came to Potrerito—and the present, October 1989, at least three Great Ceremonies have taken place. The Ishir ritual calendar has become more flexible: evidently the move to new lands and the challenge of difficult conditions has required the intensification of ceremonial time.)

GODS AND ACTORS

Once the complex time of preliminaries and warnings is over, the period of representation proper begins. To trace an elementary list of the characters that appear onstage, my guiding threads are the notes I jotted down as an astonished spectator of four great Tomáraho ceremonies which took place in San Carlos, Puerto Esperanza, and Potrerito (Peishiota), as well as the generous commentaries, memories, references, and tales of the many Tomáraho and Ebytoso informants cited throughout this book. I also use descriptions and studies undertaken by Susnik and Cordeu, the only authors who have exhaustively investigated different moments and characters of these rituals. Though Susnik and Cordeu only worked with the Ebytoso, the similarities between the groups allow me to borrow information and compare analyses.

My starting point is the sequence of presentations that I witnessed; it is a sequence organized around fragments of different rituals since, given the extension and complexity of the ceremony, it is almost impossible for a foreigner to watch the *debylyby* in continuous succession. At times I have slightly violated the sequence: the logic of exposition forced me to articulate certain groupings and, therefore, to briefly alter the procession of certain *anábsoro*. Thus I have sometimes reordered the entrance of the groups under provisional titles (hunters, gatherers, doctors, etc.) that are not intended to set up a rigorous classificatory schema but to facilitate the reading by introducing pauses in the flow of an excessively compact process: my organization is a diagram rather than a taxonomy. It would, in fact, be difficult to systematically classify the characters according to their functions since these functions continuously vary, repeat, and intersect. Each anábser can thus have multiple overlapping roles, and if a god were classified, for example, according to his gifts of harvesting, he could also come up at other moments concerned with hunting or healing.

Modalities

The aforementioned gap between the medium of the word (where myth happens) and the spaces of representation (where ritual takes place) produces notable changes in the mythical figures. The reflections, echoes, and resonances of the stage, its multiple artifices and effects mean that when converted into stage characters some gods appear disassociated, divided, or multiplied. Regardless of their status as individual entities in myth, in the ritual circle the gods appear according to the following modalities:

- alone, preserving their status as individuals (e.g., Anábser or Apépo);
- in pairs, regardless of whether they are paired in myth (e.g., Nemur and Pfaujata, Shínimit and Kaiporta);
- doubled (e.g., Pohejuvo is split into Red Pohejuvo and Dark Pohejuvo);
- multiplied (one single god is reproduced in a series of identical figures— Tiribo is represented in the *harra* by the four Tiribo; Waho is not only plural but switches gender);
- accompanied by attendants who participate in their nature, though to a lesser degree.

In this last modality, certain anábsoro are converted into the leaders— *cabezantes* or "heads," the Ishir translate insistently—of groups whose members become their subalterns. The figure of the *cabezante* has two variants. In the first the *cabezante* leads, in the second it governs:

In the case of the *webich-oso* some of the anábsoro assume and announce the role of representing the group to which they belong. These heralds appear first, emitting distinctive shouts that communicate the name of the next character. After parading around the ceremonial circle they retire, only to return leading the group. This is the case with Wichó, Wahó, Pahö, Wahé, etc.

In the second case, this model of *cabezante* is defined as mother (*lata*) of the other members of the group, who are considered her sons (*abo*) or daughters (*ebe*). There are no masculine figures, no "fathers" that lead the group; the masculine equivalent of *lata* would be *balut*, which does not mean "father" but chief, principal, or superior and extraordinary being. As discussed previously, the word *lata* indicates "mother" only metaphorically (biological mother is *ote*) and designates, instead, a superior rank and paradigm of a species. Ashnuwerta is the anábsoro *Lata:* Great Mother, anábser par excellence, and divine exemplary model, but also and for this reason the one that has power over all the others. According to translations that the Chamacoco themselves render in Spanish, she is *la patrona* (the boss), *la principal* (the principal one), or *la superiora* (the superior).

The President: Anábser

The first anábser that enters the stage appears alone and is called precisely that: Anábser. By announcing, once more, all the anábsoro that will follow it onto the stage it synthesizes them in a figure that condenses the festivity's summoning power. Anábser, in effect, has the function of coercively ensuring the start of the ceremony. The Tomáraho, when speaking Spanish, call him *el guardián* (the guardian), *el centinela* (the sentinel), or *el presidente* (the president; also *el cacique,* the chief). The last term includes the two previous ones and adds a sense of hierarchy; it also expresses the link of Anábser to civil power: in the past, the *pylota* (leaders) were the ones charged with ordering the start of the festival and rigorously sanctioning anyone who was unprepared for the start of the ceremony (Susnik 1957, 12).

Escorted by four novices Anábser enters the village and since the village is devoid of men, is greeted by a committee of silent women, the *pylota* (chief), and a representative of the *arn turnk* (ancient warrior-guardians). But Anábser does not halt before such notable people, and gracelessly proceeds on his course: he is searching for hidden men in order to punish their negligence with the staff of justice, a figure which here is given a literal meaning and has an effective reach. But Anábser not only punishes the fact that some men are not in their due places; he also sanctions the lack of readiness for the ceremony. When the feathers are not prepared and there are few masks and costumes, "the president" charges forth brandishing the staff of justice against those who have committed such a serious offense. Not even the chief is spared these blows, since ultimately he is the one responsible for what happens within his jurisdiction and must be capable of bearing the sentence imposed by Ashnuwerta and presenting an example of obedience. The women cry. (Apparently Anábser does not always appear. I have been present at ceremonies that began without his presence: it is possible that he is only required in cases of egregious negligence.)

Doctors: Wioho

While Anábser appears alone the representation of Wioho is comprised by Wioho Lata, the Mother, and the Wioho Abo, her attendants and offspring. These are gods that are allied to the human condition. They usually augur good fishing, but their specialty is curing diseases. The mythical Wioho was a great healer: he resuscitated Jolué by gathering drops of his blood from the dirt; according to Tomáraho versions, he blew on this bloodied mud, rubbing it against his potent colors or stirring it with the feathers he ripped from his own body or plucked from birds knocked out of the sky by the bolts of his lethal cries. The Wioho cure assorted sicknesses, rubbing patients with their red or white painted skins, blowing on them or sweeping their querulous bodies with the dark feathers that sprout from their backs. Among the Ebytoso, while Wioho Lata is charged with curing ills, her children surround the patient yelling their names in chorus.

Warriors and Hunters: Ho-Ho

Although Ho-Ho's assassin was a member of the Namoho clan, the representation of his numerous courtiers requires the participation of all clans. The performance of Ho-Ho begins with a happy group of youths who, starting at the right side of the village, go from house to house yelling *"boná, boná,"* asking the women thus for the domestic bags woven out of caraguata which they will then use onstage as masks. This procession through the village, called *ola ly bortysó*, takes place frequently and through it the men request the masks, dresses, hammocks, or mats which they use to dress up as the great mothers. This ritual points obliquely to the simulacrum that surrounds the great secret: ignorant that the anábsoro were assassinated, ritually the women believe that the men that appear in the *harra* are the gods that still linger in the woods, sky, somber subsoil, or underwater depths. But the women are the ones who lend their own clothes and domestic fabrics so the men can disguise themselves and pretend to be the real anábsoro. The women pretend to believe the fiction enacted by the men, and the men pretend to believe that the women believe: the ritual is a representation of a representation, the staging of a scene. Without this game of masks and mirrors, the essential deception that every culture conceals could not function: the ancient guilt that must be ciphered, the original lack or sin, the origins of redemption and desire.

The Ho-Ho march with arms stiff as soldiers'; as they move they simulate various physical defects and proffer intermittent cries. Walking thus, and shouting thus, they advance along the secret path and circle the *harra* five times. The last member of the group carries a long spear. Susnik believes that in the past this weapon was hung from the *peiwarak,* the scalp ripped from an enemy in battle (1995, 210). Each Ho-Ho has a defect that defines him or her: one is lame, the other lacks an arm or an eye; one is irascible, another a glutton; and each of these notes intervenes imaginatively in the representation of the character. At night a vociferous clamor is raised from the nearby woods to indicate the presence of another Ho-Ho group: the first group is comprised of subterranean beings, the second of woodland beings. The encounter is inevitable and the factions face each other, throwing lit firebrands which pierce the darkness and fleetingly illuminate the curves of their smoking paths. Next they trade insults: each group assaults the other one, reminding them of their various defects and pointing to their many vices. The adversaries continue their battle through screams launched from the *tobich* to the forest and from the forest to the *tobich* in an altercation of furious, counterpoised choruses. The conflict has a happy ending: at some enigmatic moment the men approach one another almost blindly, hands outstretched, until they touch and finally greet each other briefly as players often do after a game. Who knows what ancient disorder is repaired with such fiery offenses, such vocal abuse?

It is evident that this simulacrum implies the ritual elaboration of one of the ancient mobilizing principles of Chamacoco culture: war, the ultimate corollary of the *ágalo/ymasha* (ally/adversary) scheme. The Ishir say that participation in this ceremony makes the officiants strong and bold; but it also makes hunters skillful. War and hunt constitute two figures that are intimately linked in the Ishir horizon: both imply a challenge to the death to assure survival, and both require resistant rhetorical armor to process the intense intersecting sentiments at play. The fact that interethnic combats no longer have a place in spaces governed by national society means that the ritual's martial connotations have diminished even as its relation to the hunt has been stressed (although hunting is also a threatened activity). In any case, like many other forms that are driven by their own logic to survive, the ceremony continues in abridged form and having outlived its original motifs.

The Cannibal Gods: Wákaka

In general, the representation of the Wákaka takes place a week after that of the numerous courtiers of the Ho-Ho. They are ferocious gods, eaters of human flesh; the mythical Wákaka was the one who devoured the son of Syr along with other novices. For this reason they are called Wákaka Tseu, "the terrible Wákaka." And for this reason, Emilio informs me, during the time of initiation, the family of any youth in seclusion engages in ritual practices of eating, crying, and dancing to keep at bay the anthropophagous anábsoro, which symbolize all the ills that can befall youths.

The Ebytoso representation of Wákaka is nearly identical to that of the Tomáraho except that it is interpreted by two groups, the Reds and the Blacks,[2] one of which is the adversary of the Ishir while the other is their ally. The Wakaka Wys, the Blacks, cure sick women, but given their enormous power the women must be blindfolded during the treatment.

Fishermen and Fish: Okalo

The Okalo are anábsoro who promote success in fishing. To do so, in a certain sense, they themselves appeal to other figures that refer to the fish. To the Ishir fish suggest images of quantity and ensemble: they move in colonies, their schools are numerous, their species copious. They are also varied in appearance and form and exhibit a multitude of combinations and differences. The Okalo comprise a large, multicolored group. They appear with multiple voices and unequal interventions: each has a different cry which he or she emits, or falls silent, according to a personal timing so that together they produce an extravagant, trembling polyphony which is sometimes strident and always chaotic.

Cordeu offers a reading of this character through a schema that joins two basic variables: the species of fish that each group of Okalo represents and calls on, and the climatic opposition between the dry and wet seasons. This opposition is related, in turn, to the contrast between the characters' respective cries: shrill, loud, strong; deep, deaf, weak. The author concludes that the sophisticated machinery of relations and classifications staged by these characters reveals the architecture of oppositions mobilized by Ishir culture and metaphorically elaborates ideas of plurality, unicity, and difference (Cordeu 1999, 224–37).

Dogs

The anábsoro I will now discuss do not appear on the stage continuously or contiguously, but I group them here to facilitate the exposition. These anábsoro are characterized by their aversion to dogs. This attitude, however, exists in terms of affected repulsion demonstrated on the scene, rather than hatred toward a specific animal species. It expresses the ambivalence present in all Chamacoco social relations, their connections to nature, and their links to the gods: all human beings, animals, and supernatural forces are simultaneously potential adversaries and allies. The dog is a figure that is linked to the hunt, to which it is also associated metonymically insofar as it is an irreplaceable aid to the hunt. But it is also a symbol of all the animals that it helps to kill; animals that, in turn, connote both food and threat. To hunt means to conquer adversity, to turn a hostile and strange factor into a benefit. The bivalent meaning possessed by powers means that the rancor displayed by these anábsoro toward the dogs can sometimes favor the animals since they can profit from the blows.

Pui

One of these anábsoro is Pui, who is interpreted through four actors. The actors are charged with preventing the secluded youths from contaminating themselves with the filth of dog excrement (a cipher of impurity which the boys, who are learning to develop the best moments of their human circumstances, must avoid). For this reason, the Pui spill out of the circumference of the *harra* and burst into the village screaming their names like a furious choir of frogs and brandishing maces of hard wood with which they threaten, strike, or even kill the dogs they encounter.

Hu-Hu

After their entrance the Hu-Hu are divided into two groups, each of which is led by Hu-Hu Lata, the Mother, and comprised of her five sons, the Hu-Hu Abo. When the groups sprint screaming from the stage to the village they are intercepted by hunters with their restless dogs. The dogs are released and a ferocious persecution begins: a simulacrum through which the men represent gods acting as hunters and the dogs play the part of the prey they usually help to hunt down. Humans and animals throw themselves into a maddened race punctuated with shouting, barking, and panting that lasts as long as their strength does and recommences as soon as they have rested. If the animals have the courage to confront their plumed followers they receive blows, it is true, but also strength and proven valor, keen smell, and speed: all the qualities that a hunting dog desires (if he desires them, as his masters think he does).

The Gifts of Offense

The following anábsoro emphasize the moment of confrontation between different factions as expressed in insult or aggression. The staging of a dispute is one of the forms of assuming dissent and elaborating social consensus. These are not the only cases (others will be cited further on) but are those that take place most contiguously.

Holé

At this moment of the *debylyby* an especially important representation takes place: that of Holé, also called Honta. According to Cordeu, the mythological Holé were the first victims in the massacre of the gods; in order to prevent them from reaching the *wyrby*—the spring used by the gods to leap into the

A woman of the Tomáraho clan ritually confronts the *anábser* Honta Abich, who is held captive by his guardian. Puerto 14 de Mayo, 2003. (Photo by Juan Britos.)

air and cross distances—Ashnuwerta ordered each of them be tied to a man who would then inherit their clan affiliation (Cordeu 1999, 187–204).

The assemblage formed for this presentation is as follows: Holé Lata, the Mother; Honta Abich, her husband; Holé Ebe, her twenty daughters; Honta Abich Emynynsyr, the escort or guardian of the consort god; and five high-ranking shamans. Although she is not part of the entourage, another important character is called Holé Webichota or Honta Abich Otyta, the messenger charged with announcing the entrance of her master, Honta Abich. The entry of the numerous entourage of Holé produces happiness in the village because, though they represent skirmishes, they bring health, prosperity, and calm.

After the ritual presentation, the Mother and her daughters remain in the ceremonial circle while Honta Abich, the husband, and his escort or warden move to leave in the direction of the village. On their way out they are intercepted by a young woman dressed and painted in red; she is also tied to the waist of and led by another woman, her bodyguard or guardian, known as

Emynto. Thus tied, the young woman faces Honta Abich. She belongs to the Tomáraho clan, and he to the Namoho clan. He is armed with the characteristic *noshikó,* the strong male weapon; she with the *alybyk,* the female tool for defense and gathering. Bound and tightly held by their respective guardians the man and woman fight, striking the mace and stick against each other: both are made of hard wood, both are fearsome. Next they battle with gestures, and then with words: ciphers of what, for the Ishir, are weapons as dangerous as the wooden ones they have just used. They insult each other with expressive signs of physical (generally sexual) defects, and epithets whose pure sonority makes translation unnecessary and which fill the air with violence. Puffing and panting, they are hauled apart by their guardians.

The round continues, interrupted now by a woman who advances toward the *harra* and who, without crossing its limits, hands a small child to Honta Abich. He takes the child and stretches its small arms and legs to encourage full growth and promote health and understanding. These rituals of growth and the scene of a sexual confrontation between clans—a device that perhaps seeks to repair various social imbalances via symbolism—are repeated on various occasions between Honta Abich and different tethered girls and eager mothers.

Shínimit and Kaiporta

These anábsoro, who are a couple, appear together in the ceremonial circle and then leave in the direction of the village. They go to search for members of the Posháraha clan, striking on their doors to oblige them to present themselves. When the men and women of this lineage appear, eyes downcast, they are insulted by Kaiporta with words and gestures which become harsher and harsher until they culminate in simulated (and sometimes real) blows. The insulted party bears this silently: in some fashion, the offense will be repaired in a society which has so many forms, gestures, and words charged precisely with correcting abuses and reestablishing symmetry. The offenses heaped on the members of specific clans are called *enehichó.* Just because they are frequent and simulated does not mean that they do not affect those on the receiving end: those who are insulted ritually look as if they had really been insulted. Now Shínimit rushes at the frightened Posháraha children and pretends to hit them with a piece or wood or ceremonial tool.

Shínimit and Kaiporta, characters who rank highly in the myths, are presented separately among the Ebytoso. Although Kaiporta was the one who taught the women the use of the *alybyk* (digging stick), they cannot look at the person who will represent the goddess in the ceremonial scene: this constitutes another of the complexities of an Ishir counterpoint that always advances through a compensation of gifts and restrictions. Shínimit goes to the village and invades the houses of the Kytymáraha, beating on their walls and messing up their beds. Then, once back in the ceremonial circle, he confronts a succession of women from this clan with whom he wrestles with affected courage. When an opponent knocks him to the ground (which is how victory is measured) the anábser goes to the *tobich* to ask other anábsoro to help him make amends. The women remain in the circle taunting the loser. Shínimit is unable to find help among his compatriots and plunges into the woods in search of the wild ones, the *eichoso*. He returns with an army of woodland anábsoro after a few days, during the daily ritual called *dysyker labo*.

As mentioned above, this is the nocturnal ritual where a roll call of participants is taken: each character verifies his or her presence by yelling, so that the ritual turns into a deafening chorus of successive waves, squalls, and tremors of distant voices. One night the village realizes in astonishment that the cries are duplicated in instant echoes. This is because the *eichoso* allies of Shínimit are holding their own, parallel *dysyker labo* which multiplies the disquieting clamor of the first one. The predictable clash between these bands echoes the battle between the subterranean and woodland Ho-Ho's: they attack one another by trading torches and no less inflamed insults that fly back and forth all night. Originally, Ashnuwerta mediated this conflict and was able to pacify the opponents; now they calm themselves, and at dawn comprise a single, reconciled group.

Apepo

This anábser has a fleeting presence in the ritual: instead of a performance he consummates a threat, or the memory of a threat. When the mythical Apepo sprang forth from the ground, his excessively hairy body elicited the ridicule of the primitive women. Offended, the god cursed them. From that moment on women are condemned to suffer the troubles of menstruation and pains of childbirth. His appearance is, in truth, extravagant: he is covered entirely with thick strands of ostrich and stork feathers.

This character is almost identical among the Ebytoso, though his name is different: they call him Iubúbuta. According to Susnik (1957, 133), this character is the son of Nemur and Pfaujata and, therefore, corresponds to the hybrid offspring of the anábsoro (insofar as Pfaujata appears as a mortal who is deified by her union with Nemur).

Dúkusy

The Dúkusy comprise a group of about five to ten masculine characters who appear without a leader (*cabezante*). After circling the ceremonial stage they launch themselves screaming on the village as if they were an attacking enemy horde. Upon hearing the first warrior cries, the women run terrified to seek refuge in their homes or in the nearby woods. Soon, the anábsoro reach the village and strike the palm trunks of the huts to call the fugitives forth, force an entrance into their homes, or pursue them through the trees. Sometimes, they have to follow the women up the palm trees they quickly climb. When they reach the women, they hit them with force in a simulacrum that treads between the real and the represented and does not always succeed in maintaining a balance. In some representations, an older woman confronts the Dúkusy armed with her *alybyk* or with her sharpened nails.

Cordeu points out that these anábsoro act as a mechanism of internal adjustment, a necessary device in a sociocultural system that privileges the role of the women in daily life as much as it devalues it in the ceremonial arena (1999, 239–44).

Flores Balbuena offers a suggestive tale: upon emerging from the earth and facing the first seven women, the Dúkusy lived with and impregnated them. The children they birthed were therefore mestizos. They physically resembled the Ishir except for small details that gave away their mixed origins: piranha teeth, a feather here and there, a stray spot which marked the human skin with the terrible sign of the gods. To hide the signs of their promiscuity, the women pulled out their fangs, covered their mottled bodies with caraguata cloths, or painted over their spots with white ashes. But their silence could not be concealed: the children were born as mute as their fathers and this fact ultimately revealed the betrayal to the village men who, furious, set out to punish and perhaps to kill the seven unfaithful women. The women were able to find refuge in a nearby forest and, perched in different palm trees, tried to crawl into the sky which was not too high at the time. They did not succeed, but their racket turned them into *Póorch Ebe,* "daughters of the sky": the Pleiades. When the men returned to the village anxious for revenge, they decided to kill the Dúkusy. They hit them with their wooden maces and the gods fell to the ground but—as we know—did not die. They turned into ostriches and when the men spied them from afar they saw groups of these birds: larger, darker, faster. Frightened, they intuited that they were not true birds and that their feathers concealed the strength of the mute gods. They had to wait until Ashnuwerta revealed the weak spot of the anábsoro to kill them. This tale explains certain motifs that are dramatized in the ritual: the flight of the women to the woods, their climb into the trees (a theme with broad mythical resonances), the presence of the palm trees (open to so many connotations), the notion of a repairing counterbalance produced by gift and punishment, and so on.

Gatherers

Wild plants represent the only opportunity for the Ishir to ingest vegetables, just as wild game provides their only chance of eating meat. Hunting and gathering are the two pillars of the Ishir economy, as of most of the Chaco's indigenous communities. Over this duality another is discernible: the women gather; the men hunt. Coinciding with such central intersections of social activity, both hunting and gathering must be preserved through a firm symbolic architecture that imbues the ordinary tasks of daily sustenance with enigma and silence.

Many anábsoro are assigned the function of staging the task of gathering food and signaling its various meanings: the complement and tension of the sexes; the promise of desired fruits; the threat of hunger if there is scarcity or joy when there is abundance. It is true that the apparition of the gods paves the way for successful gathering, but it does so through the intricate mechanisms of poetry which are always opened to meaning and closed to a single direction: the auspicious function is only the premonition of an obscure message.

Before presenting a list of the gods of food gathering I will transcribe a brief commentary from my field notes in the hope of transmitting the atmosphere that reigns behind the scene . . . or in its depths, perhaps.

field notes

Puerto Esperanza, 15 August 1986

This morning in the *tobich* I watch the preparations for the performance of a character called Mä. It dawned some time ago, but the semidarkness created by the fog and the shadows of so many towering trees justify the bonfires. It is no longer cold but some men wear thick grey ponchos. Everyone is relaxed. While they wait unhurriedly for something I cannot determine, the Tomáraho tell stories, discuss, smoke silently. An Ebytoso group observes them from some distance away. Some of them approach, make commentaries, and join the group. It is always like this, and I suppose that this progressive and discrete way of approaching corresponds to the codes of refined interethnic protocol. Overcoming the traditional rivalry between the Tomáraho and Ebytoso requires prudent steps, though the groups are now neighbors and their differences are reasonably well controlled.

Now the preparations begin. The novices run in and out, taking or bringing different elements of ceremonial dress to and from the village: dresses, suits, and masks made of caraguata fibers provided by the women (who pretend to ignore the use to which they will be put with such conviction that they sometimes convince themselves). The novices also bring branches, flowers, and leaves that will be used in this representation, and feathers that some man forgot in a corner of his palm hut. Now another mask is missing and a sweaty boy sprints off. A bracelet is needed and another takes off running; he will soon be back, breathing heavily, will be given a new order and spring away again quickly, almost crashing into the first boy who is already back, puffing and panting.

If there are more young apprentices available, they are the ones who imprint the black bodies of the Mä with small circles they have formed with caraguata stalks. But if all the boys are occupied with fetching the various ornaments required for the performance, then the adult men are the ones to seal the dark skins of the actors. At this moment, the Ebytoso are already integrated and participate equally with the Tomáraho in the discussions on the adornments. These debates which sometimes graze doctrinaire thresholds are part of the rite that antecedes the performance in the *harra*.

The wardrobe of each anábser basically corresponds to a fixed mold, but beyond it the actors dispose of a good amount of freedom and follow their creative whims or the dictates of forces which are absolutely incomprehensible to me. This margin of improvisation, creativity, and action for unknown reasons allows for the intervention of men that help the actors, which in the case of the present Tomáraho means the presence of basically all adult males. These helpers and the Ebytoso who have joined them are especially participative today: they surround the characters and suggest the addition of a new piece to their hairdo that in this performance includes branches; they approach, adjust some bracelet that has not been tied well, straighten the plumed sticks that stand up among the branches, add details. Sometimes the inclusion of a secondary ornament leads to consultations, long deliberations, and even controversy that can be heated when the Ebytoso (whose ornamentations are different) intervene.

When all characters are ready, they line up side by side as if they were posing for a photograph; then they move quickly toward the stage.

Mä

The eight or ten members of the Mä group represent female characters that appear without the figure of the Mother. The Mä have essentially propitiatory functions since they promote the abundance of edible fruits and vegetables. But their presentation also acquires an ethical and didactic sense: their mouths are covered with their hands as an admonition that frugality must be observed even when food abounds, and as an image of the virtue of caution which must be maintained throughout life. The grass they carry in their hands is a reminder of pulchritude, required especially during the reclusion of initiation.

Waho

The next pro-harvest anábsoro who appear onstage answer to the generic name of Waho. These characters, whose number varies between eight and ten, also represent women. Like the previous group they are motherless women, which is a rare characteristic. Their performance is comprised of two scenes. The first begins with the appearance of three messengers who announce the entrance of the group; they erupt onstage surrounded by the songs of their escorting shamans and withdraw soon after, leaving in their wake the echoes of their intermittent cries and the announcements of the

Ceremonial march of the *anábsoro* Waho. María Elena, 2001. (Photo by Nicolás Richard.)

characters. The second scene involves the presentation of the entire group: the Waho advance trotting lightly, their hands placed on their hips bearing branches of *kapyla* (whose ripening they promote). The *kapyla* (wild bean) is the paradigm of gatherable fruits, the noble food that can provide for the community even in times of drought: toasted, boiled, or smoked (in which case they can last up to six months), these grains come to the aid of the Ishir during hunting expeditions and times of scarcity. Susnik says that these beans, along with eel and turtle meat, constitute the basic subsistence of the Ishir (1995, 71). For this reason, promoting the abundance of the *kapyla* is also an invocation of the community's survival.

Wichó

The entrance of the next group of anábsoro is subject to a necessarily variable regime since it depends on climatic conditions: the Wichó, a group of men, appear only after rain, so that sometimes the course of the ritual is brought to a halt to wait for the unpredictable spring rains; at other times, their presentation is inserted at another point of this tangled ritual. Bruno Sánchez explained to me that, during this representation, the land must be sufficiently humid to retain the impressions of their footprints, tracks that are known as the "trail of the peccary" and which summon prey by signaling a path that leads to the encounter with the hunter. The Ishir thus stage the fact that, according to them, animals can be easily captured after a good rainfall.

Each Wichó summons a different fruit, my informants tell me. But when an Ishir speaks of "summoning a fruit" he or she is not referring to a mechanism of prayer: he or she is not asking a superior being to grant a gift, but appealing to the favorable forces that move nature, in hope that this force may overcome adversarial ones and that the vegetables may grow and ripen despite the obstacles that can interrupt their vocation of fecundity.

Kaimo

The anábser who appears next is an important deity. Though Kaimo points to obscure and complex meanings, I have placed him among the gods which favor food gathering because the Tomáraho do so as well, and I want to follow their lead for reasons I have indicated previously. Kaimo specializes in promoting the gathering of *ajor üro* (a variety of water hyacinth) and directs, by extension, the search for roots and edible tubers that abound in palm groves in times of flood. Second, Kaimo promotes the search for edible eggs, principally those of the heron, stork, chaja, and *karau*.

Although I have obviated the description of body painting and ceremonial adornment thus far, that of the Kaimo—famous within the Chamacoco cultural horizon—cannot be ignored. They are distributed in symmetrical halves: black and white parts, counterpoised in forms and design, create an intricate game of equilibriums, confrontations, and new balances. Each black part, covered in white lines, is reflected and inverted in a white part, crossed by black stripes. I mentioned before that the checkered skin of Kaimo entranced one of the primitive women so much that she forgot her maternal duties: while she breastfed her child halfheartedly she could not tear her eyes away from the beauty of the god, crawling with contrasts, and did not notice that the cloth which covered her child had slipped, revealing his denied gender. And so the existence of men was revealed to the anábsoro, a revelation that disfavored the first women and sealed Ishir destiny. Perhaps to compensate for that unpleasant memory, the Kaimo are assigned an amiable gesture toward women: it is their place to advise them officially that the period of initiation is over and that soon they will see their sons again, whom they anxiously await.

For the Ebytoso, the figure of Kaimo is linked with other issues, some of which have been indicated previously. The ritual confrontation between the Kaimo and the men of the Posháraha clan, who appear in equal numbers, consists of two moments. In the first, the Kaimo hand over the *Kaimo ook*— the renowned scepter which is almost as prestigious as the one that represents the power of Nemur—to the Posháraha. The men cautiously wield these sticks which are painted with the same colors displayed by the Kaimo (red and black, among the Ebytoso) and which are laden with their fearsome powers.

During the second ritual act, each of the Kaimo launches himself on a Posháraha and tries to lift him from the ground in a wrestling match whose outcome is not always the one desired by the attacker. Cordeu says that, in recompense, the gods grant the assailed men the right to eat the tail and haunches of the anteater (1984, 431); such a gift confers considerable distinction on this clan in the context of the ceremonial banquet. Like other ritual performances this one strongly evokes the figures of solidarity and exchange that are so important to the constitution of primitive social consensus. And I use "primitive"

Scene from an Ishir ceremony, where the anábser Kaimo is being represented. Puerto Diana, 1956. (Photo by Branislava Susnik. Archives of the Museo Etnográfico "Andrés Barbero," Asunción.)

in the same sense as Sahlins (1972, 186), who uses the term to refer to cultures that lack a state and are defined as systems of reciprocity. The ritual stages the structure of transactions and negotiations that ensure equilibrium: the alliances between gods and mortals, between different human groups, between genders. In order for different, opposed, and even adversarial sectors to yield a community, a game of counterbalances and reparations is essential, much like the one required by the visual composition of the Kaimo's painted bodies or the ritual game that compensates the offences of a divine onslaught with edible gifts.

Katybyshé

Multiplied in ritual, the god Katybyshé is represented by four actors. The figure of the Katybyshé synthesizes essential activities of Ishir subsistence. On the one hand this god gathers eggs of the chaja, stork, a small species of duck, and a bird called *oho* which I have not been able to identify in Spanish or Guaraní. On the other hand he is a hunter: the wooden mace serves to knock down minor prey, and the jaguar crown signals his hierarchical status as a great slayer of beasts. According to Cordeu (1999, 205–11), in addition to his auspicious gifts, these anábsoro are assigned the power of language.

Okío

Two men represent the figure of Okío: a Poshátaha and a Namoho, the second of which is the *cabezante*. They are aquatic deities: they live in swamps and lagoons, streams and estuaries, and specialize in propitiating the abundance of tubers from water hyacinths, which they taught humans to gather in mythical times. Called *paë* by the Tomáraho and much appreciated in their cuisine, these tubers serve as a measure of exchange: the Okío gave them to men in exchange for snakes, scorpions, and other vermin so pleasing to the bizarre taste of the gods. This is why these characters are identified with the figure of divine gifts and, in general, with all forms of reciprocity.

Custodians of Initiation

Pohejuvo

The Pohejuvo are two men (twins according to some versions) who in addition to instruction in hunting practices (a role that is often mentioned but which lacks theatrical representation) are assigned the essential function of accompanying the novices during certain moments of the initiation: they emphasize certain events that mark masculine initiation, pillar of the Ishir culture. Thus, these anábsoro escort the boys when they are wrenched from their homes with dramatized violence. They accompany them when they enter the *tobich* to begin their reclusion, when they leave the cloister to undergo various tests, when they learn to procure food—whose governance they control—or any of the other tasks related to this phase. They also aid in the apprenticeship of various aspects of Ishir culture: the principles of an archaic knowledge, like the hollowness of words and the sayings that silence protects; ethical norms like moderation, solidarity, and readiness; the commitment to a collective destiny and diligence in the ciphered activities of the ceremony. For this reason the

Pohejuvo always trot when they move, just as the *wetern* must, to demonstrate their permanent predisposition and their willingness to serve.

Like all representations of the anábsoro, that of the Pohejuvo involves complex meanings: it constructs meaning obscurely by negotiating the adjustment of manifold tensions, imagining pacts between different terms in conflict. The Pohejuvo are instructors of certain hunting techniques and ceremonial custodians of the initiation; they are also the assassins of a primitive woman who violated the secret, the *Ös poro*, and with whose bones they crafted their macabre whistles; then in the *harra* they act as allies to the women who approach them, especially among the Ebytoso, trying to brush up against their feathers and obtain thus the gift of good birth.

This obscure ability to construct characters from various oppositions does not manifest in a privileged way in the Pohejuvo, but is very visible in their characterization. They are two: one is black and the other red, two colors that are the very model of confrontation. In the context of the *tobich,* if not in the ceremonial scene, one tends to take on the role of a mature man and the other of a youth. They are thus distinguished as Pohejuvo Ylaro, the old, and Pohejuvo Nakyrbytak, the young. The young one helps the older; the old one instructs the younger: each is defined in terms of his posture before the other. Only the young one can blow the whistle; the old one lets forth the somber sounds of punishment by emitting a whining cry.

This contrast symbolically marks the relation of difference and complement among the ages: it adjusts mutual obligations and figures rights and faculties, norms and sanctions. It is a reminder of the social place that the initiate will occupy when his seclusion is over: that of a young adult who respects his elders and commits himself to attending to them. But it also holds that of a *nakyrbytak,* an almost-child who needs to be protected by the power of wisdom the *ylaro* exhibit and that he will eventually acquire in the course of a continuous process.

The ambivalent meanings of sex and death unleashed by the Pohejuvo do not only originate in the mythical assassination of the violator of the secret (with whose bones his whistle is crafted): there is a more remote antecedent. Both Baldus (1932) and Susnik (1957, 1995) refer to a myth according to which, under the figure of a great dog, the original Pohejuvo raped Ashnuwerta and produced, in this fashion, the origin of the other anábsoro. In other narrations, the daughters of Ashnuwerta are the ones violated by two dogs: one red, the other blue (Susnik 1957, 18). None of the Ishir groups today knows these tales.

The oscillation of these meanings that signal antagonisms and correspondences in the terrain of gender, life, age, or social factions encourages us to understand the figure of the Pohejuvo as a signifier open to sheltering the different postures that intervene in the interplay of identity and alterity. They point to a logical scheme: a system of oppositions. They reveal a human question: the enigma of the same and the other.

Puut

Among the Ebytoso part of the work of the Pohejuvo is assigned to an anábser called Puut or Purt. To refer to him I will limit myself to what my informants have told me and what Susnik wrote because, since this character is absent from the Tomáraho ritual, I never witnessed his representation. In spite of his ill-favored look (he is short and hunchbacked) Puut is feared by the women and respected by the novices. He heads a squadron of men who go to fetch the youth and bring them forcefully to the seclusion of initiation, and once it is over accompany them as they go to meet their mothers with their bodies naked and painted in red with white spots. Mastering their anxiety the mothers approach, and without yet being able to look at them, they unfold caraguata mats on the ground for them to step on and enact the light genuflection which is their greeting. Afterwards Puut escorts them back to the *tobich;* some time will pass before he returns them definitively to the village.

THE END OF THE FESTIVAL

Sometimes, the sadness that the lugubrious flutes of the Pohejuvo bring also signals a certain, anticipated nostalgia produced by the end of the Great Ceremony. But, like every moment of the ritual, its culmination has ambivalent meanings. On the one hand, it leads to a gentle state of collective sadness; on the other, it opens onto times of collective euphoria. The ceremony has brought mourning to a close, reestablished different equilibriums, rectified the reactivation of the social contract, and hastened the season of new harvests. Often, then, the end of the festival takes place at a time when the air is refreshed and the cold currents of June and July and the withered lights of the northern wind of August suddenly yield to light breaths and warm transparencies. "It smells like Tsaat," the Ishir children say, not unlike the Paraguayan children who will say, "It smells like Christmas," when they sniff the aroma of the first coconut flowers.

That is its name, Tsaat: this ambiguous final stage which is charged with vivifying energies and shadowed by the disquiet that every consummated cycle leaves in its wake. The Tsaat expresses the climax of the ceremony: it signifies culmination in the sense of the triumphal pinnacle of a process, as well as the closure that reveals a limit and names death. By putting them onstage, rites intensify human experiences: they emphasize the satisfaction before the accomplished task and the despondency before the closed circle. The Tsaat exposes a radiant and fateful, feared phase. It manifests an accelerated time, which condenses the libretto of the rite, shortens the intermissions, and hastens the time of representation. It implies, therefore, a complex moment made up of different representations that are enumerated in the following pages.

Ashnuwerta

The great goddess initiates the ceremony's complicated close. She presents herself in the ceremonial circle escorted by a retinue of five daughters who are dressed like her but with simpler adornments. They wave small sticks to frighten the dogs and prevent them from dirtying her path. Sometimes the character splits into Ashnuwerta the red mother and Ashnuwysta the black. Both appear surrounded by respective attendants of daughters.

Kyshykyshe

The anábser Kyshykyshe splits into four male and female characters: Hartok (or Kashta), Manume, Hiaha, and Ñana, whose interplay precipitates dense meanings linked with the principal spaces of Ishir collective practices. This representation constitutes, in effect, a synthesis of the questions that always obsess the Chamacoco and that the rite must hasten to resolve; almost as if the beginning of the end forced the extraction of conclusions on the meaning of the great themes at stake: food, health, power, social alliance, difference, beauty, death. The moment of the dramatic denouement approaches.

After an aestheticized choreography in the ceremonial circle the four characters move toward the village. There they are awaited by four initiates who lean against trees whose positions correspond to the cardinal points. Rigidly, solemnly, the youths hold staffs crafted from the wood of fruit bearing plants. Each anábser approaches a novice, leans over with unexpected elegance and lightly touches the staff, pretending to fight for it with a gesture that is so stylized that it reminds one of a courtier's gesture of reverence rather than the expression of an archaic struggle. This movement, according to the Tomáraho, implies a magician-like gesture that brings abundance in food and relinquishing of power: the anábsoro transfer to the novices, the quintessential apprentices, their knowledge, power over nature, and cure for young death. This minimal and essential act also exposes the scheme of a conflict, the fight for power around food, and reveals political cartographies, economic outlooks.

When the Kyshykyshe withdraw some fathers approach their daughters, painted with the colors of Ñana, in order to bestow upon them the gift of her powers and keep sicknesses and other threats at bay. The goddess lifts the children and deposits them back on the ground in a single movement that seems to happen at lightning speed like all the performances of the Tsaat.

Wo

The next character, who responds to the laconic name Wo, also signifies a compendium of fundamental questions. The Wo are numerous—as many as are practicable. In the past, many villages joined in so that the maximum possible number of male actors represented Wo.

The requirements of quantity spare this performance from other requirements; any initiated male, regardless of clan affiliation, physical condition, or age can play the part of Wo. On the one hand, such a large number of actors makes it inevitable that they have different positions: there are fishermen and hunters, gatherers, artisans, healers, and chiefs. There are actors of all clans and of all ages: sometimes as a reminder Wo Ylaro, the ancient, appears onstage. But there are also female and male Wo: although normally they are organized through a system of male leaders or *cabezantes* (they use three *webichoso*), there are occasions in which they are governed by a Wo Lata, Mother of

The characters on both ends personify the *anábser* Wo, who appears gagged with great ropes of ostrich feathers (symbols of the ceremonial secret). In the center an adorned shaman shakes the maraca. All carry cylindrical bags, laden with their nomadic equipment. Karcha Balut, 1996. (Photo by Juan Britos.)

the Wo, and even others, in which there are so many Wo that three mothers are required.

The figure of multiplicity that the Wo suggest points to diversity as well as to profusion. On the one hand it is evident that they are a metaphor of variety of all kinds: one could almost say a celebration of the complex or, at least, a staging of the plurality of activities, sectors, and individuals that constitute the social, as well as the natural species that populate the environment. But they also reinforce the idea of desired providence: the profusion of fruits and honey, prey and fish; the abundance of plumes, the opulence of goods.

The *Kadjuwerta*

In this moment of denouement—of conclusions and condensing images—
an essential ritual is inserted that begins to close the circle of the drama and
knot its various issues. During the representation of Wo, some of the few
males who do not participate in it begin to prepare a cryptic ceremony in the
tobich. A man of the Dyshykymser clan begins to braid a thick rope which is
tied on one end to a tree. He uses threads of caraguata fibers that an assistant
of the Tymáraha clan brings after having acquired them from the old weavers
in the village. The rope, which is called *dugorik,* is dyed red. When the Wo return to the *tobich* after having finished their performance, they take off their
bracelets and earrings, their many skirts of ostrich feathers and heron feathers,
their crowns and diadems, their plumed sticks and necklaces. Next, aided by
novices—as many as are available to help such a multitude of participants—
they ceremoniously deposit all feathered ornaments on the *lëbe* (rush mat) at
the side of the Dyshykymser man. All the shamans approach, each singing
their song and agitating their maracas until the air is filled with a resounding,
off-key, disquieting clamor. As if he does not hear it, the man proceeds diligently in his task: he ties an end of the rope to a tree and begins to hang all
the plumed ornaments on it, producing an ensemble that is exuberant due to
the sheer number of ornaments from the Wo performance. First he arranges
the red or pinkish feathers, then feathers of other colors, and lastly the red
ones again so that they cover the piece—or at least impose their tone—so that
the resulting, full-bodied artifact takes on a reddish hue.

The opulent mass of feathers I describe is called *kadjuwerta.* The term
kadjá refers to a powerful concentration of forces that ends in an explosion;
the word *wert,* to reddish tones. So that *kadjuwerta* means something like a
crimson discharge of power. This important ensemble suggests a critical moment capable of condensing and then liberating, with the force of a lightning
bolt, all the energy accumulated by the interaction of men and gods, cosmic
forces, feathers and colors, screams and maracas during the course of the
debylyby.

Now the shamans approach the strange mass and spit on it to increase the
powers contained in its feathers. The Ishir, be they Tomáraho or Ebytoso, say
that sometimes the spit falls in the shape of venomous creatures: serpents,

scorpions, and spiders; all of which are food to the anábsoro and *woso* in its ominous phase. They say, because I have not seen it, that at other times the *konsaho* spit out their cries converted into blood on the extravagant bundle of feathers; this transmutation, linked with the red mark of the Osíwuro, Masters of the Pleiades, signifies the maximum display of power that a shaman can offer. Thus, laden with the powers that the feathers of the ceremonial circle bring, and which increase as they are interlaced; equipped with the powers that shamanic saliva adds, converted or not into poisonous insects or reptiles; and strengthened by the blood of the *konsaho,* the *kadjuwerta* becomes a plethoric matrix of various faculties. In Ishir thought such an intense concentration of *woso* implies both beneficial powers and adversarial currents.

This ambivalence—a characteristic of the numinous according to Cazeneuve (1971, 141)—determines that the *kadjuwerta* mobilizes opposite values and precipitates divergent feelings. The *kadjuwerta* represents fresh breezes that replace the scarcity of winter with budding sprouts, humidity, and warmth; it promises vigor in the hunt and the bed and installs the purifying relief of a new cycle; it initiates a stage exempt from mourning, guilt, and the negative energies accumulated during a difficult year (and all years are difficult in the Indian Chaco). But the *kadjuwerta* is also filled with dangers: if a woman or noninitiate looks at it, it can cause sterility or impotence, blindness or death; if touched accidentally it can produce a deadly discharge on the careless person; if waved incorrectly it can drag the incompetent man toward madness or a flight among stars, alternatives that do not differ much in the Chamacoco cultural horizon.

After the shamans have watered this great bundle with potent saliva (and perhaps even with their blood), it is time for the ceremony the Ishir call the "dance of the *kadjuwerta,*" which is reserved for adult men. The young men— even the novices and initiates—are strictly prohibited from watching while the men, at a distance of twenty meters from the group, whirl the voluminous mass of feathers over their heads; as this strange operation begins, therefore, the young men run off. Sometimes they throw themselves on the ground, covering their eyes with their hands, keeping their heads glued to the ground.

After a vibrant silence, a chorus of shamans bursts into the air opposing the *kadjuwerta* with the power of their deep cries and the dull thunder of their maracas. A man from the Tahorn clan approaches at some exact moment, takes the piece from the end of the rope and begins to spin it around his head

Tomáraho man spinning the great feathered bundle called *kadjuwerta*. Puerto Esperanza, 1989. (Photo by Cristián Escobar Jariton.)

in circles like a windmill, slowly first, and then furiously. This operation is repeated (three times) by a representative of each of the remaining clans: after fulfilling his heavy task, the last one places the plumed body on the rush mat and, followed immediately by the others, begins to strike it with all his strength. In this way the Chamacoco metaphorically defeat the adversarial forces absorbed by the feathers and nourish themselves with the beneficial ones also harbored by the feathers. They feel relieved, clean, blessed; they can continue the last part of the ceremony that will finish purifying the village and will lodge within it, for a while, the elusive calm of unity.

On occasion, during the time of the ceremony, the village is threatened by drought; on occasion there are cases of madness, where people become unhinged by such a concentration of energy. If so, another ritual takes place which is formally similar to what I just described (its similarities and oppositions make it its counterpart). The ritual I described manifests red power; the alternative ritual manifests black power. It is the same power, perhaps, considered in different, sometimes inverse, moments. But they are not equivalent: the bundle of red feathers is more potent, efficient, and therefore dangerous than the bundle of black ones (it is comprised of mainly black, grey, and blue feathers).

The Tomáraho relate the *kadjuwysta* (black mass of feathers) to the figure of Totila, the mythical crazy woman; for this reason, the ceremony during which it is whirled through the air is called *Totila Teichu,* "the ritual of the crazy woman." During this ritual, while the bundle of feathers flies through the air the men become crazier and crazier until they lose all control and begin to howl outrageously. From the village the women attribute these screams to the powerful Totila who wanders, lost and crazed, through the palm groves and forests of the Chaco. It seems that the thundering din that rises from the *tobich* is able to disorient the crazy woman or the very cosmic forces over which she has inexplicable influence; but whatever the case may be, what is certain is that the power of the feathers and yells (an image of thunder) unleashes real storms and brings abundant rain.

Wahé

In this stage of final urgency the events tangle together or their borders almost overlap. At the same time as the serious ritual through which the *kadjuwerta* is dismantled, the preparations for the presentation of the Wahé (also Wawé, or Wawá) begin. They form a numerous group—not equal to the Wo, but numerous all the same—perhaps to take advantage of the profusion of feathers collected in the *tobich* at that moment, perhaps to suggest the abundance of fruits their presence is supposed to summon.

In the ceremonial plaza (*harra*) various women await them. These women are stationed in equidistant points of the circle, their backs to the center, and they shout to the anábsoro: "Come here, come to my side." Responding to the invitation, each Wahé places himself with his back to hers. Then they perform a stylized simulacrum of a stolen harvest: the women inch their hands backwards and with affected nonchalance rob the fruits of the branches each god bears in his hand and then throw them in the direction of their houses. Obviously, this brief representation serves to underscore the harvesting function of women. But like any rite (and like all art forms) it does not do so lit-

Scene from the ritual of Wahé: symbolic dispute between men and women for the fruits the latter have collected. Puerto Diana, 1956. (Detail of a photo by Branislava Susnik. Archives of the Museo Etnográfico "Andrés Barbero," Asunción.)

erally, but rather through multiple suggestions and twisting turns that name the culture/nature opposition and the male/female difference through the enigma of the figure and the complicated detour of poetry.

Nemur and Pfaujata

The last act of the ceremony is in the charge of a prominent and terrible couple. He is Nemur, fateful lord of guilt and punishment, tragic cipher of Ishir extermination; she is Pfaujata whose shining gaze can kill or madden, steal the power of speech or annul the power of sex. We already know that the Ishir gods have more than one face and that the gifts offered by these figures end up compensating for the misfortunes they bring. Nemur is a hunter and warrior and incarnates the archetype of masculine activity. Pfaujata is a food gatherer and represents a model of women's labor. The goddess is also the one who introduced the caraguata, the bromeliad whose fibers the Ishir use to craft domestic and ceremonial cloths: all Chamacoco culture is wrapped in caraguata fibers. Vengeful and laden with gifts, feared and venerated, both Nemur and Pfaujata are good examples of the divine caste and worthy of the grand conclusion.

If Nemur and Ashnuwerta act as face and counterface of the divine power that installs the essential code, Nemur and Pfaujata represent two opposite and complementary sides of certain tasks that are no less important for being ordinary: utilitarian routines of subsistence, technical skills, and social practices. The first opposition, proposed in terms of myth, mobilizes an ethical normativity; the second, performed in the space of ritual, stages prescriptions whose reach is basically economic and social. The fact that one issue is dealt with in a mythical register while another is approached through ritual is arbitrary and does not signify, obviously, a division of jurisdictions. It is taken for granted that the differences between myth and ritual are formal rather than material (and I employ the distinction in its Aristotelian sense): it is not a division of abilities; they simply treat the same subject from different places. And these different places require different expressive, rhetorical, and aesthetic resources. Thus the figure of Nemur when faced with Pfaujata does not emphasize his ministry as the Lord of Punishment so much as his role as the instructor in the arts of war and skills in hunt.

Just as Kaiporta is the one who teaches women how to use the *alybyk,* Pfaujata is the one who introduces the caraguata. According to the Ishir logic which tends to create formal relations on the basis of successive counterpoints and equilibriums, the Tomáraho say that Pfaujata first taught this fundamental technique to the men, who at that moment lingered on the outskirts of the initiatory grounds, but once they supplanted the women as porters of the secret the women inherited the work of the caraguata. From then on the men cannot intervene in the process of gathering caraguata, making threads, and weaving cloth. If they did so Pfaujata could leave them impotent, crazy, or mute for life: the imbalances generated by Pfaujata are irreversible.

Thus, not only does she institute the figure of the caraguata and its multiple applications, she also sanctions the forms that organize its use. Pfaujata compensates for Nemur's vindictive side: if he provokes panic in women (they cannot even look at his representation), she spreads terror in men. The inexplicable deaths of hunters who have died without signs of violence, the disappearance of men on expedition, as well as stuttering, paralysis, and epileptic crises suffered by novices are all attributed to Pfaujata.

The withdrawal of Nemur and Pfaujata from the stage marks the end of the great ritual. Surrounded by shamans who shake their maracas melancholically, a group of men of different clans enters the ritual circle, empty now of gods. The Kytymáraha, those of serene action and indispensable words, proclaim simply the words *debylyby tsaatyk,* "the ceremony has finished."

A Tomáraho shaman, Aligio Estigarribia. María Elena, 2002. (Photo by Nicolás Richard.)

THE PATH OF THE SHAMANS

THE KINGDOM OF THIS WORLD

As I have had occasion to note in previous chapters, the shamans act in another dimension than that of the gods. These planes do not contradict each other—in fact, they can intersect—but they are fundamentally different. The shamans do not busy themselves with religion and its cults and do not, for this reason, project their actions onto dimensions that transcend the human condition. On the contrary, they are dedicated to traveling the complex terrains of the human condition to facilitate the advent of the designs that shape it.

The spaces of human experience are traversed by alien forces. The human body itself is a stage moved by foreign powers. Since these can either be friendly or hostile, the Ishir must progress by dodging obstacles, trying to secure the favors of nature and history, and staving off many evils. They do so by balancing and countering forces, negotiating with the obscure energies that inhabit their natural surroundings, and making deals with the unknown impulses that propel their own bodies. Left to their own devices the Ishir men and women would not be able to successfully undertake such a great enterprise. They would not be capable of successfully manipulating the almost infinite repertoire of *woso,* and would succumb under the weight of adversity. They need, therefore, the assistance of exceptional individuals.

Shamans, the *konsaho* or *áhanak,* are human beings equipped with extraordinary qualities. They are, therefore, capable of controlling the forces that affect the community by intercepting or encouraging these forces. The shaman is the strongest individual in Chamacoco culture, the one who best embodies the value of the personal even if the shaman also condenses a certain collective spirit and interprets obscure ciphers of the entire community. Few warrior chiefs attain as exceptional a status—one in which they truly stand out from the rest of their community—as do the great shamans.

The jurisdiction of the *konsaho* does not involve religious / transcendental levels but rather centers itself intensely on the temporal and bounded terrain of organic, historical, and existentially situated human experience. The markers that point out the paths taken by culture stand in relief against the background of the everyday; they border on the exceptional, the unusual, and even delirium. Shamanism explores the exacerbated edges of the human, those that graze madness and death, desire and the excesses of obsession, those that refer to critical experiences and radical situations: hunger, pain, fear, pleasure, the rebellious disquiet of the mortal who knows and refuses his or her destiny. As privileged representatives of human action, the *konsaho* push themselves to the limit, crossing it ephemerally in a furious fit of ecstasy, only to fall back into the causality that regulates the pulse of the cosmos. But not all shamanic activity bears this dramatic sense of primordial limits. To arrive at existential and natural limits the *konsaha* (singular of *konsaho*) must follow a routine marked by prosaic necessities and everyday demands. For this reason the "path of the shaman," to use an image frequently employed by the Chamacoco, also comprises minor questions. Shamans help to summon the food eaten daily, cure minor illnesses, remove small disillusions, and alleviate the fatigue of hunters and gatherers.

On this basis, it should be clear that the professional equivalents of shamans in our culture are not priests (with whom they have often been compared) but rather psychoanalysts, poets, doctors, artists, visionaries, and the maddened prophets that illuminate and conceal (drive and twist) the course of Western culture.

The shamans are also the equivalents of philosophers and wise men. Shamanism is deeply linked to the idea of analytic and sensorial development. The formation of the *konsaha* requires, in effect, not only arduous training in different disciplinary practices (ecstasy, healing) but also a long process of reflection and apprenticeship, maturation, growth in sensibility, and *eiwo*. Eiwo can be translated as the entire intellectual apparatus—including thus both the "understanding" and "reason" of modern philosophy—and is linked, in a Lockean sense, to the idea of "vision," which allows the perception of the totality of things.

Some shamans use wooden swords called *anarak*. The hilts of these symbolic weapons are etched with two points that represent eyes and that, according to Susnik, refer to the intense and shining gaze of the star-men. Susnik interprets this representation as a metaphor of the shaman's need to see simultaneously in all directions. This global vision is understood as the capacity to see in extension, in depth and intensity (Susnik 1957, 96). For the Chamacoco the dream-vision is a medium to profound and total knowledge. It enables the shaman to perceive "absolute truth" or, as the Chamacoco say, *"what is today and what can still be tomorrow"* (Susnik 1995, 220). Considering the function of different human faculties in shamanic discourse, Cordeu maintains that according to the Ishir, the *eiwo*—"whose use leads to wisdom or *oso eiwo* and whose abuse leads to madness"—is located in the brain.[1] "This is why the shamans who have prevailed in ecstatic combat slice off the head of the defeated and devour their brains, the place of thoughts, to appropriate them" (Cordeu 1986, 109).

The world of the shamans constitutes the other great stage of aesthetic, mythic, and ritual forms, parallel to that of religion (the world of the anábsoro). To a lesser extent, everyday social life also erects a scene that brings into play aesthetic signs. But the activities directly linked to domestic life, subsistence, the exercise of power, and social contract require less rhetorical effort and demand less theatrical mise en scène: disguises and masks, simulacra. The flares of light and the darkness of spaces are coupled to the representation of the gods and the ministry of the shamans.

This chapter will approach the world of the shamans through the accounts and tales of the Ishir themselves, which are so complex and sophisticated as to make analysis and explanation superfluous. I will therefore only briefly indicate some themes necessary for an elemental introduction to the Ishir shamanic world.

ACTIVITIES AND DUTIES OF THE SHAMANS

The main categories of shamanic activity are as follows.

THERAPY

Most shamans develop medical and psychological competency. Through song, suction, the use of professional tools, medicine, and enigmatic acts performed during trances and dreams they prevent and cure physical illness and mental disturbances. They even recover the spirit that has recently detached itself from the corpse before it is taken definitively to Osypyte, the kingdom of the dead.

PROPITIOUS MAGIC

One of the most common and important functions of the *konsaho* is related to their capacity to act upon natural, psychological, or social forces that condition the life of the Ishir. The shamans can halt or unleash rains and storms, avert plagues, turn away or defeat enemies, seek alliances, arouse the collective spirit, promote good hunting and fruitful gathering, and even ripen slow fruit.

Certain issues must be kept in mind when considering shamanic magic; I will merely indicate them here since they exceed the scope of this book. It is important to admit that the meaning of certain forms of indigenous culture is unattainable to us. It is impossible to determine the mechanisms of certain propitious or therapeutic practices, and even the meaning assigned by the Ishir to such actions: this meaning is quite possibly obscure to the Ishir. Even the most rationalist cultures assume that not all of their instances can be explained in logical/causal terms, and know, or intuit, that their borders are confused by the shadows of neighboring enigmas. It is thus useless to clarify the intimate apparatus that activates magic.

Secondly, the mechanisms of magic—like aesthetic, mythic, or ritual mechanisms—cannot be interpreted literally. Its gestures and invocations respond, to a large extent, to rhetorical artifice. They are powerful metaphors of the "real world" whose complexity disallows direct interpretation.

Finally, the level of shamanism's "real" efficacy should be taken into account. Jensen argues that, in a strict sense, only the extraordinary personal aptitude of the shaman, capable of precipitating phenomena within the context of his culture, constitutes a case of real magic (1963, 214–40). It is evident that the shaman's vigorous personality—the force of his psychological abilities, his great power of concentration and suggestion, his uncommon sensibility and exceptional intellectual development—have a great impact on the life of his community. The impact is all the greater because he is so tightly bound to the community; he interprets, concentrates, and mobilizes the ideas, values, desires, and images that integrate the social body and trace the outlines of the community's representations.

VISION

The development of an intense vision that enables shamans to understand and foretell phenomena, as well as their ability to communicate with birds (prophetic entities par excellence), allows shamans to make predictions and omens. They can give advice regarding distant presences; identify threats, contact dead shamans, anticipate storms and natural disasters; and pinpoint the direction of prey, the location of the best fruits, and the most promising site for the village's next move. The ability of the *konsaho* to forecast what will happen, be it good or bad, can also come through revelations transmitted by powerful figures in dreams. Finally, the vision of the shamans also includes his or her capacity to know the truth of things simply from the perspective granted by flights of ecstasy. The shaman increases his knowledge by skimming the bed of the river, tunneling underground, or lifting himself above the clouds to reach Osiwuro, the mysterious and titillating homeland of the star-men. The distance allowed by flight produces a vision of totality, and the comprehension of objects that can be entangled in relations, or discrete.

RITUAL ACTS

Shamanic rites are not as impressive as religious rites. The rites do not need to represent a primordial time, but to assist in acts of healing, vision, and beneficence; the rites also give them strength to combat other shamans, accompany the community, and bring it good fortune through the power of voices and dream instruments. The most important ceremony is called the *shu-deich* and literally means "the defeat of the sun." On occasions that require a great surplus of collective energy or the reinforcement of the valor of some *konsaha* who will undertake a difficult task (usually combat), all the shamans of the community gather in the *harra* (ceremonial circle) and spend the night singing their own songs and shaking their maracas.

Another rite that brings the shamans together and raises a chorus of voices and rattles is known as *áhanak techu* ("song of the shamans"). It takes place on the eve of the start of the *debylyby,* the Great Ceremony, in order to bless the village, stimulate the collective spirit, and predispose the Ishir for the great expenditure of collective energy demanded by the ritual time. The shamans frequently appear throughout the *debylyby.* They do so not to act (they do not represent the gods) but to accompany and encourage the community. During certain propitious religious acts the shamans sing from a distant spot to reinforce their efficacy. On other occasions, such as the beginning of the ritual game of *póhorro,* the shamans will also gather and sing in chorus.

The forms implicated in certain professional dramatizations (healing, blessings, propitiatory gestures, etc.) do not require too many flourishes and are reduced to precise, indispensable gestures that mark the shaman's shadowy vocation. By way of example I will describe the capture of the soul of a recently deceased youth, as told by Flores Balbuena. Susnik (1957, 106) cites a case that coincides remarkably with Balbuena's account, and I draw on it to complete his notes. In the first place the shaman must identify with the youth. To do so he lays himself down beside the inert body and encircles its neck in an embrace that symbolically likens him to the *ágalo,* the youth's companion. He falls into a trance and while the animals assisting him breathe onto the recently extinguished body, the shaman through ecstatic convulsions lifts off in search of the spirit that advances already toward Osypyte, drawn by the noise of the dead as they play their deadly games. When the shaman intercepts and captures the spirit with his *lepper wolo* (crown of duck feathers), he returns it to the body by blowing and filling it up. Now the spasms of his trance have ended and the shaman must imitate every movement of the resuscitated person, imitate even his uncertain breathing. The two are "as one," say the Ishir. The basic senses of the deceased must be reawakened: to do so the *konsaha* sweeps his strand of ostrich feathers first over the nose, and then over the still, glassy eyes and dry mouth of the youth, thus opening them. Memory—which has until this moment remained erased—must be recovered next: the shaman wraps a caraguata rope around the youth's chest so that the youth will feel the constricted flow of his own blood. The consciousness of this vital flow helps him return to life and disperse the forgetfulness brought on by death.

FLIGHT

To fulfill their tasks, shamans must take leave of their bodies in dreams or ecstasy. Dreams unlock the fullest instance of revelation and bring the shamans
into contact with the forces to be controlled. The dream opens up the "path
of the shaman": the elevated road shamans must take to soar in the flight of
wisdom, search for recently detached spirits, communicate with dead shaman
friends, and battle with enemies that interrupt their progress. The *konsaho*
also achieve metamorphosis through dreams. Shamans can identify (the principle of *cet*) with an allied or contrary force to assume or usurp its strange
powers.

The second means of access to flight and metamorphosis is trance. Generally, shamans reach ecstasy by concentrating intensely on the repetition of
their songs and the rattle of maracas until these sounds and rhythms, reiterated obsessively for hours, allow them to enter a dimension that is parallel to the
organic causality that governs their body. The shamans of a certain category—
byrbyk posyro, the "eaters of honey"—can enter a trance state by ingesting hallucinogenic honey. According to Cordeu (1986, 104), some shamans can reach
a trance through a particular way of breathing. The psychic state of some
konsaho is already so close to what is conventionally considered "abnormal"
that they can cross the threshold between these dimensions without much
effort and achieve the degree of alienation that leads to ecstasy.

THE SHAMANS' TOOLS

Shamans use a variety of tools, depending on the requirements of their tasks.
The following is a list of the basic ones.

CORPORAL PAINT

The colors and designs that are painted onto the bodies of the shamans reinforce the efficacy of their tasks, especially magical/propitiatory ones. The development of these paintings follows Chamacoco iconography—coloring
with red, black, and white; and comprising designs with lines, spots, circles,
distribution in planes, specks and spills of paint, palm imprints, etc.—but the

fact that these motifs and shades depend on personal revelations introduces an element of variety. Consequently, the corporal paints of the shamans are looser and more varied than those employed by the actors of the religious ceremony (this difference is more pronounced among the Ebytoso shamans). The ceremonial representation of the anábsoro demands fixed patterns, although there is some room for particular variations and improvisations. The individual nature of shamanic paintings accents the fluidity of their meaning: the same motif can assume different semantic corollaries according to the individual who uses it and the occasion on which it is used.

Typologically, the feathered pieces employed in shamanic dress are identical to those worn in the ceremonial circle—not all of which are used by shamans—but the meanings of these pieces differ in the different contexts. While the feathers used in the ceremony seek to complete the images of the gods, those used by the shamans are meant to augment their powers or function as vehicles for the powers. Ebytoso and Tomáraho shamans share the basic feathered trappings: crowns of black feathers from the muscovy duck (*lepper wolo* or *manon wolo*); strands of ostrich feathers (*pamune*); feathered sticks (*báteta* and *shak-tern*); different kinds of earrings, bracelets, and crowns crafted with braids from the hair of widows (*kuhu* or *katy*) from which twigs dangle.

While this repertoire is common and indispensable to both the Ebytoso and Tomáraho, there are differences between the shamanic dress of the respective groups. The dress of the Ebytoso shamans is more uniform, and circumscribed in a stable repertoire even when they incorporate some ornaments unknown to, or at least unused by, the Tomáraho: skirt-belts composed of large feathered sticks (*or yrrote*), crowns comprised of birds' nests (*pem-uk*), and large caps called *or uhür*. Tomáraho shamans display a great variety of forms and flexibility in their dress, and loosely manipulate a diverse array of feathered ornaments that vary according to dream revelations or personal preferences.

The real songs are revealed in dreams or trance states to the *konsaho,* who are also referred to as *áhanak* insofar as they are singers. Each *áhanak* has his own *teichu:* his own *polca* (polka), as the Ishir sometimes translate it, forcing Spanish to name something that lies far beyond its domain. Songs serve to punctuate shamanic activities: healing, trances, propitiatory practices, and the battles they sometimes fight through the pure force of their sounds and the arguments woven by their intoned words.

Susnik deals with the conflict created when two shamans sing the same *teichu,* which is meant to be an individually assigned "signature" (1957, 90). The complaint must be resolved in an oneiric or ecstatic plane and end in the discredit of one of the shamans if he plagiarized the song, or an alliance if they both have legitimate rights to it. If the two allied *konsaho* ever need to journey the same "shamanic path," they warn each other so as to avoid bumping into each other in the landscape dreamt out of the same tone. Sometimes, the co-proprietors of the *teichu* help each other detain the spirits heading to Osypyte.

The shaman who sings until his throat bleeds proves his extraordinary professional vigor. Such is the case of Wylky, a Tomáraho shaman, whose hoarse voice and almost inaudible words attest to his prestige as an outstanding *áhanak.*

PHYSICAL IMPLEMENTS

The shamans make use of various physical implements that are also meant to reinforce the efficacy of their flights, cures, and propitiatory acts.

Anklets that serve as percussion instruments (*polasho*) are composed of animal hoofs, seeds, or small turtle shells. They are formally identical to those used in the Great Ceremony. The movements of the shamans turn these pieces into rattles whose crackling rhythms encourage flight, exalt the spirit for combat, and emphasize the song that requests gifts from the forces of nature.

Maracas (*peikara*) are made of small round gourds filled with different seeds. The rustle of the maraca is an indispensable accompaniment to the shaman's song. Its light or nervous vibrations mark the tempo, introducing pauses or stressing the arguments of the rising and falling words.

The staff-sword (*anarak*) is a symbolic weapon made of wood (generally palo santo), approximately forty centimeters in length. It is the instrument used by shamans—especially those of celestial rank—to soar and surmount their enemies in flight. Susnik says that the term *anarak* also designates the tail of a comet, which is considered to be the wake of the "furious passage of a stellar shaman in the yellow strata" (1995, 223). The two seeds on the hilt represent the sword's eyes, symbolize the shining gaze of the star-men, and constitute—as mentioned previously—a metaphor of the profound and extensive gaze of the shamans. Some informants assure me that these seeds represent the eyes of the storks that help the Master of the Osasërö, the birds of storm and rain. (In fact, there is not much difference between the versions: the star-men as well as the Osasërö correspond to mutations of the primitive men who were marooned in the sky after the fall of the cosmic tree.) In order to confront their rivals, the shamans can also bear other weapons like the *noshikó*, a powerful mace crafted from the carandá palm, or the *pik*, crafted from wood of the carob tree, but these are not specifically shamanic weapons.

The smoke of a wooden pipe (*monyak*) is used to bless the village: it animates collective energies, expels evil, and drives away outside threats.

A suctioning tube (*potytak*) is used by shaman healers to suck out ills that damage the body, confuse and mislead the understanding, or impair the spirit with fear and melancholy.

Whistles (*potak* or *dóshibyt*) of wood, poppy stems, or bird bones (generally stork or heron bones) are used to call the animals that help the shaman and to convoke the aid of allied forces.

A woven mat, rolled into the form of a tube, becomes a sheath or case (*lëbe*) that holds the aforementioned tools as well as feathered adornments. This bundle brims with power and is the shaman's greatest treasure. On certain occasions, a bag of caraguata fibers serves the same function.

SHAMANIC CATEGORIES

On this subject I have decided to follow Bruno Barrás's classification, which I will lay out in more detail further on.[2] There are certain remarks I want to make at this point. In general, shamans are distinguished according to jurisdictions—sky, surface of the earth, underground, or underwater—but this classification intersects with one that distinguishes them according to the origins of their shamanic powers. According to the figures, which act as magisterial and protecting models, the shamans can be, for example, of the sun (*konsaho Deich jilo*),[3] of Osasërö (*konsaho Osasërö jilo*), of Iolé, of Lapishé, of Hoshta, etc. The separation between religious and magical domains promotes the fact that such superior figures emerge in shamanic mythology and not anábsoro mythology (except Pfaujata who, in any case, is considered a deified mortal). Certain references by Susnik link Ashnuwerta with the "shamanic path": she refers to the ancient *konsaho* of Ashnuwerta (1957, 74), a category that no longer exists today, and mentions that this goddess protects the sky shamans (1995, 200). Cordeu, moreover, states that Nemur grants powers to sky shamans from his abode in the Third Sky (1992b, 231–32). But these intersections between gods and shamans are isolated instances. Nemur, Ashnuwerta, and Pfaujata are the great mediators between different moments of Ishir culture: they can open doors between different dimensions, but this does not mean that the distances that separate these dimensions are annulled.

SHAMANIC MYTHOLOGY

The stories about gods can be understood as a single narrative corpus—the Great Myth of the anábsoro—but it is impossible to articulate the shamanic tales in an organic set. There are too many unequal and dispersed moments. Some narratives are life-stories, accounts, summaries, chronicles, fables, legends, and minor tales, while others are serious myths that suggest ethical and cosmic consequences, which approach the central questions of Ishir culture in a different key from the god-stories. Both registers of myth share forms and figures, of course. They are both concerned with rhetorically justifying norms and sanctions; with explaining (through the obscure turns of poetry) the great operations of Ishir logic (classifications, identifications, oppositions, etc.); and with forcing discourse to include the obscure themes that transcend it. Both mythical dimensions also share a sense of great cultural heroes. The anábsoro on the one hand, and the mythical protoshamans on the other, are civilizers, not creators by fiat. They bring the value of the symbol, and consequently the restriction of the norm. Faced with meaning, mortals realize that the light of understanding always takes place against the backdrop of an enigma. This paradox pushes them to the fictions of language: intense, twisted truths of myth, ritual, and art.

Since my endeavor is to suggest the complexity of the shamanic path through figures rather than through concepts, this chapter will present a series of myths concerning shamans. I include here small fables and grand epics, tales filled with cosmic reverberations, narrations brimming with hermetic ethical and existential signs. Three fundamental shamanic myths were laid out in chapter 2: the origin of the colors (the woman and the eel), the origin of feathers and death (the cannibals), and the red color of feathers (the woman and the caraguata flower). I have also previously relayed four minor tales on the origin of corporal painting in chapter 3. These tales should be kept in mind and confronted with the ones that follow. And as I mentioned in the Introduction, while I have scrupulously followed plot and narrative content these tales are freely transcribed.

THE CYCLE OF THE SUN AND MOON

The Lessons of the Sun

[Narrated by Tybygyd (Luciano Martínez), a celestial Tomáraho shaman. Translated from Ishir to Spanish by Bruno Barrás.]

The primordial Ishir climbed to the sky to collect honey through the great tree that linked it to the earth. The daughter of Laguylta, a powerful shaman and widow, was bothered by these honey-seekers and complained constantly to her mother. On one occasion Laguylta lost her patience and, furious, turned into a termite (or a legion of termites) and gnawed at the base of the tree until the trunk began to sway from side to side as it was about to fall. Given its great height, the men and women still clinging to its trunk and crown were thrown and scattered great distances. This dispersion created the different Ishir peoples (Ebytoso, Tomáraho, and Horio, as an ancient Ishir group was called). The daughter of Laguylta, cause of this cosmic cataclysm, fled, transformed into the germ of all epidemics, whose ills she disseminated in all villages that crossed her fateful path.

The sky, which had been held up by the tree's highest branches, moved away from the earth. Deich, the Sun, moved closer to the earth to counteract the imbalance provoked by this phenomenon. As it did so his colors soaked the sky, which became yellow (that is, luminous). And so a new cycle, the time of the Sun, begins.

On earth Deich, the proto-sky-shaman, gathered the dejected Tomáraho who had been brutally separated from their people and deprived of the tree that allowed them to reach the celestial nectar. "I will give you the knowledge to seek other foods, but to gain this knowledge you will have to submit yourselves to severe discipline." Deich began to give instructions that the Ishir followed with attention and diligence. This provoked the jealousy of a wise shaman, the first Chamacoco shaman, who decided to leave his village. Deich tried to dissuade him because he needed an assistant, but the shaman was indignant by what he considered the betrayal of his community and insisted on leaving. Before going he turned and cursed his people: "The knowledge that Deich gives you will bring disgrace; it will be incomplete and its costs will be too high. You will pay with death." The Tomáraho laughed at this bizarre and extravagant curse. "What is this death?" they asked, shrugging their shoulders.

Since the shaman did not want to act as the Sun's assistant, Deich decided to ask Pyne (Moon) his younger brother (or, in other tales, a young nephew). Deich said to Pyne: "The first lesson I will teach the men will be to chase ostriches properly, because without this knowledge they do not take advantage of their meat. You have to pay close attention to my method of hunting so you can then repeat it in front of them." Deich then ate the wild lemons (*jylychy*) and palm flowers (*osëro*) favored by the ostriches (*ñandúes*) and turned into an ostrich himself. He lay down underneath a carob tree and began to emit the cries of the ostrich. Soon a group of thirty or forty ostriches surrounded him, watching him cautiously without daring to come too close to him. Vigilant and tense, they asked him who he was. "An ostrich, like you," answered Deich. "But you are so much bigger than we are," they replied suspiciously. Then the Sun answered that he was bigger and stronger because he knew a place filled with prodigious foods. Eating them had given him extraordinary powers. "If you want," he said, "I can show you this place." The birds asked him for proof of what he said. Then Deich took off running at great speed and as he ran he expelled bursts of gas, as ostriches do, as well as the residues of the announced fruits. When they saw this the birds were convinced of Deich's sincerity and let him guide them to the site of the supposedly exceptional lemons and palm flowers. Once satiated, the ostriches decided to rest. Deich took advantage of this and killed twenty by twisting their long necks. He arrived at the village laden with his feathered prey, gathered the people, showed them how to eat the meat of unknown taste, and instituted the restrictions and taboos linked to it.

As the people dispatched the new meat, Deich called his brother and ordered him to repeat the tactic that he had used exactly. So Pyne did, or tried to, since once he had eaten the lemons and flowers he was tempted by the fruits of the cactus (*nyme*) and wild bean (*kapylá*) and could not resist his desire to eat them. He glutted himself and when later he tried to convince the other ostriches of his ostrich-self through the aforementioned farting demonstration, his supposed kin discovered the residues of human food among the fruit. "It is a man disguised!" they shrieked together, throwing themselves on him and pecking and stomping him to death.

Worried by his absence, his older brother went in search of him the following day. When he found the dead body of Pyne he stepped over him three times and blew softly on him to revive him. Deich was a *konsaha pa*, a great shaman, and was able to bring him back to life. "Give me another opportunity," said his brother as soon as he could speak. Deich accepted, but decided to show him another hunting method. He found a large wild dog in the woods (there were no domesticated animals then), approached her, and looking straight into her ferocious eyes blew on her muzzle, jaws, and ears, and thus tamed her to hunt ostriches. The dog took off with the speed of the wind, because Deich had infused her with that ability, and launched herself on a band of ostriches (*ñandúes*) and knocked down enough to feed the village for several days. "That is how you must proceed; don't approach the ostriches until the dog has finished with her task," said the Sun. But his younger brother could not control his impatience and clumsily erupted on the scene and began to gather the bodies of the fallen prey before the dog had finished hunting. Furious, the dog turned on him and tore him to pieces. Again, his brother the sky shaman blew on him softly and brought him back to life.

Pyne's unrestrained greed continues to bring him misfortune and mishaps, which Deich reverses throughout many episodes detailed meticulously by Luciano. Pyne does not control his avidity in his shamanic invocations to fruits, which then pour on him and bury him; he is discourteous to the Masters of the Animals who, offended, mortally wound him; he is caught in his own net, which Deich invented to hunt ducks, and so on.

Tired, finally, of his younger brother's mistakes Deich set out to teach the Ishir the arts of hunting and collecting himself. When he finished he instituted the category of sky shaman and told his brother: "We need to go now, because they now know how to supply their own necessities." They walked away across the endless plains of the Chaco. Exhausted, Pyne sat down under a carob tree. "I no longer have the strength to keep going," he said to his brother. The Sun sank into the fields and returned the next day with a white horse.[4] He helped his brother ride it, and so they continued their long journey: one riding, one walking.

They arrived at a place that was so distant that not even the clouds passed overhead, and prepared to enter the celestial sphere to continue the journey that they had until then undertaken together. Pyne proposed that they part ways: he did not want to accompany his brother any further. Deich was opposed: "You are too clumsy, you will not know how to cross such large distances, you will make mistakes and have problems every day." The younger brother reminded him that as inept as he was he had abilities his brother did not have: he could see through darkness and through the heaviest clouds. And he could cross great distances galloping on his white horse. Their separate movements would thus allow them to take turns so that one could rest while the other walked. Deich accepted with the condition that they meet at regular intervals. (And so the brothers coincide when the Sun decides to control the Moon during an eclipse. This way, the sun prevents the blunders that the moon's immaturity could cause during the Chaco's long nights.) After they had bid each other farewell, the Moon rushed to the north. The Sun shouted to him, "Slow down, don't be so reckless! We need to move on an east/west axis, because if we move north/south our cycles will take too long. The seasons will be delayed and the children will suffer hunger." So the Moon corrected his path and they parted again.

During one of their encounters, long after they had left the earth, the younger brother asked the Sun: "Don't you think you should put a limit to human life? If they do not die, and continue to reproduce, the earth will not be able to sustain them." The older brother agreed, grabbed a fruit and threw it at the earth. "The fruit is not an appropriate sign," the Moon said, "it will leave seeds behind and the cycle of life will recommence." The older brother agreed again, and threw a stone that was swallowed by the pond it fell into and disappeared forever. And so the first shaman's prophecy was fulfilled.

Note on the Lessons of the Sun

This myth, whose first episode coincides with the tale of the origin of the colors of the sky, belongs to the cosmic cycle, which coincides with the shamanic dimension, and is therefore not connected to the world of the anábsoro. In this dimension the supreme shaman, the Sun, plays the part of the cultural hero that Ashnuwerta played in the dimension of the anábsoro. It is evident that this tale is influenced by the Guaraní myth of the twins, according to which the Sun (Kuarahy) displays wisdom and the Moon (Yasy) clumsily makes mistakes, which represent the many accidents of the human condition.

The Helpers of the Sun and Moon

[Narrated by Opserse (Emilio Aquino), expert in Ishir culture and myths. Translated from Tomáraho to Spanish by Bruno Barrás.]

When the great principles and norms were already established among the Ishir the Sun and the Moon decided to leave the earth. But there were many important details humans still had to be taught: minor codes of hygiene, courtesy, civilized eating habits, interclan and intertribal etiquette, and so on. Therefore the Sun and the Moon left two representatives behind: Nerpyrt the dwarf and Júut. Both were Ishir but were very wise since they had been given special instruction by the celestial bodies. They taught the others how to clean their bodies properly, to separate the edible parts of the prey, to help in childbirth, and to cover their genitals (which had until then been exposed).

Nerpyrt and Júut were the first shamans of the solar category: that is, the first konsaho Deich jilo, anointed by the Sun with its own powers. They gathered the people together one day and said: "Now we will teach you to decipher the cries of the birds. If a charata (Ortallis canicollis) sings during the day, be alert because it is a warning that enemy forces are nearby. If the bird sings at dawn it is a serious omen: the village must relocate." It happened that, on a certain occasion, the village heard the charata sing at dawn and picked up their belongings and left. But they could never establish themselves anywhere because as soon as they were about to do so they heard the bird's cry at dawn again. The shamans then told them: "There will always be adverse forces that will follow the community. They must be kept at bay. We will instruct the wisest of the village so that they may be shamans." So they did, and these new shamans could detect the presence of malevolent spirits and expel them from a site so they could inhabit it.

The first shamans still spoke to the people. "Be careful of the jaguar: it is a human cannibal transformed into animal form and knows therefore the habits of humans," Nerpyrt said. "Family members must help each other," Júut added, "when one of them brings fish, animals, and fruit, these must be given first to the elderly members of the family, then to the rest of the family, and finally to others. Never sell food that was obtained in the woods." And day after day both gave instructions the Ishir tried to memorize.

"New couples must live apart. Women should not be sold; but giving the father of the bride a *kuña premio*[5] of hammocks, feathers, hunting dogs, or pottery is fine. If the youth is valiant the marriage should be permitted even if his parents have no gifts to offer. There are certain signs that allow the parents of each of the future spouses to determine the value of the other: a young man is a good candidate for marriage if he is courageous and can fish an eel with his bare hands, extract honey with the traditional axe, and control gluttony, greed, fury, fear, and his words. A woman will make an ideal spouse if she speaks justly, is tempered in her eating habits, and diligent in work; she must know how to collect fruits in the wood and weave with caraguata."

And so the first shamans spoke, repeating the Sun's commands for months. ("But this advice," Emilio says calmly, "is followed less and less with each passing day. The closer the Ishir are to being Paraguayan, the less Ishir they are.")

One day Nerpyrt bid the people farewell and left. Only Júut remained. He gathered the people and spoke to them: "Listen, Ishir, I am leaving now to travel to other villages but I want you to wait for me. I promise that I will return." The Ishir agreed to wait for him and they did so during days, months, and years until they became convinced he had deceived them and decided to emigrate to other lands. When Júut returned and found the place uninhabited he became furious, struck the ground with his wooden staff, and cursed the Ishir: "You will now be condemned to constantly wander without lands of your own, and when you have lands, to lose them. And for this you will be forever unhappy."

The Moon's Helper

[Narrated by Nintyke (Palacio Vera), Tomáraho shaman of the category "of the far ends of the earth." Translated from Ishir to Spanish by Clemente López.]

The Sun and the Moon lived among the Ishir, teaching them the correct uses of things, the techniques for hunting and gathering, and the forms of kinship and clan order. They also instituted behavioral norms, classification schemes, and systems of organization. The Sun was strict and rigorous; the Moon was more affable and understanding, but also more prone to human error. For this reason, the younger brother acted as the mediator between the Sun, too distant and serious, and the Ishir. The older brother dictated the precepts and instructions and the younger one transmitted them, making them more accessible to mortals.

When the astral brothers withdrew from the earth the humans were not very confident in their ability to provide for themselves. They had, in addition, forgotten the details of certain instructions, which prevented them from following them exactly. The Moon had told them that if they ran into problems they could seek out some of his relatives who lived in a village on earth. To reach his relatives they would have to feed on *pähä* (an aquatic potato) and follow the path indicated by the presence of these tubers.

The Ishir did as he said and tramped up streams and estuaries in search of the indicated food. In the process they came upon a mysterious village of hermetic words and looks. For the first time they saw people that differed from themselves, but having received instructions to never succumb to fear in such encounters they followed the presence of the potatoes and discovered a succession of nations, each different from the others in physical appearance and customs, some very extravagant and all very strange. They lived for a time with each new group of people and exchanged words, suspicions, and ways of hunting, dressing, and eating. Once they met a people who already knew the clothes of the Paraguayans: they used pants and dresses of cloth and leather shoes on their feet. They were hospitable. After journeying for so long they realized that all peoples, as different as they were from each other, had been taught by the Sun and the Moon, for they shared knowledge and abilities that they recognized as having come from the celestial bodies.

Once they encountered a people of affable manners and distracted gazes. By the paleness of their skins and their nocturnal habits they understood that these stiff men and women belonged to the Moon's family, as he had announced. "How beautiful they are!" the Ishir commented among themselves, and set up camp beside these new people. One day, a dwarf presented himself to the Ishir. He was called Nerpyrt and had been designated by the Moon to complete the training of the Ishir in difficult cultural practices. Until then, the gaze of the Ishir could not reach very far. Nerpyrt taught them to focus their vision on objects that were farther and farther away until they learned to recognize distance. "You must think in order to see well," he told them.

Nerpyrt appeared one morning leading an unknown animal by a rope. "This animal is a dog," he told the wisest Ishir, "it will help your people hunt ostriches and other prey." The dog, which was large and had powerful fangs, was called Poitite. At the dwarf's signal the animal took off running at great speed, overtook a band of ostriches, launched herself on them and knocked down some birds. The Ishir realized that Nerpyrt had given them a valuable gift.

Trained by Nerpyrt, the wise Ishir was becoming a shaman. He was already a *konsaha porro,* an apprentice. Nerpyrt taught him how to control the hunting dog and the man was doing it well, but on one occasion he rushed in a little too quickly to pick up the dead prey when Poitite was still in her hunting trance. Furious, the dog turned on him and devoured him. The wife of the *konsaha porro* was worried because her husband did not return. At dawn she saw the dog sleeping beside the fire with a full stomach and she suspected what had happened. She called her people together and laid out her fears before them: she wanted them to kill the dog and look for pieces of her husband in the dog's stomach. The Ishir divided themselves in two, those who found her demand just and those who were opposed to it. The first group prevailed and Poitite was sacrificed. Nerpyrt approached them then and blew on the remains of the unfortunate shaman apprentice, which had appeared in the body of the dismembered animal.

"We have recovered our countryman but at the cost of our hunting dog," said the Ishir when the man had come back to life. Nerpyrt told them that that countryman was in the process of becoming a man well versed in the knowledge of the Moon. "He will be able to teach you how to catch ostriches through tricks and ruses, which is the best way of hunting them," he added. The dwarf took the apprentice into the woods to finish initiating him in the shamanic mysteries. After a long time of apprenticeship and arduous tests the new shaman learned how to turn himself into an ostrich. He approached a flock but the birds quickly discovered the deceit and attacked him with their sharp beaks and feet. Nerpyrt, the shaman instructor, had to revive him again.

"Where did I go wrong?" the man asked as soon as he had returned. "When you turned into an ostrich, you appealed in dreams to the Moon and you forgot to brush off the Moon's chill when you awoke. The animals sensed the low temperature of your body and recognized what you were. Before approaching the flock you must warm yourself by the fire," the dwarf answered. "Let's try it again."

And so the following morning they tried again. After nourishing himself with lunar powers in his dreams and recovering the warmth of his body near the fire, the new sky shaman transformed himself into an ostrich (*ñandú*) and was able to successfully imitate his supposed kin. He lay himself down with a band of ostriches to rest under a carob tree and when the animals slept as they do, stretched out on the ground like people, he threw himself on the closest ones and was able to kill a fair number. Nerpyrt plucked the feathers off the fallen birds and gave them to the novice *konsaha* to use in the implements and ornaments his new position would require. Afterwards, both shamans carried the meat in their large *boná* (caraguata bags) and returned to the village. There Nerpyrt taught the people how to cook and eat ostrich meat and laid down the restrictions and taboos that accompany it. Then Nerpyrt the dwarf shaman took his leave. "Now you no longer need me; you already have your own shaman," he said before disappearing forever.

THE SLAYER OF THE MISTRESS OF THE ARMADILLOS

[Narrated by Luciano Martínez, a Tomáraho sky shaman. Translated from Ishir to Spanish by Bruno Barrás.]

A woman who had gone in search of food was astounded when she discerned the unusual shape of a giant armadillo in the middle of a great plain. As she hurried back to the village she ran into a group of hunters and told them falteringly what she had seen. The group decided to go verify the identity of the strange being and asked the woman to guide them. When the immense animal saw them arrive it shook itself; its body was so huge that the earth shook and trembled. It then began to dig amidst huge seismic convulsions and buried itself underground. The men dug rapidly in the direction the colossal animal had disappeared but they could not find the creature, which zig-zagged toward the center of the earth.

The hunters dug for days and were about to give up on their obsessive quest when they felt the earth move rhythmically and heard an echoing sound that rose and fell. Following these signals they finally came upon an enormous cave near a subterranean river. They had found the armadillo's hulking body. The exhausted, monstrous animal was resting and its panting shook the cave with vibrations, chasing away the silence of those nether regions. Raising its head the animal addressed them in somber tones: she was Amyrmy Lata, the Mistress (or Mother, or Owner) of the Armadillos. Before they killed her she wanted to pass on certain essential warnings and prescriptions. "A great catastrophe is coming. The world will be covered in a flood and you will only be saved if you build a giant tower." She gave them instructions on how to erect the refuge and how to organize themselves and repopulate the world, which would be depopulated after the destruction wrought by the waters. "Many will not believe and will mock you. It will be so much the worse for them; they will drown and be turned into the spirits of unknown beasts." The hunters asked, "What will we eat?" "My body," answered Amyrmy Lata.

Then the strongest and most daring hunter stepped up and killed the armadillo. Laden with copious amounts of meat the hunters began the long journey back up through dark and suffocating tunnels. They walked and climbed for days without being able to distinguish night from day and when they reached the surface they found that the trees were greening. Spring had arrived, but the air was dark and heavy with the smells of impending rain. Realizing that the flood was near the men quickly summoned their village as well as the neighboring villages, but many of the people thought they were crazy and not only ignored their warnings but jeered at them. Accompanied by those who had decided to follow them, the hunters began to build a tall tower out of wood and adobe, all the while eating the meat of the sacrificed animal, which never spoiled despite the time that had passed. When the tower was several kilometers high—enough that its upper reaches disappeared into the clouds—the rains began. During the long and dreary months of rain the survivors continued to feed themselves with the meat of the armadillo, which never rotted. On the day it stopped raining the men saw from the heights of their refuge that the entire world was covered in water. One morning, the call of a chaja on the top of the tower showed them that that bird was the only external survivor of the catastrophe.

According to the directives of the Mistress of the Armadillos, the tower contained a system of great plugs vertically lined at ten-meter intervals. Once the rain ceased the armadillo-slayer controlled the level of the waters by removing one plug with each change in the Moon's cycle. When he removed the last piece and only mud oozed through they knew the danger had passed. All began to shout and sing joyfully and wanted to run outside immediately. The armadillo-slayer, who had been anointed by the Mistress of the Armadillos as the leader of the group, advised them to leave the tower prudently and to avoid looking immediately at the Sun because they had not seen sunlight for so long and could be blinded by it.

The group's leader summoned the people, dazed by their long enclosure in the tower. So much time had passed that a new generation had been born. This new generation was marked by the strange conditions of the only world they had ever known and their bodies, skin color, and facial features were different from those of the older generation. Some were darker than others; some had rounder, and others narrower eyes; some had frizzier hair, and others longer limbs. The killer of Amyrmy Lata classified these families in different groupings according to the new attributes that identified their offspring. The family that had given birth to brown-skinned children with smooth hair would go south. Those who had produced thin, white children would go east. Those whose children were tall and darker would go west. And so—according to the hair, facial features, and skin of their children—the family groups were assigned different directions and told to go off and repopulate the world. Before the flood the earth had not been very large and each family left the tower thinking that they would not end up too far from the others. As they walked, however, they discovered that the horizon had receded and that the world had acquired the dimensions it has today.

"I will go north," said the leader. "And I will carry a photograph of our savior, the Mistress of the Armadillos." ("A photograph?" I ask Bruno, who is translating for me. "Well," he responds, "a drawing or a token." And then, after a moment of thoughtfulness, "An image.") Walking toward the north, the armadillo-slayer found a strange people that had survived by clinging to the tops of tall trees. Their skin was yellow and they looked sick and puny. At their invitation, the wise pilgrim halted. After some days he observed that although his hosts were skilled fishermen (of all the animals, only fish had survived) they lived off of honey dissolved in water. "Solid food makes us sick," they said when he questioned them on such a curious custom.

He was walking one afternoon on the banks of a river when he saw a child strip himself naked for a swim, and noticed that the child had no buttocks. As he lifted him to inspect him, he saw that he lacked an anus. "Your child has no ass!" the astonished man told the mother. "What is ass?" she queried. He realized then that the bodies of all the villagers were like the child's, and understood why they could not eat solid foods: since they could not expel their wastes, it caused them great discomfort and pain.

By this time, guided by the words of Amyrmy Lata, the man had become a shaman. He summoned the village and spoke thus: "Your problem is that you are underfed. You cannot live off of honey alone, and the lack of an exit prevents your body from taking in fruit and meat." He lifted the child, turned him over, blew on the place where his buttocks should be, and traced a line with his index finger on the flesh that was now as soft and malleable as wax. In the middle he punctured a hole. He spent many days drawing lines and perforating the skins he had softened with his breath until he had fixed every villager. "Now," he told them, "you can eat the fish and fruits that I see you harvest so ably." But they answered that no, they could not: the food he had seen them gather was given to bodiless woodland beings, shadows that prowled around the village and required this tribute, threatening to wreak misfortune on the people if they failed to do so.

The killer of Amyrmy Lata decided to investigate what was happening. The afternoon sun was waning when he stationed himself behind a tree and saw that the food was quickly seized by misty silhouettes that then fled. He knew who these spectral beings were: the incredulous people who had not sought refuge in the tower and had been changed into nameless, shapeless beasts. The next day he returned and when he felt their anxious panting and smelled their distinct presences he blew on them, one by one, until he gave them individual forms and assigned them a diet. And thus appeared animals that had not existed before: wolves, coatis, foxes, rabbis, jaguars, and deer. And since each was assigned their own food, he warned them that many of them would be destined to serve as food to men, and that they would have to flee from man always.

"And so this tale ends," says Luciano, through Bruno's words.

BRIEF TALES BY FLORES BALBUENA

[Here I transcribe various *mónene*, small tales or anecdotes, told on different occasions by Flores Balbuena (Ogwa), an Ebytoso expert in shamanic mythology. He expresses himself fluently in both Guaraní and Spanish.]

Crazed and Resuscitated Shamans

There was once a shaman protected by Pfaujata. In dreams she had imparted to him the forms and colors of his corporal painting and the motifs of his songs. In dreams he also accompanied her on her trajectory through the skies. Both shone with intermittent lights: like powerful fireflies, like airplanes with blue lights. The people who saw them pass swiftly overhead were frightened. "They are bad lights," said one. "They are shooting stars," thought another. But the wise men knew that Pfaujata and her protégé had passed.

There was a shaman much beloved by his people who died before the Chaco War (1932–1935).[6] After burying him the people returned to their village grief-stricken. In the middle of the night they were awakened by a thundering sound. The newly revived shaman was opening up a path by parting the ground like an earthquake, knocking down trees, frightening animals, and setting off whirlwinds of dust. When the villagers felt the earth opening they ran to the woods and saw from afar the earth split open and the shaman shoot out amidst smoke and flame. They returned the next morning and found an enormous chasm, still smoking, whose bottom was too deep to be visible. When they heard the sound of rushing water they backed off again and saw it gush up and up until it became a great river. This was the origin of the Riacho del Pollo, which stretches between Puerto Pollo and Puerto Diana. The people were still heartbroken until on one particularly stormy afternoon they heard the voice of the shaman speaking to them: "You need no longer mourn me nor fear storms: Pfaujata freed me from Osypyte, the Land of the Dead, and brought me to the domain of Osasërö Balut, the Master of the Storm Birds. Now I will protect you from bad weather. If the men sing at dawn I will calm the storm's rage."

In dreams, or after their deaths, the sky shamans are transported on clouds as if these were boats or airplanes. The Ishir call them *Osasërö póorra*

Ramiro Jara, Ebytoso shaman, painting his body for participation in the ritual "The Defeat of the Sun." Potrerito, 1989. (Photo by Ticio Escobar.)

("the ship of Osasërö"). Sometimes the shamans in Osasërö's retinue go mad: the vertigo of speed, intense lights, and thunder make them lose their reason. This is why at times, in the midst of a storm, a shaman astride a cloud will throw himself at the earth at great speed and kill an Ishir in a flash. The body of the slain person remains on earth but his or her spirit is encased in the cloud and converted into a splendor that briefly illuminates it from within, or is transformed into a beat that makes it quiver ever so slightly. At other times, some of the crazed shamans throw themselves from above and hit an Ishir without killing him or her completely. The victim is left weak and dazed and needs another sky shaman to fight the thief and recover the stolen piece of his or her soul.

On other occasions the shamans fight to appropriate for themselves another's spirit. One incident that took place some years ago near Puerto Caballo is still remembered. Two sky shamans from different villages had agreed to duel. Their respective villages performed the *shu deich* ("the defeat of the sun") ceremonies, songs, fasts, and vigils. At dawn the adversarial shamans lay down to sleep at the same time, separated in space by many leagues. They fought in dreams, transformed into a stork and vampire. The shaman who lost—who had taken on the form of a vampire—did not awaken. His spirit was captured and detained in a *pamune* (bundle of ostrich plumes) borne by his enemy. From the uncertain place of dreams he saw his woeful mourners, barely recognized his widow, and watched from afar as they buried his body. The shaman who defeated him unrolled the *pamune* and freed his spirit, but he could no longer take embodied form. Converted into *dykchybich* (ghost) he wandered through the world for some time and eventually headed to Osypyte—the land of death, located in the direction of the setting sun—under the land near Bahía Negra. There the dead, both old and new, wander weightlessly—barely scraping the ground with their ethereal figures, almost floating—in a land of ambiguous lights at whose center stands a lugubrious *samu'u* tree.

The Boat of Rains

In the first celestial stratum (*Póorch pëhet*) lives Osasërö Balut, Master of the Storm Birds. When he organizes a storm, he decides that the clouds must condense to the form of a great boat in which he and his court will travel. His son Lapishé; all the shamans of his category; his auxiliary birds, the storks; and the four kinds of birds that comprise his army (the birds of lightning and thunder, those of downpours, those of torrential rains, and those of hurricanes) accompany him in this great boat. The four kinds of storm birds are the mutated primitive men who were stuck in the sky after the cosmic tree fell. Some of them became star-men and others Osasërö's birds.

When this great boat tears through the sky—driven by strong winds and trailing smaller clouds—the shamans on earth must call on all the strength of their songs to protect the village from the damage that storms and rains can produce. Sometimes they negotiate with enemy shamans traveling on the boat; sometimes they fight them.

The Shaman and the Wasps

A shaman once received the power of wasps. In dreams they tell him: "When you need us, paint your body in such and such a way, sing, and we will come." He can swallow wasps and spit them out as he sings. He has the ability to cure any wound or pain caused by thorns, sharp objects, insect bites, and venomous plants and animals. In his hand he has a *noshikó,* the prototypical weapon of the Ishir. To better summon the power of the wasps, he wears a sash woven over a caraguata rope, covered with seeds from the shiny black fruit called *byrbyr.* The wasps that protect this shaman are members of a species called *bërpërch;* on some occasions, enemy shamans attack under the protection of another species of wasps (adversaries of his wasps). Whoever has more *woso* (power) and can wield it more effectively wins. What counts is not so much strength as the ability to wield it.

The wasps carry the shaman to the sky as he dreams. They give him the power to extract honey, harking back to the time when men collected honey in the sky.

The Battle of Words

Two shamans are fighting in their dreams. They fight with their voices. One sings and launches words; the other replies with thundering verbs. Both sleep far apart on earth but battle in their sleep through the content of their songs. "I am a deadly serpent," sings a shaman, shaking his maraca. "I am a bird whose sharp beak can cut off the head of a serpent in a single blow, no matter how strong the poison," the other responds. They can spend hours until one of them runs out of words, overcome by the other's discourse. Sometimes neither of them wins: the verbal battle is a tie, and they become allies despite the physical distance between them. When they meet on the path of the shamans they look at each other and can recognize each other as companions.

A shaman invoking the power of the wasps. Drawing by Flores Balbuena.

The Three Shamans and the Warrior

Basybeké, the famous Ebytoso chief, frequently engaged in aggressive incursions against the Tomáraho, Ayoreo, Caduveo, and white men. Three shamans of different ranks were part of his court. At night the shamans blew their whistles and then brought the whistles close to their ears. This way they could hear the sounds of their enemies and the families that had stayed behind in the villages and foretell the positions of the ones and the well-being of the others. During the day birds helped them with their flights and cries, giving them information on the distances that separated them from their enemies, the presence of game or water, and the best paths to tread.

"A hawk sang this morning: the enemy is near," they warned the chief one morning as they camped near Kyrkyrbi (near Florida, beyond Filadelfia). Basybeké decided to go out to meet the Caduveo who approached. Quickly his men dug trenches and planted stakes. When the attackers arrived they were greeted with a thick shower of arrows. They tried to retreat but Basybeké had come up with the plan to light a great semicircle of fire behind them, and they were surrounded and defeated. The great warrior began to cut off the heads of dead enemies and collect their weapons. "We have to go immediately," said the shamans, "we have heard the sounds of mourning in the village through our whistles." They knew that the wife of one of the warriors had died, but wanted to shield him from the pain during the long march home and did not tell him. This warrior, the recently widowed one, died in a skirmish against the Ayoreo soon afterward.

The Manon Wolo

The *manon wolo*—a crown of black muscovy duck feathers, called *lepper wolo* by the Tomáraho—has great powers. On some occasions these crowns haul the shamans during their dreams, lift them high, offer them the inspiration of a song, and grant them specific healing powers. When a shaman awakens, he sings what he saw in his dreams and knows how to use his *manon wolo* to sweep away madness and other ills of the lost spirit.

The Shaman of Many Animals

Part of a shaman's powers is the capacity to identify with a certain animal. In dreams the shaman acquires the features, force, and abilities of an animal so that if another shaman confronts him he does so under the form of a beast and with equivalent or superior forces. Some shamans can take the shape of more than one animal. According to the circumstances, they choose to identify with a peccary or turn into a hawk. Strengths are not always the same in the territory of dreams as they are in the natural world: in dreams a stork can fly more swiftly than a hawk or prove stronger than a jaguar.

Near Bahía Negra there lived a shaman with great powers of mutation. He could turn himself into a caiman, a monkey, and almost any snake and bird. No shaman could best him in dream battles because none of them had the capacity to present such varied forms. In general, the shaman who is linked with a species can not only assume its form and abilities but can determine the behavior of that species. This shaman could, for example, order a snake to bite anyone. He could also spit snakes from his mouth and cure any wound created by their bite.

The Shaman's Tools

Lëbe is the name of the mat that is folded into cylindrical form and houses shamanic instruments. This bundle concentrates an enormous amount of energy and is a respected and feared piece. When a shaman dies his *lëbe* is buried with him, but since it is a powerful object there are risks involved. If the dead shaman had a malevolent side his tools can escape as adversarial forces. One solution would be to burn the bundle ("the suitcase," as Flores sometimes translates). But this is also a dangerous operation. If unleashed, the powers of the *lëbe* could fly off in the form of smoke and take physical form in fateful impulses. For this reason, when a shaman much feared for his dark disposition died one day, the men of his community decided to tie his *lëbe* to a large rock and throw it into the Paraguay River. But the feathers of his crown, bracelets, anklets, rattle, and other tools turned into malignant beings; they emerged from the water and launched themselves on the community disseminating anguish, disease, and misfortune. The inhabitants had to seek out another great and powerful shaman whose own instruments were thrown against those of his dead colleague until he defeated them one by one. But not all were defeated; some sought refuge in the woods.

The Two Shamans

There are three characters in this tale: a young man, his adopted son, and his uncle, who is an old man. The young man and his old uncle are shamans, but despite their family ties are great rivals. The plot begins when one morning these three go fishing. The old man realizes that once again the child has stolen one of the owl talons that they use as hooks. The next day as the trio readies itself to go fishing again the uncle, who specializes in snakes, summons a rattlesnake and orders it to curl up in the bottom of his fishing bag. When the child reaches in to rob another fish hook the snake bites him. The young shaman shouts for his uncle, who is the only local specialist in healing snakebites, but the older man only allows himself to be found once the child is dead. Despite the uncle's exaggerated display of sorrow the young shaman understands that he has caused the death of his adopted son and decides to seek revenge. He attacks his uncle in dreams, shaking his maraca. His uncle's maraca defends itself. The messages of defiance and challenge fly back and forth in the night like Morse code. "I am a shaman of Osasërö Balut, Master of the Storm Birds," says the nephew's maraca. The uncle's maraca replies that he has the same rank. "I am the protégé of Tenhía, Mistress of the Thunder Birds," warns the nephew's maraca. "My Mistress is Botsyrbo of the Torrential Rains," replies the old man. And so each power put on display by the nephew is met by an equal or greater one by the uncle, until he finds a specialty the older man lacks. "I am the shaman of the otters," the youth's maraca transmits. And the old man's falls silent because he does not have a shamanic link with these animals.

The old man is depressed; his nephew has discovered an instance of superiority over him and could destroy him at any moment. He warns the young man: "If you destroy me, I will attack you from the ship of storms: the spirits of the dead shamans possess superior powers to dreaming shamans in the kingdom of Osasërö." The youth is not daunted. During a hunt he orders an otter being chased by dogs to plunge into his uncle's body. As soon as she does so the dogs tear the old man apart.

Days later the young shaman goes out in search of honey. He hears a red macaw sing and is frightened: the bird announces a fierce storm. He sets off running but is not able to reach his house. The ship of storms appears overhead—thundering, dark, flashing with lightning—and his uncle gallops on one of the clouds escorting the ship. He swoops in low and hits his nephew with a bolt of lightning. Since the youth also belongs to the shamans of Osasërö his spirit is soon installed in the first celestial stratum where the Master of the Storm Birds lives. The uncle and nephew meet again, and the young man challenges his son's killer. "No," says the old man, "if we battle now, our storms will bring catastrophe to our village." The young man agrees and their hostilities cease.

TALES OF THE REGION OF LUCERO

Iolé (version 1)

[This tale, as the whole of the preceding section, was narrated by Flores Balbuena.]

A group of men slept in the open air at night during a long hunt. Each morning one of them, a shaman apprentice, watched the celestial vault, which in the Chaco is imposing and seems to crush the plains. With his face to the sky this *konsaha porro* anxiously searched for the brightness of the morning star. When he spied it he contemplated it, entranced, finding in this daily vision the forces required by the harsh life of the hunt. He was obsessed with the *póorch abo* ("the daughter of the sky"); he was in love with her. One morning he overslept. His companions shook him and shouted at him but could not wake him. They left him sleeping on the ground and went off in search of game. He was finally awakened by a frozen caress. He thought he was dreaming. Before his eyes was a beautiful, radiant, shining woman, glittering with blue jewels. "I am Iolé," she told him, "the star you seek every morning. I have come to wake you." As she felt insecure on earth, she took him up to the sky to make love to her. They met each morning until one day the man said he did not want to separate from her, and offered to bring her with him to the village. The star became a concentrated point of light in the young shaman's maraca, which he sealed with wax and stowed away in his caraguata bag, the *peikara pich* (a special bag to carry rattles). And so he carried her near him all day long, and exalted by her nearness his songs burst out with strength. One night the youth told his sister the story of his secret love. "I need to go hunting tomorrow morning," he told her, "please care for this small caraguata bag and never leave it alone."

One morning a herd of wild boar attacked the village. The women protected themselves by climbing the trees, and in the chaos and confusion the hunter's sister dropped the small bag, which was trampled underfoot by the boar. Indignant, Iolé flew off to the sky and sent a flood that destroyed the village. When the hunter returned he found his lover gone and his village destroyed. He went back to watching the sky every morning.

Iolé (version 2)

[Narrated by Luciano Martínez, a Tomáraho sky shaman. Translated from Ishir to Spanish by Bruno Barrás.]

A woman was fascinated by the beauty of an *oikakar,* the feathered bracelet of a powerful shaman. Taking advantage of a moment of distraction, she crept into the shaman's cabin and stole the ornament. The shaman called to her but she refused to return the stolen piece. This unleashed a violent encounter that involved both of their families and ended with the death of the shaman at the hands of the woman's brother. The incident was a serious one not only because of the crime itself but because it had affected a powerful sky shaman. All of the men gathered at the *tobich* and once their judgment was reached the accused was declared guilty and condemned to death. The assassin was, however, also a shaman, and he was not willing to suffer the sentence. He leapt into the air and disappeared from the *tobich.* Flying east he reached a celestial stratum where the stars, the *Pilío,* barred his way. "You killed a sky shaman," they told him, "we can not give you shelter." He tried his luck elsewhere, taking other paths, but whenever he reached some kind of celestial dimension ("a planet," Bruno translates) he was expelled for his crime. He finally reached the frontiers of the land of Lucero, the kingdom of Iolé, and was overcome by sleep and exhaustion. A young girl with shining eyes found him and brought him to her mother, Iolé, who took pity on his situation and miserable state and allowed him to stay in her land of cold blue lights. With lowered head he confessed his crime and was pardoned. "You have already suffered much," the Daughter of the Sky told him, "you can stay here and live with us until you recover and your crime is forgotten."

So it was. And well fed by Iolé and her three star daughters the man recovered his strength and health. After some time, despite the attentions he received in that extraterrestrial abode, he found himself wanting to return to earth and take up his daily routine and practices. Iolé told him to wait; she turned her powerful star-eyes on the earth and observed that the village still sought the fugitive. This was reiterated many times, and so the years passed since the man had reached the region of Lucero.

It so happened that Iolé had fallen in love with the stranger and was delaying his return to the village. The man realized what has happening, since human beings always know when they are loved, and he begged Lucero to give him the ability to see great distances. As vulnerable as any mortal being before the demands of the beloved, she agreed to his request, even as she knew that it was not in her best interest. The daughters of Iolé washed his face and exchanged the warm spheres of his human eyes for the frozen blue stones through which the star creatures see. With much effort at first, but increasing confidence, the man threw intense glances toward his village until he could see with clarity the entire course of a peaceful day. "It is time to return," he said. Iolé piled him with gifts to bring to his village: jewels and strange feathers, unknown glittering stones, new weapons made of hard minerals that gleamed faintly. He himself was decked out in luminous feathers and painted an icy blue. And so he appeared before his people again with blazing eyes, opaline skin, and laden with celestial gifts. Many years had passed and though some of the dead shaman's family members invoked the old sentence, the village forgave him.

He took up his old life, enriched now in his shamanic ministry with the abilities given to him by Iolé, which allowed him to spot prey, enemies, and visit friends at great distances. But the man was no longer comfortable in his village. His strange powers of sight made him feel like a stranger in his own land, just as he had felt a stranger in Iolé's sky. He returned therefore to Lucero, where he married Iolé; but he did not feel at home there either. And so he came and went many times—missing the earth when he was in the sky and the sky when he was on earth—until one day he disappeared from the village forever.

HOSHTA

[Narrated in Chamacoco and then translated into Guaraní by Clemente López, an Ebytoso. This myth coincides almost exactly with those recounted by Flores Balbuena and Enrique Ozuna on different occasions. According to the Tomáraho version told by Palacio Vera, Hoshta is a beautiful wild woman who takes on the shape of a turtle to provoke collective lust. The figure of Hoshta is related to the ritual orgies.]

The protagonist of this myth was a skilled hunter. His prestige extended to neighboring villages and in times of scarcity he was called upon as a savior and much lauded when he returned with great amounts of food. One day however he began to lose his famous abilities, and after he returned various times with empty hands he became an object of laughter and scorn. Humiliated, he decided to recover his lost fame by chasing the largest animal that existed: an immense turtle called Hoshta that no one had ever been able to catch. He left in search of Hoshta and after traveling the woods and plains for many months, exhausted and about to give up he came across the gigantic tracks of his prey. A few days later he found her. She was monumental and from the sides of her head, at the height of her temple, sprouted two *báteta,* rods adorned with the white feathers of a stork or heron, which she could twirl at will. The animal immediately realized that the man was there to kill her, and asked him his motives. The man explained that he had lost his reputation and that he would be able to recover it by hunting such a monumental animal. "If those are your reasons then you do not need to kill me, because I can teach you infallible hunting skills," Hoshta answered. She told him to braid a caraguata rope, rub it softly against her shell, and then place it over the tracks of any animal. The man followed her instructions and discovered with astonishment that he was able to summon tapirs, anteaters, or deer depending on where he laid down the rope charged with Hoshta's *woso* (power). She told him then: "You can spend all day hunting the animals you want and return triumphantly to your people." But the ambitious man was not satisfied with using the turtle's gifts only once and decided to take the monumental creature to the village. "That is not a good idea," she said. "You will bring chaos upon your village." But he did not listen, and dragged her behind him with a thick rope.

He entered the village to great commotion. Everyone came up to the man who had recovered his status as a hero, praising the game and circling the giant turtle curiously. But something unexpected took place. Slowly the animal began to twirl her *báteta,* the plumed wands she had instead of ears, and this movement provoked a gradual but uncontainable sexual ardor among all the villagers who ended up entwined in multiple copulations that transgressed all limits of modesty, age, and family ties. The faster the turtle twirled the wands the greater the frenzy that possessed all lovers. During this promiscuous collective orgy some couples fell to the ground exhausted, and in the houses babies protested their abandonment and hunger. The hunter, swept away perhaps in some irrepressible tangle, ordered the animal to leave the village. And so, with their desires satiated at last, the people untangled themselves and turned their attentions back to less exciting but indispensable routines. The village recovered moderation but at the cost of losing the prodigious gifts of Hoshta. Even so this situation led the hunter to acquire shamanic powers and he became a *Hoshta jila,* inheritor of Hoshta's power, whose mercies he invoked through his songs. "My grandfather was a shaman of Hoshta," Clemente says proudly, "and I aspire to be one too."

According to the versions of Flores Balbuena and Enrique Ozuna the communal orgy ceased with the hunter's demand that Hoshta stop twirling her *báteta.* The turtle remained in the village for a while, promoting the abundance of game until the greed of one man broke the caraguata rope by rubbing it frenetically against her great shell. Furious, she fled and was captured by the Caduveo, to whom she gave prosperity and occasional raptures of collective lust. According to Ozuna she left and was captured by the Bolivians during the Chaco War.

THE *SAMU'U* AND THE ORIGIN OF FISH

[This tale contains a motif that is common to the Ebytoso and Tomáraho. I organize this account around a version narrated by Emilio Aquino (Tomáraho), which Bruno Barrás translated into Spanish. Its structure coincides with those related by Luciano Martínez and Palacio Vera of the Tomáraho, Flores Balbuena and Clemente López of the Ebytoso.]

The *kymychyló,* one of the most important ceremonial games among the Ishir, is a club-throwing competition. Once there lived a true champion in a certain village: no one could beat him at this game. When he had defeated all the men of his community, players from other successively distant villages came, only to be defeated as well. On one occasion there arrived a foreigner who was almost as skilled as he was: he was a respectable competitor. Careful to not lose his scepter, the champion gathered all his strength and threw the club so far that no one could see it. He went off to look for it the following morning, but though he tried to retrace the club's itinerary for many days he could not find it anywhere.

Exhausted, he finally decided to return to the village. He was hungry and thirsty and it seemed impossible to find food in the desolate lands around him. Suddenly he saw something unexpected: a small puddle, signals of recently flowing water in the middle of a sandy clearing far from any lagoon, estuary, or spring. The man followed the wet path until he reached an enormous *palo borracho* or *samu'u*. Water dripped to the ground. Following it he found that it trickled from his club, incrusted in the fleshy wood of the tree. He pulled on it with all his strength and was knocked to the ground by a formidable waterfall that surged out of the tree, brimming with fish. The water gushed so strongly the man realized that the land would soon be flooded. Desperate, he plugged up the hole with his club, blocking the flow of liquid and fish. He looked around him and saw the ground strewn with animals with gaping mouths: cold and covered in brilliant scales. For the first time a human being—or an Ishir, at least, which is the same thing in myths—saw a fish.

The man roasted and ate one of the fish. It did not taste bad. He filled his *boná* (caraguata bags) with as many fish as the threads could hold and stumbled back to his village under the heavy burden. The people were astonished to see these animals without feet or hair, without feathers and almost without heads, but driven by hunger they agreed to try the white meat and some of them found it to be delicious. So much so that when the feast ended they asked the man to return the next day and replenish their stores with these strange victuals. Then he told his people about the origin of the fish and organized an expedition to gather them.

When the men had set up a small camp near the *samu'u*, eager to gather up the tree's slippery bounty, the leader gave instructions to lift up a great net that would retain the fish as they poured from the tree, and ordered that the prodigious collection be done only collectively and under his leadership. His orders were followed, and all were satiated. From then on whenever the village wanted to eat fish or needed to, due to the scarcity of other foods, they traveled to the tree and carefully followed the instructions of the leader.

But the greed and gluttony of a spiteful woman in the village who sought to be a shaman brought problems upon them. One night she went alone to the tree to stock up by herself on its gifts. Ignorant of the correct method, once the club was pulled out of the tree she was knocked down by the force of the jet of water, thrown to the ground, and dragged by the roaring current. She was barely able to stand and climb a nearby guayacan as the water level rose. Soon the waters reached the village, putting out fires and flooding the houses. The Ishir realized that someone had betrayed the agreement and suspected the woman since she was known to be selfish and disloyal. One *konsaha pa* ("shaman of legitimate powers") sent a crow to find out what was happening.

The bird returned with the news: the hole in the tree was wide open and great torrent of water streamed from it shining with silver fish. "Did you see a woman nearby?" asked the shaman. The crow answered that he had seen only seen a fox clinging to a tree. "It is her," said the shaman.

They had to swim to the place and the *kymychyló* champion had to dive deep to search for the club that would stop the torrent of water. He did not find it in the bed of the river that was being formed. He stopped the men who were about to kill the fox. "Wait, she must know where the club is." The fox told them that she would reveal the position of the club/plug only if they let her live, and helped her to climb down the tree. After they had agreed and deposited her on firm ground, the fox gave them a wrong location and lost herself in the woods. The shaman ordered the crow to fly overhead until he found the club. He found it hanging from a branch of the very guayacan tree where the fox had found refuge; she had put it there without knowing what to do with it. The crow brought the club/plug to the shaman and he gave it to the champion who, swimming through the fierce current and wriggling fish, managed to stop up the breach.

The group of men waited on a small island for the waters to lower. There they found the fox, wet and trembling, and killed it. A few days later, back in the village one of the men saw the fugitive shadow of the animal who skulked around the houses. "Treason never dies," pronounced Emilio.

THE SUN, DEATH, AND THE SHAMAN SPIRIT HUNTERS

[Narrated by Bruno Barrás (Ebytoso).]

"I will tell you a story the great Boggiani[7] used to tell us in the *tobich*." When the Sun, accompanied by his brother Moon, still lived among the primitive Ishir—teaching them about hunting and gathering, social norms, and essential techniques—human beings did not yet die definitive deaths. Their souls would detach themselves from their bodies and take off in the direction of the setting Sun, but after wandering around for a while in the shape of a shadow they would return to the buried body and reanimate it. The Ishir would then return alive to their village carrying the objects that had been buried with them.

When the Sun considered his mission on earth complete he gathered the mortals together and announced that he would return to his dwelling place in the seventh and last celestial stratum, and that he would continue to shelter them from afar through his protégées, the *deich jilo,* the shamans who invoked his figure and his words.

Before bidding them farewell, he instituted two essential figures: definitive death and the shaman spirit hunters. In the first case he gathered all the resuscitated souls and installed them forever in Osypyte (also called Kululta), the land of the dead located on the western horizon. From then on all who died would go to this place and not return. But in order for this change to be less radical, he invented a category of shamans who would be capable of capturing recently deceased souls and returning them to their bodies. For this reason when someone is dying he or she requests the presence of these *konsaho* who dress in the appropriate feathers and paint their bodies with the necessary colors while the entire community maintains absolute silence. As soon as the dying man expires, the shaman launches himself in search of the spirit making its way to Osypyte. If there is not enough time to call the *konsaha* and he arrives several hours after the person has died, it is less likely that he will recover the spirit since it moves away very quickly.

When a thunder is heard and there are no clouds about, the Ishir know that it corresponds to the racket of the dead in Osypyte. "The dead are playing: they are calling us," say the old people.

SHAMANIC CATEGORIES
The Report of Bruno Barrás

Bruno Barrás (Ebytoso) proposed this classification of shamanic categories, without claiming that it is systematic or exhaustive.

The *póorch oso* shamans—sky shamans—belong to the highest rank. They have dominion over atmospheric phenomena, meteorological cycles, and seasons. They can intervene in the movement of bodies in space, rains, storms, and the ripening of plants. Some of these shamans reach the status of *konsaho pa* ("true or maximum shamans"). In a dream or trance state, the *konsaho póorch oso* can detach their spirits from their bodies and take long journeys. With the help of their swords (*anarak*) they reach the first celestial sphere where the Osasërö—Birds of Rain and Storm—live. From there they are capable of influencing weather conditions. They can also chase lost spirits (those of the dead or demented) and establish contact with the spirits of dead sky shamans.[8]

These shamans are divided into subcategories. One such subgroup is comprised by the astral shamans, the shamans of the Sun (*Konsaho Deich*), a superior category that has disappeared now, and those of the Lucero (*Iolé jilo*). Another subgroup is constituted by the shamans of Osasërö (Birds of Rain and Storm), who are also subdivided into different hierarchical orders. Among them, the highest rank are those of the *Konsaho Osasërö Balut jilo* ("shamans of the Master of Osasërö") whose jurisdictions include all kinds of meteorological activities: from innocent showers to furious hurricanes. Next are the shamans of Lapishé (*Lapishé jilo*), whose master and protector is the son of the Master of the Osasërö; they have great powers over rain. Minor ranks are those of the *Konsaho Tenhía jilo* and *Konsaho Botsyrbo jilo*. The first can assume the form of giant swallows and control (unleash or detain) torrential rains. Identified with small swallows, the second group has powers over electric storms. These last *konsaho* do not have good relations with those of the great rains whom they generally confront, engaging in terrible battles that shake the sky and disturb the earth.

The *konsaho nymych urros* (literally, "shamans of the ends of the earth") have jurisdiction over phenomena on the surface of the earth. Given that most illnesses originate in this world, they are good healers. They extract sicknesses by sucking them out of the patient's body through the *potytak* (suctioning tubes). Among the Ebytoso Robert Candia belongs to this category and Justo Alverenga is in the process of becoming one of these shamans. Among the Tomáraho Wylky, Luciano, and Palacio Vera are *konsaho nymych urros*.

The *konsaho niot ut oso* ("shamans of the waters") have jurisdiction over rivers, streams, and lagoons. They receive songs, visions and dreams, powers and appearances from the waters. Simplicio Miranda (Ebytoso) belongs to this category; he does not eat fish because he receives his powers from them. Some of these shamans belong to the subclass of *Debylybyta jila*. The great Mother of the River is their advocate. She inspires their songs, gives them designs for their corporal paintings, and strength to act underwater and overcome whatever ills arise from there.

The *konsaho nymych ut oso* ("shamans of the underground") act in the subterranean world. They are healers of all infections, pests, and parasites that emerge from the subsoil, and fight against these powers as well as against rival shamans of equal rank. They sleep facedown so their breath maintains contact during the night with the telluric forces that feed their dreams.

There are no great shamans today who belong to this category, to the detriment of the vulnerable communities. The last great shaman (*konsaha pa*) that exercised subterranean powers was Capitán Pintura (Captain Paint). In truth, he belonged to three categories: he was a shaman of the sky, the underground, and the waters. When he died in 1971 he asked to be buried facedown.

Alongside all these, there exists a category of shamans called the "honeycomb eaters," the *konsaho byrbyk posyro*.[9] *Byrbyk* is the name of a hallucinogenic honey. Its ingestion requires a long and difficult initiation because it can lead to madness if done improperly. The shamans of this kind cure mental illness and deep anguish ("the confused sadness," says the literal and literary Bruno). These shamans have the trust of their communities, never speak more than is necessary, look at people only when they are fulfilling their professional functions, and see across long distances with their eyes closed. Among the Tomáraho Aneryhë (called Lucas in "Paraguayan") belongs to this category. Cirilo Pintos, Bruno's grandfather, was the last of these among the Ebytoso. When Bruno was born Cirilo lay him on his knees, stretched his limbs, and anointed his body and face with his saliva and breath. This was a ritual he repeated every so often. "So that you become a prudent leader," Cirilo used to tell him.

The Report of Enrique Ozuna

Enrique Ozuna is Ebytoso, and spoke about the different shamanic categories in Spanish, a language he speaks with ease.

There are *konsaho* that have many specialties. One notable case is the grandfather of Bruno Barrás's wife, the famous Capitán Pintura (Captain

Paint), whose Ishir name was Chúebi. He was a sky, aquatic, and subterranean shaman, and qualified in five subjects: preventing infections, for which task he summoned a species of spider capable of destroying infectious principles; eliminating worms and other parasites that cause disease, including appendicitis; summoning the black fruits of the *porosuó,* much appreciated in the Chamacoco diet; controlling gentle rains and electric storms by summoning the corresponding Osasërö birds: the Echyrbo and the Botsyrbo; and exercising dominion over caimans.

On one occasion his wife went to the river for water, accompanied by her favorite dog, which was devoured by an alligator. In the face of his wife's affliction Chúebi decided to punish the alligators: he stopped singing, provoking in consequence a great drought and the death of many of these creatures. His countrymen, including his wife, pleaded with him to lift the sanctions, because they were causing great upheaval. Then Chúebi sang again to the Echyrbo, Birds of Gentle Rain, which brought rain to the region and replenished its rivers and lagoons.

Some types of shamans have disappeared. For example, there are no longer any *konsaho kadjuwerta jilo,* followers of the force of *kadjuwerta.* These shamans used to receive their powers from Ashnuwerta herself. There are also no longer any shamans affiliated with the power of Hoshta, the principle of carnal desire. The grandfather of Clemente López was a *konsaha Hoshta jila* and could provoke uncontainable amorous impulses; he could also regulate and calm them with his songs and even console unhappy lovers. ("And Clemente?" I ask. "He is in the process of becoming one," says Ozuna.) There are no longer any water shamans (*niot ut oso*), "inheritors of the powers of Debylybyta" (*Debylybyta jilo*); the last Ebytoso who bore this title passed away not long ago. He was Ozuna's father, and called Kyrpese. He had much power over the underwater world: its species and its negative forces. He could not drink cold water; even in the summer his wife always heated his water.

The *Pfaujata jilo* are also scarce now. They are favored by the fearsome Pfaujata and her followers in their ecstatic flights. The shamans who follow Pfaujata have jurisdiction over the sky and as such can extract sicknesses as if they were infected thorns. Faustino Rojas does this; he specializes in snakebites, and when someone is bitten he extracts the venom that has been transformed into a thorn.

STORIES OF SHAMANS

A Shaman's Journey

[Narrated in Spanish by Bruno Barrás (Ebytoso).]

One of Bruno's grandfathers was called Andrés; one of Andrés' cousins, named Pascual, was like him a honeycomb-eater. On a certain occasion they met in a community located near Puerto Mihanovich, and the *konsaha* Pascual approached his cousin and proposed that they travel together to Puerto Guaraní to watch the celebration of the *debylyby*, the Great Annual Ceremony, which was taking place there. "We should hurry," he said, "because the ceremony is already approaching the moment of the *tsaat,* an occasion that requires the presence of greatest possible number of men." Andrés replied that it would be impossible to arrive in time; it would take them several days to cross the 300 kilometers to Puerto Guaraní.

Pascual answered: "I am surprised, cousin, that you would doubt a shaman of my rank; remember that I know how to eat honey without dropping into madness." Andrés assented, asking for forgiveness, and accompanied him to his cabin to assemble his tools. Pascual was putting them away in his *lëbe* (rolled mat or "doctor's bag," as Bruno explains) when his grandmother Shypyteu came into the cabin. When she discovered what they were about to do, she began to cry. "This is madness. You will never get there!" she moaned. Pascual held her by the shoulders and looked into the depths of her eyes. "Grandmother," he said, "I know what I do: calm yourself." The old woman's anxiety subsided and both took their leave of her. It was afternoon.

On the outskirts of the village, after night had fallen, Pascual asked his cousin to wait for him. He moved fifty meters away and began to dress in feathers and paints. Andrés heard the maraca's rustle, the shaman's whistles, and the sounds of a strong wind that approached, agitating the palms. Then he saw his cousin walk to him with closed eyes. Pascual gave him a poppy-stalk whistle (keeping the stork-bone whistle for himself) and an *anarak* (sword/staff) of palo santo wood (keeping the one of quebracho wood for himself). "Take these and do not let go of them during the whole journey; walk without looking," he told Andrés without looking at him. They began to walk in the dark, and in silence. Andrés followed the pace set by Pascual, which was not too fast. He never ceased to be aware of the wind pressing at his back but did not feel it pushing him. He simply walked, clinging to the sword and whistle: without looking, without thinking of anything. After a while, which he found impossible to measure, the wind died down. The shaman told him: "Open your eyes." It was dawn and they saw the bonfires of Puerto Guaraní nearby. All that day, Andrés could still hear the sound of the wind echoing in his ears.

Eshpei's Threat

[Narrated in Spanish by Enrique Ozuna (Ebytoso).]

Not long ago one of the last shaman spirit hunters died. His name was Eshpei, and he was a sky shaman of the category of the Master of the Osasërö. One day he was working with a group of laborers in a place called Ashemá, near Puerto Ramos. The work was arduous and they had not received sufficient rations to sustain themselves. They were thus weak with hunger and fantasizing about grilling one of the heifers of the farm they were working on. "Do it," said Eshpei from where he was sitting. The Ishir did not dare, however, fearing punishment at the hands of the Paraguayan military. "Do not worry. Kill the heifer, barbecue it, and eat in peace. I will claim responsibility." The men hesitated no longer: they killed the animal and sat down to a one-course feast among the palm trees.

The next day a squad of ten soldiers trotted up and imprisoned the Ishir with many shoves and insults and took them to the military barracks. They did not dare touch Eshpei; he inspired fear from afar. But he presented himself at the barracks and spoke to the lieutenant: "I am the only one responsible for the animal's death. I demand that my men be freed and that I be imprisoned in their place." And so it was. The shaman was handcuffed and thrown into a dungeon whose doors were bound by strong chains and double locks. Two men were stationed in front of the door.

At dawn, the guards opened the dungeon to offer him food but the small room was completely empty. They went in search of him and found him in front of his house drinking maté with his wife. They entered the village violently, ransacking the houses and mistreating the women and children. One old woman was thrown to the floor, her last teeth knocked out, her mouth bleeding. Eshpei appeared then and was so imposing that the soldiers did not dare approach him. When some overcame their fear and tried to hit him they felt their arms go stiff and their bodies become paralyzed. The shaman looked into their eyes with the frozen and fiery gaze of the celestial *konsaho* and spoke: "If you dare return to this village you will all be struck down by lightning." In the distance thunder rumbled, emphasizing his words and the men took off running, their bodies no longer paralyzed. They reached the barracks panting and recounted the incident to the lieutenant, who told it to the judge, who told it to the bishop. But thanks to Eshpei's great fame none of them dared disturb the renowned Ishir of Ashemá.

A Shaman's Crime

[Narrated in Spanish by Enrique Ozuna.]

A shaman—even a wise and powerful shaman—can unfortunately be driven by human weakness to turn against his own community. This is what happens in this tale. In a centric land called Noseluta lived one of the last sun shamans (*konsaha deich jila*). His name was Herse, and he was the son of a captive Caduveo. He was a severe, serious man but on occasion fell prey to pride and lust. He sometimes boasted of his powers. "Who will dare defy the son of the sun?" he provoked the men as he strutted through the center of the village with arms extended and eyes closed, as one who only needs to look within to obtain all necessary certainties.

Tired of his arrogance, a young shaman apprentice challenged him one day: he grabbed a club and readied himself to throw it against Herse. But as he lifted the weapon he felt his body go rigid and he was completely paralyzed. The shaman blew on him and the youth recovered his motion but no longer dared to defy him. After a while another man accepted the challenge. On that occasion Herse turned into an incorporeal being so that his rival's arrows passed harmlessly through his body as if it were smoke. No one dared cross his path after that incident and the villagers resigned themselves in silence to his boasts.

On one occasion something so serious happened, however, that it could no longer be tolerated. Herse was obsessed with the wife of his nephew, but as she spurned his advances he raped her. All the wise men gathered to judge the shaman; they declared him guilty and condemned him to death. The problem, however, was how to apply the sentence since the shaman was invincible and would not submit to the decision of the jury.

All the *konsaho* of the village gathered but none of them was affiliated to the sun and when any of them attempted to kill Herse an astonishing phenomenon took place: dark and dense clouds swiftly covered the sun producing a quasi-nightfall, and when the men tried to light bonfires a cold wind from the south disrupted the delicate task.

The villagers had thus to seek out shamans in other villages. The tale enumerates the many frustrations in their attempts to fulfill the punishment. Finally a foreign shaman, of the same solar category as Herse and possessing equivalent if not superior powers presented himself. The shamans confronted each other in the space opened up by their ecstatic trances. Shaking with rage and delirium they fought, transformed into felines—*ylypió wert* (puma), *ylpió* (jaguar), *tatyo* (wildcat), and *húsho* (ocelot) successively—until Herse had exhausted his repertoire of metamorphoses. As he no longer had any fighting animal to turn into, he used his last chance at mutation to escape: he took on the features of a light bird called *houporo*, which flew away at great speed and could not be caught. He could not turn back into a man because, technically, he had been defeated in combat and his powers of transformation had run out.

But Herse still possessed shamanic powers and, feeling great resentment against his community, he sent a forest fire in their direction, which devoured the grasslands and trees in its path. When the sparks began to fly near the village and the men and women felt the suffocating heat and smoke Herse's wife took her small child in her arms and went out to meet the circle of flames. The shaman who observed the scene from above halted the fire's assault. And defeated once more, he flew away forever.

MOTIFS OF SHAMANIC SONG

The Songs of Pfaujata's Shaman

[This is a testimony of Faustino Rojas regarding his personal experience as a shaman. It was taped in Puerto Esperanza in August 1986, when Don Faustino was 79 years old. He died in Puerto Esperanza in 1993. Clemente López translated this into Spanish.]

One night Faustino dreamt of a large woman with shining eyes and the wings of an ostrich. Light streamed from her eyes and mouth "as if they were lanterns." She taught him the use of certain shamanic tools and inspired him to compose his own songs. When he awoke he knew he had dreamt of Pfaujata, and that he would be her follower, a *Pfaujata jila*. Following the instructions of his new mistress he crafted a headdress that ended in a long stick crowned with red feathers. His body was coated with Pfaujata's colors—red or black, depending on the occasion—and covered with white dots. Finally, he prepared the adornments and instruments.

Soon after he began to fly in dreams and trances atop the great winged body of Pfaujata. When he cures brain hemorrhages, stops the course of poison, or banishes exhaustion he sings the songs learned in dreams. He sings to the brightest stars, to the spiders spinning their shining webs, to the crazy Totila who wanders crying through the woods without knowing the cause of her cries or the end of her wanderings. And in his songs he sings what the sun tells him in dreams, "If it were not for me the men would not be able to see"; what the darkness tells him in dreams, "If I were to desire it, the sun would no longer appear and it would always be night"; and what the rain sings to him in dreams, "When you summon me with your voice I will come to soak the earth, bringing water to your people and hastening the season of pink fruit."

When on one occasion he was bitten by a snake (he points to the scar that has enlarged and darkened his left ankle) he was saved by his mistress and protector who came in his fevered delirium and extracted the poison, sucking it with her strength and knotting a string of ostrich plumes over it. After this incident Faustino specialized in curing poisonous bites: when he was summoned to help he encircled his wrist with a snakeskin and his ankle with ostrich feathers, crowned himself with a headband armed with the spongy nests of certain birds, and raised his voice singing to bring down the powers of his fearsome advocate.

Throughout his long training under the guidance of Pfaujata he learned to undertake protracted flights of ecstasy. His cap of duck feathers allows him to visit the beds of rivers and lagoons, journeys that add to his wisdom. His long feathered wand acts as a compass during the flights he undertakes independently. His skirt of sticks covered in hawk, owl, ostrich, and white heron feathers allows him to summon rains and cure certain sicknesses (especially those related to intoxications). His *anarak* (staff/sword) "gives strength to the spirit." From it hang smaller versions of itself, the *anarak abo* ("sons of the sword"): powerful amulets whose small dots, etched into their hilts like eyes, shine during his nocturnal flights. The principal piece ends in a belt of red feathers or in a red scarf: this is used to scar the "dangerous sores" and infected wounds. "When you don't use it," Pfaujata told him, "hang your sword in your house: it will protect your family from malign influences and keep snakes, scorpions, and spiders at bay."

Pressured by the New Tribes missionaries, for a time he set aside his feathers, rattle, songs, and powers. "And then," he says, "I could not cure snakebites, nor call upon rain in times of drought, nor gain in wisdom by flying over the earth and following the paths of fish, nor defend my family from evil. Then I decided to go back to using my shaman's tools. Only when my wife dies will I leave it again, to die with her."

The Furtive Songs of Jazmín Gamarra

[This is an account of Jazmín Gamarra, an Ebytoso shaman apprentice, of his personal experiences as a shaman and the themes of his songs. Jazmín speaks in Guaraní and Spanish.]

Jazmín receives instructions, suggestions, encouragement, and strength from the Masters of the Animals and various figures of nature in his dreams. The themes of his *teichu* (shamanic songs), which specialize in summoning calm rain and preventing hunger, are inspired by these forces that unfold in nocturnal scenes or the impossible place of ecstasy.

In a song, the Master of the Dragonfly (Posháraha Balut) incites him to saddle and ride the Osasërö birds like cloudy colts and gallop through the Ishir skies in order to provoke beneficial rain or detain powerful storms. Riding and swallowing the fecund celestial winds can satiate the hunger produced by the journey's rigors. Another of his songs tells of an invitation by the Master of the Kingfisher to fly over the best places to catch fish; or the offer made by the Master of the Surubí of the white flesh of the fish he shepherds. Fog speaks in another song: "I come to interrupt the frost, so your people do not suffer cold."

When the missionaries came (he refers to missionaries of the New Tribes Mission) they decided that these ridiculous songs and this shameful "equipment" (the shamanic tools and adornments) needed to be expelled from the new evangelized space. One missionary, Wanda Jones, threatened him with the ambiguous torments of hell and with the specific punishments of epidemics and famine if he and other shamans continued their practices and did not cast aside the attire that offended the cults of Christianity and civilization. But Jazmín held on to his maraca and his songs in secret, their muffled sounds mimicking the sounds of the Chaco. "I need to sing," he explains, "because if I do not I will never cease to be tormented by my lost dreams."

The author records a myth narrated by Palacio Vera and Wylky as translated by Bruno
Barrás at the initiation site. Potrerito, 1989. (Photo by Cristián Escobar Jariton.)

THE HISTORY

THIS text has wandered around an elusive theme attempting multiple, lateral, occasionally intersecting, and generally unsystematic approaches. In that spirit, my intention in this chapter is to delineate some traces that indicate the other side of the scene. I am not trying to deal here with the ethnocide of indigenous peoples: I have done so in a previous work and have little to add. Nor am I venturing ethnohistorical approximations: such attempts exceed my competency, and have been the object of admirable works by Susnik, Cordeu, and Chase-Sardi, among others. I restrict myself to transmitting various references regarding the concrete lives of (mainly Tomáraho) men and women, the strange figures this book addresses. I proceed through an unorthodox recourse to different documentary fragments—writings from my field diary, annotations, transcriptions of indigenous peoples' accounts and stories, quotations, references, and clarifications—all to suggest an intense and remote history that is sometimes painfully close and almost always astonishing.

FRAGMENTS FROM A LETTER
TO AUGUSTO ROA BASTOS

Asunción, 11 May 1990

You ask me how my entanglement began with this dark world that obsesses me and interests you. Well, it started at the 1983 São Paulo Bienale. In the context of the exhibitions there Osvaldo Salerno [director of the Museo del Barro] and I visited a stupendous show titled Arte plúmaria do Brasil [Feathered Arts of Brazil]. And there we came up with the idea of curating a similar exhibition in Asunción. During two intense years we visited numerous indigenous communities, missions, homes of *indigenistas,* and offices of anthropologists, and managed to put together an interesting collection. This, along with some additional objects and obsessions, were the basis of what would later become the indigenous collection of the Museo del Barro. The project was essentially artistic in nature, since the forms of this artwork with feathers are exuberant and constitute an expression of striking aesthetic impact. But it also had a political aim: presenting the indigenous peoples not through what they lack (and they lack much, of course), but rather through what they make (which is among the best art produced in Paraguay) as a way to support their right to difference.

We had found feathered objects of nearly all seventeen ethnic groups who live in Paraguay, but we lacked Chamacoco examples. I had studied the subject for a previous project (*Una interpretación de las artes visuales en el Paraguay*), and I knew that the Chamacoco had developed one of the most powerful expressions of featherwork in Paraguay. I also knew that, due to their condemnation by fanatic missionaries, the ceremonies for which these feathered ornaments were made had been definitively abolished. Officially, Dr. Susnik had recorded the last ritual in 1957 among the Ebytoso, a Chamacoco subgroup; but we wanted to obtain at least one piece that spoke of the ancient Chamacoco splendor.

One morning in April 1985—on the advice of Miguel Chase-Sardi—Osvaldo Salerno, Line Barreiro, and I went to the locale of the Asociación Indigenista del Paraguay, located near Luque. There I met Bruno Barrás, who discouraged us considerably. "There are no more pieces being produced today," he said, "and there are no antique ones left." We were leaving as an old but vigorous man approached us: it was Clemente López, whom you later met. "I know of a Chamacoco group that lives in the jungle and still practices the ceremony," he said. "They only have contact with the Compañía Carlos Casado, for whom they work. They flee the missionaries, the Mennonites, and Paraguayans in general, for they feel they will forbid their ceremonies." This ceremony, he explained, helped them survive as a different culture but was leading them to extinction. In order to preserve this ceremony, they were living in inhuman circumstances: exploited by the tannin company, malnourished, and ill.

After the Chaco War ended (1935) and they lost their original territories, the Chamacoco had to negotiate with colonial society for land. They did not have much room to bargain, of course, and lost almost everything. The different Chamacoco groups living in the vicinity of their ancient grounds are exploited and have had few opportunities to reconstitute their devastated imaginaries. The Tomáraho withdrew and preserved the matrix of their identity but paid a high price for their insubordination. After many go-arounds, Clemente López finally put me in contact with them. Or rather, he put both of us in contact with them: Mito (Guillermo Sequera), who was then living in Paris and working in Asunción, became so involved in this matter that he ended up being absorbed by it and returning to Paraguay definitively . . .

fragments from field notes

Asunción, 14 August 1985

After Clemente López confirmed a month ago that a ceremony should be starting by now in San Carlos, I began to look for a plane since it is difficult to get there any other way. Carlos Colombino managed to convince Ferdinand Stadecker, a businessman, to lend us a four-passenger single-engine plane, piloted by his own man, Rubén Granado. Last week, we were about to take off when the sky rapidly darkened. We found ourselves in the midst of an unexpected storm that forced us to cancel the flight. Today we tried again. Clemente slept at my home last night, and he and I met with Mito early in front of the VICRA hangar where we drank maté while God knows what time-consuming procedures were being carried out. We were supposed to take off by 6 a.m. but were delayed permission to do so every ten minutes, even though we had fulfilled the many requisites the airport demanded in order to authorize the flight. At 8 a.m. they told us we could not leave: the president, General Stroessner, might need to use the runway and it had to be available for him. All flight orders, therefore, were automatically suspended. "Aren't these adverse signs?" I wondered quietly.

San Carlos, 12 April 1986

With Beto (engineer Roberto Vera Vierci) I managed to find not only a plane but his personal piloting services. He personally flew the small single-engine plane on a long trajectory whose course was at times dictated through observation from the plane itself, since we lacked other coordinates. Clemente would tell him: "Keep flying over the river until that tributary. Now take a right. Follow the dirt road until we get to the forest. Cross the clearing and keep to the road again." And so on, as if he were giving directions to a taxi driver. We were flying as low as we could, following the itinerary Clemente drew with his precise indications. Finally we arrived at San Carlos where we were expected, since our visit had been announced and our landing authorized.

In spite of mutual wariness we were received almost courteously by the people in charge in San Carlos. "Do you want to go to the village now?" Yes, we wanted to do so immediately. They drove us in a truck on roads that were not much wider than they had seemed from the plane. Night had fallen by the time we got to an open ground (I would later learn that we had arrived at the *harra*). Everything seemed confusing: the campfire shrouded and revealed features, screams and silences came and went with the breezes; whispers approached, strange whistling sounds.

I think we were a bit disappointed.

San Carlos, 14 April 1986

After the first night's perplexity in a scene veiled by shadows and dustiness and shaken by screams; after yesterday's vertigo and stupor before the eruption of the plumed and painted bodies, absent glances, anxious spirit; after our disturbance when faced with the misery and abandonment in which the Tomáraho live; after so many shocks, today we finally had a quiet moment that allowed us to speak. A representation in the ceremonial circle—an open clearing in the dense forest—had ended and the men had washed each other, effacing the trace of paintings, exchanging their radiant garments for proletarian shirts and pants.[1] Then we began to talk—or rather, they talked. We were still stunned by the impact of this incomprehensible, radically beautiful, and fierce world. And they woke us by brutally naming their misery.

EMILIO'S ACCOUNT

[The following account is an excerpt from a long disquisition by Emilio Aquino. It was recorded in San Carlos on 14 April 1986 by Guillermo Sequera, translated by Bruno Barrás, and copied by María Lis Escobar in Asunción.]

Clemente López asked him to explain the present Tomáraho situation, and Emilio answered thus:

Our people, who were numerous back then, lived without contact with the Paraguayans. But these encroached more and more on Ishir lands. Our elders knew they would need to talk with the whites eventually in order to negotiate the guarantee of land. The cacique of the village of Ohuytá, a place close to Olimpo, was called Tukusía. For a long time he had participated in discussions about the necessity of establishing a dialogue with whites and decided one day he would leave the hills and approach a Paraguayan village. As soon as he did so he felt several shots echoing around him. He ran back into the trees and to his village and told the others what had happened. The Chamacoco were not familiar with firearms and became very frightened. After many months Tukusía, still obsessed with the incident, said, "I will go and see what this thunder is about." His father decided to follow him—and so did his grandfather, and also his *ágalo* [companion], and his *ágalo*'s father—and so a group formed to go discover the origin of those incomprehensible sounds. They encountered, for the first time, a group of Paraguayans. These were in turn surprised because they thought the Ishir—naked and covered in feathers—were unknown animals or birds, or hybrid beings perhaps. They readied their weapons to shoot, but when they realized that the Chamacoco were lifting up their arms in sign of peace they signaled the Chamacoco to follow them into a military settlement called Fortín Galpón. The Indians stayed there for some time, learning some of the Paraguayan customs: eating beef, drinking maté, the use of firearms and Western clothing. The Paraguayans said: "If you come and work with us we will teach you many more things. We will guarantee you the use of forests and we will give you food and clothing."

When they went back to the village they found their women shaved and mourning: they thought they had been widowed. That night they all sang together until dawn to celebrate the return of the men who arrived with gifts of clothing, utensils, and strange foods.

After a while they went to work for the Paraguayans. They were not interested in money since they knew nothing of its value; nor were they interested in Paraguayan food for they preferred the honey and meats of the hills. They were not interested in clothing since they could move more freely in the hills in their own minute loincloths; nor in houses, for they felt better in their own huts. Thus, they worked for free. In exchange they only expected that the Paraguayans would not forbid them access to their means of subsistence: the forest that was once entirely Chamacoco. In hopes that the Paraguayans would value their work they wandered through different settlements offering their able bodies for labor. They went to Puerto Sastre, avoiding the villages that scared the elders.

On an occasion when they were headed to Pitiantuta they encountered a squadron of soldiers. "What are you doing here?" they asked. "This is our land," the Ishir answered. Then the soldiers told them to protect themselves, for the Bolivian enemies were advancing: it was the time of the Chaco War. "We will protect you if you serve as our guides. If not, the Bolivians will decimate your villages," threatened the Paraguayans. The Chamacoco accepted. They received the food, clothing, shoes, mosquito nets, weapons, and horses the whites gave them, and helped them seek out roads among the thorn-infested hills, plains, and palm groves. So it was that our grandfathers helped the Paraguayans win the war. Some of the great caciques who fought were Chicharrón, Nicasio, Julián, and Sosa: they fought with bows and arrows, and clubs, and used crowns of jaguar skin because they were brave chiefs and warriors. They opened paths, pointed out roads unknown to the Paraguayans; they discovered water reservoirs and forest foods; they even built bulletproof palisades. The birds pointed out enemy tracks to the Ishir (and not to the Paraguayans) so that the Ishir could capture or kill them. But when the war ended, the Paraguayans did not even thank them. "Settle on the river banks," they told the Ishir. But our grandparents did not take heed, and returned to the hills.

During the war many Paraguayans had married our women; but while these were still pregnant they abandoned them. Mestizo children were born. They were a little different from us—they had different hair, a different gaze—but when they talked, they spoke our language. One of these mestizos was called Konionyke. One day, people started dying and nobody knew why. Konionyke said: "This is a Paraguayan illness called measles. I will go look for a vaccine in a white settlement." But he himself died on the way there. After this first epidemic ended and had devastated a large part of the village, a group of Paraguayans approached our people and spoke thus: "You will all die due to illness. Come and work for us and we will give you vaccines, food, and land." But there was a great cacique called Konit who vehemently opposed this. He said: "The Paraguayans are liars. They will give us nothing and will infect us with other illnesses. They will marry our daughters, and we will have more and more mestizos until our grandchildren have other faces." The shaman's remedies could no longer cure us because our people's blood had been intermixed. Many of us were no longer Ishir, but we were not Paraguayan either. This is why Konit did not want to have any contact with the Paraguayans. "I do not need firearms," he said, "I can slay a tiger with my spear." But our people could not resist much longer. After the war the Paraguayans—as well as many foreigners—increasingly occupied our lands, and we lost our chances of surviving. We had to approach the logging camps to secure protection and so we did. We have been working in the Compañía Casado logging camps since 1955, cutting down the quebrachos. We are not ensured permanent work; we roam from camp to camp according to whether we are hired or fired. Sometimes we are out of work for long periods of time, but we always linger around the *quebrachales*. If we are fired we have nowhere to go and we wait at the edge of the forest.

We are paid 12,000 guaranis per hectare cleared, and we need three people working for three days from 7 to 11 a.m. and 1 to 5 p.m. to do so. We also build posts (we are paid 200 guaranis for each), and clear trails (we are paid 4,000 guaranis for every 100 meters).[2]

At this point Palacio Vera, also called Tatié, interrupts:

From the moment of our first contact with the Paraguayans an arrangement was made: we would work for them and they would take care of us, for we had lost nearly all of our lands. But the whites only wanted to make money from our work. We had decided to leave the hills to live in better conditions, but that was not the case: we are worse off than we were before. They think we are stupid because we do not speak their language or know their customs. The center of our territory is called Pitiantuta, which means "anteater." This name has its history: our ancestors had lit a large circle of fire there to hunt for wild rabbits and then, instead of finding rabbits, they had found an anteater that had died of asphyxiation. This is an animal that sleeps deeply, and it had died without being able to escape. With the war we lost this great territory of ours and had to leave it even though we had also fought on the Paraguayan side and had suffered many casualties. We abandoned our lands and went to Olimpo to meet with the Paraguayans: we had to meet with them since we had no more land. We thought that since we had fought on their side we would be accepted as their allies. We were wrong. As soon as the war ended we were Indians once again.

When Bruno Barrás and Walter Regher worked on a census of all the Chamacoco, we sent a representative there in hopes of sharing the Puerto Esperanza territory with the Ebytoso. Now our territory is that of Compañía Carlos Casado. That is, we live there but it isn't ours: it does not belong to us, and has become an enemy place that is killing us off. Before we were brave and strong, but cohabitation with Paraguayans has tamed us. This is why my father never wanted to leave the forest.

Emilio resumes:

Before, the Tomáraho were numerous. Now there are only eighty-seven of us: thirty-one women, twenty-seven children, and twenty-nine men.[3] Our situation is serious because we have neither land nor food and we can no longer have chiefs. And because we work badly. The people who contract us to work promise they will employ us with social security, but this is a lie; we prefer to work in temporary jobs because they do not live up to their promises. They say, "You are also Paraguayan." That is a lie, we are indigenous people. And as indigenous people we are treated badly. We are forbidden to hunt in the land of Casado; we do so clandestinely but the scarce and furtive prey is not enough to feed the whole group. The wild plants are not enough, because to be fed properly children need meat. We have to go to Boquerón to work in clearing land, but they pay us badly. We work bravely from sunrise to sunset; we men work cutting down trees, our women wash their clothes and clean their houses. What do they give us in return? They give us food, sometimes donated by the agency Charitas: old bread, *locro kya* and *kumanda vai*—dirty *locro* and bad beans, in Guaraní. And what they give us is not even abundant:

it is not enough to feed us for half a month. They pay us with vouchers that are useless, with the very instruments we use to work for them, with the medicine that foreign missions send. And they pay us with alcohol, which we did not know before. We do not even ask for sugar; wild honey is enough for us.

We have vouchers that the Compañía Carlos Casado gave us in exchange for our labor. But we will burn these papers: they are useless. And they still insist that we owe them more work. That is why we cannot leave, they tell us. But we will leave anyway; the lumber yards are destroying us.

Some time ago, there was an abundance of leftover, spoilt flour in the Compañía Carlos Casado. They threw it away among the trees and our women went to pick it up; they wanted to use it for cooking even though it was rotten. That is how great our hunger was. They mocked us: "They are used to eating filth, like pigs." What could we do? We were hungry. We do not eat filth in the woods: we eat the clean meat of peccaries and anteaters, turtles and armadillos, eels and fish; we eat the fruit of the carob tree and the wild bean, we eat pure honey and fresh heart of palm.

Only when we are very sick do they improve our ration of food. "We do not have energy to work," we say, and they look at us with suspicion. When they see that we are indeed very ill they add some meat to the menu; but if those who are sick are old men, they do not worry since after all, they can no longer work.

We work all day and they tell us we are slothful. "They are Indians," they say, "and Indians are lazy." If the work is clearing land, we have to do a hectare in three days. We do it, but they are never happy. "They are lazy," they continue to say. But we are not lazy; we only dislike work if we are not paid. We don't intend to earn as much as the Paraguayans, just enough to survive.

We do not separate: when one of us finds work that will allow us to survive for a while, we go after him. And so we live united. When someone falls sick our doctors [shamans] cure them with songs and wild herbs. But many herbs can no longer be found here. And there are no songs to protect us from the new diseases. When someone dies—and many die—we mourn together. When we have a bit of food we share it. And we share our hunger always.

Here in San Carlos our settlement is too precarious. We do not have cabins with walls of palm and roofs of straw like the Paraguayans and even other indigenous groups who live elsewhere. We all live under tents that are open on all sides and already ripped. If someone does not fit under the tent he or she must seek shelter under the trees when it rains. And if it rains too much we strip off our clothes and use them to protect the children. When it is cold we awaken huddled together around the fire. And this is not new: since we arrived in San Carlos it has been like this. Our old people catch colds and die. Our children grow a bit and die too. Each year there are fewer of us. Some days ago, seven of us died. But before, many others died. We die like dogs and they bury us like dogs: we cannot even have a cemetery like the Paraguayans that die. Not long ago one of Wylky's children died and we buried him there where we were working. And during epidemics when several died each day we did not even have time to bury them. We had to continue to work so as to not die ourselves.

When a Paraguayan is hungry, he or she sells something and buys food with the money. But we have nothing to sell.

We have been dying out since we arrived here: we need to leave. We want to go to Puerto Esperanza, to Ishir land. There we can hunt and fish and gather fruit in the woods. We will be able to work for the Paraguayans and learn to plant. But we cannot do it alone, we need help. We owe money to the people who contracted us to work, money they gave us in advance for tools, food, and medicine.

Clemente López interrupts, asking if they don't have a leader who will help them overcome the situation; he remembers that when he was in a Tomáraho village in 1951 he met the great chief Chicharrón. Emilio's account continues:

Chicharrón, my uncle, was a great chief and a wise and prudent man. He was called Koächina and was the last representative of the Dosypyk clan. He fought for Paraguay in the Chaco War, but the Paraguayans never recognized his status as an ex-combatant. "He is an Indian," they said. When we began to work in Compañía Carlos Casado he defended us. He had learned to read and write during the war and ensured that they respected our rights: hours, pay, social security. The Compañía Carlos Casado never paid well, but at least Chicharrón guaranteed that they fulfilled the little they promised.

When he felt he was dying he called the people together and spoke like this: "I have to die now. My body is burnt by the sun and drenched by too many rains: my body has endured cold and hunger and no longer resists. Our land was Pitiantuta, but now we lost it because the Paraguayans took it. As an ex-combatant I asked that they reserve at least a fraction of that land for my

Portrait of Vicenta Maura. San Carlos, 1986. (Photo by Guillermo Sequera.)

people, but they did not listen to me. 'He is only an Indian,' they said. But you must remain together, and together you must find a way to survive without separating." So spoke our grandfather before dying.

This illustrious grandfather died in 1964 in Puerto Casado. And then we lost all hope that someone would defend us. There was a Paraguayan who worked in the Compañía, called Mario, who tried to help us, but he was fired. We do not know how to read and write, and they write our bills however they want. They give us half a kilo of locro and write that they gave us a full kilo. "You owe us," they say at the end. But why would we owe them if we are always working and what they give us is never enough? Before, we could hunt and ease our hunger; but when animal skins became more expensive we could no longer do so. They became the owners of the animals, of their skins. That was when our greatest suffering began. Because if we can't stand the hunger and go hunting we are denounced to the mayors of San Carlos (Florentín, López, and others) and are imprisoned. The soldiers treat us badly: they hit us with batons or with their rifle butts and make us strip the bark of the quebracho tree that they then sell to the Compañía. When we lived in Puerto Casado we were more respected. There, some even called us "countrymen."

But when we arrived at Toro Pampa and later San Carlos they called us "Indians" and despised us.

Clemente interrupts again: "When you came to Quebracho Poty there were many children. Two years ago I saw children that I no longer see . . . "

Emilio responds:

They died. They died quickly. From 1977 until now [1986], six hundred Tomáraho have died. Last year measles killed thirty people in three days. We are ending. All the youth who were my son Crescencio's age also died. He is the only one of his age: he no longer has companions. We have survived a little longer. When disease comes, the people panic. Many run off into the woods. But they die anyway.

Clemente asks, "Haven't you tried to approach other Paraguayans?"

Emilio responds:

Once a priest came and promised medicine; but we know that he will only give it to us if we go to the mission. And there they will not allow us to perform our rites. They will prohibit the *debylyby* just as they prohibited it among the Ebytoso. I wanted my sons to learn to read and write so that the Paraguayans would not harm them so much. So I sent them to schools in Toro Pampa and Quebracho Poty. But they suffered a lot and only learned nonsense. I sent Crescencio to the Paraguayan military barracks after he passed through the barracks here [he is referring to masculine initiation]. He learned to speak Guaraní and to read and write. But he also learned mischief.

Clemente asks: "Can't you build better huts? There used to be a good forest here, there was plenty of wood, and the palm groves are not far . . ."

Emilio responds:

Do you think a machine knocked down the trees? We did it. The manager of Compañía Carlos Casado told us that if we cleared the trees they would build us a village with wooden walls, but as soon as we finished our work they built houses for themselves and sent us packing into the woods. They do not even allow us to use the wood to build our own houses.

Author's Commentary on Emilio's Account

At this point Emilio's account turns into a dialogue in which more and more men participate. The real issue that had brought us here, without our knowledge, is raised: the possibility long contemplated by the Tomáraho of moving to Enishte, Puerto Esperanza, and their request for help to do so. Clemente, an Ebytoso, acted as an intermediary, possibly after an agreement between them. Now they openly discuss the possibilities of sharing a territory of 21,300 hectares that INDI—Instituto Nacional del Indígena—had bought for all the Chamacoco. To some degree, Emilio's detailing of his people's suffering is intended to promote solidarity for the move. The Tomáraho fear that their historical rivalries with the Ebytoso will produce a crisis in Puerto Esperanza. Clemente assures them that there will be no problems; each group will occupy their own space and the communities will support each other mutually. They decide to nominate a commission to go with Clemente to visit Puerto Esperanza to study its potential as a future Tomáraho home. Marcos Maciel, Crescencio, Dionisia, Toti, and Minina are nominated as members to the commission. They decide to discuss the issue among the Tomáraho once the delegates return. They discuss the necessity of keeping the Tomáraho and Ebytoso apart. Emilio, Palacio, Bernal, and Wylky insist that Clemente, in the name of his people, assure them that they can live apart, continue to practice their cults, and have a guarantee that they will be neither persecuted nor exploited.

Clemente is a good example of the ambivalent relation that links and separates both groups: on the one hand, he ardently supports the Tomáraho cause; on the other hand, he has caused numerous skirmishes and rivalries between both groups, and pressures the Tomáraho. He promises support and does so sincerely. And he played as fundamental a role in this early stage as he will later play in the discord that will prompt a new exodus.

The Comisión de Solidaridad con los Pueblos Indígenas [Commission of Solidarity with Indigenous Peoples], founded in 1986 in Asunción to accompany self-sustainable indigenous demands, promoted a specific program called Campaña por la Vida de los Tomáraho [Campaign for the Life of the Tomáraho] to aid in the logistics of their move from San Carlos to Puerto Esperanza. From September 1987, the ACIP (Apoyo a las Comunidades Indígenas del Paraguay) [Support for the Indigenous Communities of Paraguay] took on the tasks of tracking the resettlement of the Tomáraho in Puerto Esperanza and developing programs of medical attention and agricultural technical assistance.

ACCOUNTS

Account of Dr. Juan Carlos Chaparro Abente

[Dr. Chaparro Abente was sent to San Carlos by the Comisión de Solidaridad con los Pueblos Indígenas.]

Asunción, 8 May 1986

We have inspected twenty-two indigenous children whose ages range from three months to thirteen years of age, and in general we have found evidence of the same pathology in all of them: an advanced state of clinical anemia, parasites, and malnutrition. Teeth and mouth examinations show that most of them have an alarming state of dental deterioration. With regard to adults we have undertaken twelve clinical examinations: six men, six women. We have found venereal diseases (gonorrhea) and detected four cases of a high probability of tuberculosis; given its serious implications we advised that these four move to the capital for better diagnosis and treatment. We consider the state of health of the examined community to be a consequence of the surrounding chaos, the current impossibility of a space to constitute a more or less stable habitat, the crowding, and absence of minimal conditions of health (contaminated water, precarious alimentation).

Fragments of an Account by Ticio Escobar

[This account was sent to Indianerhilfe und Tropenwaldschutz Dr. Binder at the request of Dr. Edelmira Recalde and on the basis of an appeal by Pedro Vera, chief of the Tomáraho since 1994. The chief was interested in finding support for technical instruction in agriculture. Since their move to Puerto Esperanza, the Tomáraho mix hunting with light cultivation, artisanal production, and occasional small jobs.]

1 September 1998

Convinced of their right to their own culture, the Tomáraho were being extinguished. Exploited in the lumber yards, the population declined rapidly and the women had ceased to become pregnant. When Guillermo Sequera and I entered into contact with them in 1986 there were only eighty-seven people: the last survivors of a particular experiment in civilization, of a particular way of conceiving and expressing the world. Even in the death throes of this culture they continued to preserve their rich mythical corpus and rites: an exuberant world of corporal paintings, dance, featherwork, and performance.

On this occasion, they asked us to help them obtain lands to establish themselves and attempt to ensure the continuity of the group. They were aware that INDI (Instituto Nacional del Indígena, an official Paraguayan entity) had 21,300 hectares for the Chamacoco in Puerto Esperanza. There was a group of Ebytoso established there already who had migrated from Puerto Diana, and who had stopped performing the ceremonial and initiatory traditions. The Tomáraho proposed the following: they would establish themselves in a place in Puerto Esperanza with the guarantee that their cultural rights and religious difference would be respected. Once we returned to Asunción we entered into contact with indigenist and anthropological organizations and accompanied the Ebytoso leaders—representatives of a sector that was willing to help the *silvícolas* [wild ones]—and Tomáraho delegates to claim their own piece of land in Puerto Esperanza. The negotiation was very difficult due to the intransigence of INDI (traditionally hostile to ethnic self-determination) as well as the suspicion of some Ebytoso, who invoked old intergroup rivalry. After long discussions and the help of anthropologists such as Oleg Vysokolán and Miguel Chase-Sardi, we gained authorization for the Tomáraho to move to Puerto Esperanza.

In May 1986 the Tomáraho moved to Puerto Esperanza, near the Ebytoso group. The process of settling in the new lands was difficult: the new arrivals had to practice new forms of survival and learn to live near their traditional rivals, among whom there were allies but also detractors. Some interethnic friction was produced but the project continued with the decision of the Tomáraho to install themselves in a more distant part of Puerto Esperanza; that is, they would leave the riverbanks to live and build their village in the woods. And so they did: they established a village of palms called Potrerito (Peishiota).

Now the arrival of the Tomáraho produced a strong commotion among the Ebytoso. The rituals of the new arrivals—their religious fervor, their cults and dances, their songs and invocations—touched the depths of Ebytoso memory and produced a notable event: many of them began to practice again the *debylyby*, the traditional annual ceremony. Thus, when the Tomáraho moved to Potrerito they were followed by a group of Ebytoso who wanted to recover their religion and who established themselves alongside the Tomáraho. Obviously, this nearness generated friction again, but at that moment it proved a rich experience for both communities . . .

[In the years since then] the Tomáraho had to confront the challenges of strengthening their population, living with ancestral contenders, negotiating spaces with national society, and learning new cultural forms. And all this work had to be done without sacrificing either their self-sufficiency or the symbolic nucleus that sustains it . . . Currently the Tomáraho live on their own piece of land called María Elena, located forty kilometers north of Olimpo in the traditional habitat of the Chamacoco. The property has 3,873 hectares, of which 2,000 are apt for agriculture. The Tomáraho basically plant manioc, sweet potatoes, beans, corn, squash, and watermelon. They also engage in crafts, fishing, hunting, gathering honey, and the sale of carandá palms. Today 130 people live in Santa Elena. The accelerated process of mortality that was decimating the group has been halted, and thirty-five children have been born. The group has grown with the influx of some Chamacoco who lived in other villages. The Tomáraho have many difficulties: there is no community in Paraguay—in Latin America—that does not. But today they are an autonomous group: politically and religiously independent and economically self-sufficient. They continue to practice their ceremony enthusiastically and they continue to have their own shamans and beliefs that orient the community's path . . .

Selections of an Account by Miguel Chase-Sardi

[The following account is derived from Miguel Chase-Sardi et al. (1990, 52ff.).]

"With the boom of the lumber yards and the tannin industry [the Chamacoco] were poisoned with alcohol, their only salary, in the industries of Casado, Sastre, Pinasco, and Guaraní. The Toba-Maskoy, Angaité, Sanapaná, and Guaná were in the same situation. During the Chaco War they had to prostitute their women to the troops and were subsequently decimated by venereal diseases. The crash of the international market for natural tannin produced a kind of diaspora that moved into the zone of influence of the Anglican Mission and the Mennonite colonies. No one knows why, but the Chamacoco in general did not migrate . . . [T]he one group that conserved a certain autonomy and ethnic identity was precisely the Chamacoco, the only one that, as mentioned, has not migrated en masse . . ."

Yet, "the expansion of the colonizing frontiers of the Paraguayan national society, which takes the form of razing forests to make room for cattle ranching," promotes "the search for contact with global society." Even so, the Tomáraho, called "Fierce Chamacoco," resisted the colonizing expansion longest and most aggressively. Chase-Sardi believes that the Tomáraho were the ones who "committed a series of offenses and deaths that the Paraguayans always attributed to the Moro or Ayoreo." Such indigenous groups "were in permanent hostile defense before the advance of colonizing frontiers of national society."

The Tomáraho resistance prevented their swift deculturation at the hands of the missionaries. The Ebytoso, however, suffered ethnocide at the hands of various Christian missions. "Since the 1920s, the Salesian missionaries began to work in Puerto Mihanovich. And at the beginning of the 1940s, the New Tribes missionaries moved into Puerto Diana. The Ebytoso abandoned their cultural norms under the pressure of the constant scorn displayed by the Salesians toward the Chamacoco rituals, which they called *payasadas* [clowning around], and as a result of the systematic deculturation that the New Tribes missionaries forced upon the younger generation through a model of directed leadership."

Between April and August of 1986 the Comisión de Solidaridad con los Pueblos Indígenas undertook the Campaña por la Vida de los Tomáraho [Campaign for the Life of the Tomáraho], which actively supported the "migration of the Tomáraho from the lands of Carlos Casado S.A. to lands that the INDI had bought for the Chamacoco in Puerto Esperanza. Under the exploitation of that company, the last eighty-seven Tomáraho lived in subhuman conditions in the vicinity of San Carlos. The situation was clearly one of ethnocide and genocide, until the cited commission intervened. From that point on a process of cultural revalorization began, which spread to the Ebytoso group already located in Puerto Esperanza."

"Despite the fact that wage relations—with the Carlos Casado S.A. tannin company—have taken root in the Tomáraho group since the 1930s . . . the Potrerito members have managed to maintain their traditional cultural values and ethnic identity intact. They perform their rites and religious ceremonies with astonishing regularity, given the depressing situation in which they found themselves. Their influence sparked a revalorization of the mythology and traditional religion in their Ebytoso neighbors and today they celebrate their ceremonial feasts together . . . I note good social cohesion and consolidated leadership in the sociocultural realm."

field notes

A meeting of Tomáraho and Ebytoso *cabezantes* takes place to discuss the delicate issue of the cohabitation of their respective communities, which has lately become almost impossible: in the face of constant friction between the groups, a considerable number of Tomáraho have decided to return to San Carlos. This is a serious turn of events and both communities are prepared to face it. A list of the principal problems is drawn up: the boasting of some Ebytoso; a ferocious brawl between women caused by the aggression of Pichunga to a Tomáraho woman; the discussions on ceremonial protocol and mutual interventions in the internal affairs of each village. There are also issues that weigh on everyone's mind, even if they are not spoken aloud: the strife produced by the shared daily routine of neighbors who are strangers to each other, and the archaic reservations that memory imprudently insists on invoking.

For a society like the Chamacoco, endowed with sophisticated mechanisms of social mediation between sectors, the lack of mechanisms capable of compensating unforeseen imbalances is disconcerting. The Tomáraho/Ebytoso cohabitation is an unprecedented historical situation in Ishir culture, which does not have adequate resources to repair this strange discord. It will have to force its mythical and ritual articulations, its images and ideas to resolve a new conflict. As time passes it is increasingly obliged to do so more and more. The settlement in Potrerito requires adaptations in other arenas as well: it requires a model of political leadership different from the one demanded by an autonomous and separate community. Now Crescencio Aquino (Apytal), son of Emilio, is the new chief; he is a young man, capable of adapting himself to the necessities of a new time.

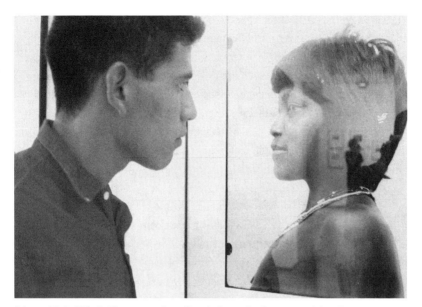

Edgar, chief of María Elena, examines the photograph of a woman taken by
Guido Boggiani in 1901. (Photo by Arístides Escobar, at the 2004 exposition of
Boggiani photographs, Centro Cultural de España "Juan de Salazar," Asunción.)

But just as all Western cultures dispose of certain figures (like tradition,
equity, or doctrine) to confront the emergence of events that lie outside their ju-
ridical horizon, Ishir culture also has means to deal with unexpected collisions.
The Chamacoco are agile manipulators of the verb: they can argue for hours
and negotiate with skill, with the flourish of consummate swordsmen. "Negotiation through words" is an indispensable mechanism of the Ishir world and
wielding it an art. They asked us to act as moderators. But our ministry was
unnecessary. The Chamacoco speak at length with no interruptions. When one
person stops speaking a brief and necessary pause ensues while the words
settle and then another person begins to speak unhurriedly. This dynamic is
maintained even in heated debates: the interlocutors listen attentively to each
other so that the crossfire of their discourses does not overlap. Each orator is
given all the time necessary to present his or her ideas and affirm them, to justify his or her arguments and refute adversarial ones, to illustrate the claim
with long examples, and to conclude by gliding down in gentle spirals or plung-

ing suddenly. The speaker also has time to veer off from the course of the discourse he or she is weaving, to meander and take parallel paths and abruptly return, enriching his or her reasoning with strange figures and suggestions. Thus, now Wylky refers to a tale that serves, through a very long detour, to attempt another access to the intricate subject. He narrates a mythical tale concerning the confrontation between the Ishir and the Ayoreo. The myth acts as an exemplary reference that clarifies a confused issue; but also as a rhetorical mechanism that can unlock the dialogue. The Chamacoco know that sometimes a detour is the fastest route.

Clemente is next. He has a propensity to argue through performance rather than syllogism. The histrionic gesture is also an ally of the word. After him, Palacio Vera speaks with exaggerated gravity; perhaps to refute Clemente's convincing show through a performance of his own. And so the afternoon passes as they speak and fall silent in turn until some unknown element thrown into the mix suddenly brings about a conclusion. They decide to create a Tomáraho/Ebytoso instance of discussion and consultation; at a later meeting the proposals will be discussed. No one answers my question on when this reunion will take place.

Potrerito, 3 March 1991

During the long discussions that take place these days about the crisis of the Tomáraho/Ebytoso cohabitation I have verified the malleability of the Ishir language, which can position itself in different terrains: jumping from one language to another and creating neologisms with great syntactic liberty and astonishing ease. When we came into contact with the Tomáraho, only some of its leaders spoke Guaraní and none of them spoke Spanish. Now all of them express themselves fluidly in Guaraní and most can communicate clearly in Spanish, some with notable ease. And to facilitate communication they have no problem inventing words, introducing hispanisms and forcing shifts from one language to another with carefree insolence. I have noted some examples:

> *cabezante* [head]: chief or leader
> *cuartel* [barracks]: the tobich
> *doctor* [doctor]: shaman
> *equipo* [equipment]: the set of shamanic utensils kept in the *lëbe* (including the maraca, feathered ornaments, suctioning tube, etc.)

fútbol [football]: ritual game of *póhorra*

mariscar [to fish]: to hunt

partido [political party] or *club* [club]: clan; they will say for example that Auir's *partido* (or *club*) is Tahorn

payaso [clown]: anábser; this term was adopted from the missionaries who used it insultingly, but it has been purged of negative connotations

pinta, a noun created from *pintar* [to paint]: corporal painting; for example, "Kaimo's *pinta* is based on alternating colors"

pista (de baile) [dance floor]: the *harra*

polca [polka]: *teichu*, shamanic song

presidente [president]: *pylota*, chief

recluta [recruit]: *wetern*, youth during initiation

rifar [to raffle]: to copulate

valija [suitcase]: *lëbe*, the rolled mat shamans use to guard their tools

Benjamín's Account

[On 14 August 1998, Benjamín Vierci, chief of the Ebytoso community of Potrerito, was in Asunción on errands for his community. He drew up a picture of the current distribution of the different Chamacoco groups, which I transcribed almost literally. (See map on page 7.) It is a condensed and oscillating map: the different groups continually change their locations, driven by their old nomadic impulse, the pressures of survival, or expulsions by new landowners. This picture coincides basically with one that Ojedo Benítez laid out on 26 March 1997 in Asunción, where he had gone with his grandson Ticio Rafael Benítez, who needed medical attention.]

The Ishir are divided in distinct communities:

María Elena is a parcel of land of about 4000 hectares in extension located forty kilometers north of Olimpo, and 100 kilometers from Bahía Negra. One hundred and thirty-five Tomáraho live there. Their chief, Pedro Vera, is trying to obtain the title to the land. They engage in agriculture, hunting, gathering honey, and fishing. They also work on crafts: wood carvings, cloth from caraguata fibers, and baskets from carandá palms. Sometimes they work in neighboring establishments, but right now all are in the village. They celebrate the *debylyby* every year in October and November. Their main shamans are Alicio (Ikyle), Gregorio (Wylky), Palacio (Nintyke), Isabelino (Wytsyke), Máximo Martínez (Balihybyt), and Juan Torres (Híit). They have two female shamans: Aparicia and Nyerke.

Potrerito (Peishiota) is a fraction of approximately 600 hectares situated twenty-five kilometers north of Puerto Esperanza.[4] The Ebytoso group that lives in Potrerito followed the Tomáraho from Puerto Esperanza, and recovered the annual ceremonial celebration in 1987 under their influence. This group is now only fifteen families, some seventy-five people who identify strongly with the Tomáraho, with whom they are considering the possibility of meeting annually to perform the *debylyby* together. Their chief is Benjamín Vierci. They have two shamans: Meneto Vera and his brother Luis Vera, a healer of great renown. Their productive activities are essentially the same as that of the Tomáraho.

Puerto Esperanza (Enichte) is a settlement located thirty kilometers south of Bahía Negra, on the Paraguay River. Since 1983, there are approximately sixty Ebytoso families living there. The *cabezante* is Sindulfo Ferreira. They no longer celebrate the *debylyby* but some members join the ceremonies that take place in Potrerito or Carpa Cué. Their shamans are Juan Romero, Bonifacio Frutos, and Ojedo Benítez (they tell me that Faustino Rojas and Roberto Candia have died). This group used to dedicate itself to hunting caimans, but the pressures of different national entities has forced them to diversify. Thus, its inhabitants cultivate orchards (manioc, sweet potato, corn, beans, watermelon, squash, and sugar cane), crafts, and some light cattle-raising. Seasonally, the men abandon the village and offer themselves as day laborers in the area: they strip posts of quebracho (that boats take down to Asunción or Bahía Negra), make wire fences and roofs, and till the land for neighboring farms and lumber yards. The tourists that arrive at this port leave some money (the Ishir dress up as themselves for the tourists and ape their own galas and songs).

Carpa Cué is a small settlement located thirty kilometers from Puerto Esperanza. It corresponds to an ancient campground of woodcutters belonging to the Compañía Carlos Casado. Five Ebytoso families live there, engaged in odd jobs and crafts. They celebrate the ritual with their small population and any visitors from Puerto Esperanza, whose shamans they use.

Puerto Diana is located less than a league south of Bahía Negra; this is the largest Chamacoco community and includes some four hundred people. They are almost no longer Ishir: they are Catholics and Protestants. They no longer have shamans or rituals, and do not know myths or indigenous legends, Benjamín says.[5] Their methods of subsistence correspond to the basic ones of other present-day Ishir groups: traditional models (hunting, fishing, gathering) with transculturated forms (in this case: agriculture, cattle-raising, horticulture, jobs in lumber yards in Pozo Azul, domestic service in Bahía Negra, and the sale of wild animal skins and crafts).

Karcha Balut is a new settlement comprised of seven Ebytoso families. It is found in a place known as Puerto 14 de Mayo, on the Paraguay River south of Bahía Negra. Bruno Barrás, after a long process, was able in July 1998 to have a territory of 8000 hectares adjudicated to the Ebytoso community under his leadership. This place has great mythic importance: the "Great Shell Deposit" (which is what Karcha Balut means) was the site of the original *tobich* and anábsoro hunting grounds. Since its population is so small no *debylyby* takes place there, but some of its members go to Potrerito, Carpa Cué, or even María Elena to take part in the celebration. Karcha Balut has three shamans: Clemente López, Simpricio Miranda, and a very old woman called Bringa Ferreira. Their work with palm leaves—making hats, fans, and containers— is especially good. (Bruno Barrás is erecting a museum on the site with various pieces of Ishir traditional art.)

Buena Vista, in the vicinity of Fuerte Olimpo, is a settlement of about thirty Ebytoso families. The Salesian mission has been efficient with them and produced a group that believes neither in its own truths nor in foreign ones. ("There are no Ishir or Christian truths," says Benjamín.) They have neither ritual celebrations nor shamans, but are good artisans with carandá palm leaves. They have some animals, and like all Ishir periodically offer themselves as cheap labor in lumber yards and neighboring farms. Their chief is called Chano Vera.

Interview with Pedro Vera

[The following is an extract of a conversation I had on 13 April 1998 with Pedro Vera, called Mbochana and nicknamed Peíto (Kytymáraha clan). He had come to Asunción on some errands and was accompanied by Feliciano (also called Túkule, of the Tymáraha clan) and a youth called Mbolud (Tymáraha as well). On this occasion they were silent and only Peíto answered. He was not very talkative; perhaps he was tired or in a hurry, perhaps my questions that day bored him, or perhaps he was preoccupied.]

T.E.: When you abandoned Potrerito, did you go directly to María Elena?

Peíto: First we went to Puerto Caballo in 1995, and then we moved to María Elena, where we live now. The land is ours: 3,873 hectares located north of Bahía Negra (40 kilometers north of Olimpo) on the Río Negro, close to the Three Frontiers (Paraguay, Brazil, and Bolivia).

T.E.: How many people live there?

Peíto: There are 225 people, the majority of whom are Tomáraho, but there are also some Ebytoso. There are 35 children under eleven years of age (born after the move to Puerto Esperanza). Here all the Tomáraho are concentrated: none of our countrymen live in other settlements.

T.E.: How do you sustain yourselves?

Peíto: We have an orchard. We cultivate beans, corn, sweet potatoes, manioc, squash, watermelon. We also hunt iguanas (to sell their skins) as well as peccaries, anteaters, turtles, and armadillos (to eat). We gather fruit and honey. We fish eels and other fish in the Paraguay River. Sometimes we return to work in San Carlos. We make posts for barbed wire fences; sixty men work sporadically as woodcutters.

T.E.: Isn't it a risk to return to San Carlos after all you suffered there?

Peíto: No; now we have our own land. Anyway the men sometimes want to go to San Carlos. ("They miss it," he said literally in Guaraní. I thought of the nomadic impulse, the desire to leave the village, the intense weight of a history of dependencies knotted into their culture.)

T.E.: Aren't there restrictions on hunting iguanas and selling their skins?

Peíto: No, iguanas abound and there are no restrictions on hunting them.

T.E.: Do you continue to perform the annual ceremony?

Peíto: Every year during two months (between October and December) the *debylyby* is celebrated. The initiation of the youth lasts eight months. Even now there is a young boy in the "barracks" (the *tobich*): he is called Romualdo Martínez, Kohyrby, and he is twelve. Last year there were four new initiates. In María Elena there is enough *ostyrbe* (hematite) to paint them red.

T.E.: Do you have enough equipment (clothes made of caraguata, feathered ornaments)?

Peíto: Yes.

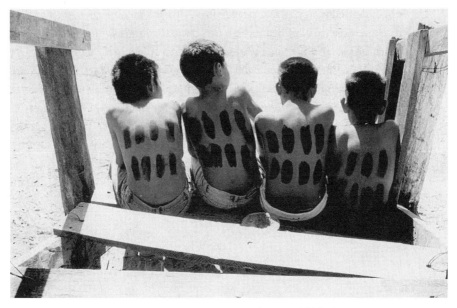

Children whose backs are painted with black lines. María Elena, 2003. (Photo by Arístides Escobar.)

T.E.: Who are the shamans that currently live in María Elena?

Peíto: Alicio, Wylky, Palacio Vera, Luciano, Isabelino, Máximo Martínez, Sánchez Vera, Zacarías Bolsón (new), Juan Torres, Aparicia, Nyerke, Ramona, Aurelia Agustín (Palacio Vera's wife), and Calí Acosta (a new shaman, Wylky's wife).

T.E.: Do you have Paraguayan sicknesses that cannot be healed by the shamans?

Peíto: Yes, flu and skin and teeth problems.

T.E.: What are your most urgent necessities? Do you have enough clothes and food?

Peíto: We need a mill and are negotiating to acquire one. We lack winter clothes. Sometimes we lack food; we indigenous people do not know an abundance of food.

I WAS tempted to ask if this handful of men and women would survive; that is, if their intense gazes and irrefutable silences would continue; if their words of condensed materials and strange forms, their fearsome cries, their radiant plumes, their weather-beaten skin preserved through essential colors would resist the passage of time. I wanted to ask if they would have the strength to ward off the shadow of guilt and fear that can suddenly darken the Ishir horizon: if a Kytymáraha capable of belying the primordial sentence would survive. I did not dare, of course. Peíto thrust his hand in the bottom of his caraguata bag and extracted a bracelet of crushed feathers. "It is for your son Cristián," he said. "I owed it to him for a poncho he gave me in San Carlos." He got up, checked his watch, and distractedly checked the sky: "Come," he told Túkule, "it will rain this afternoon." I glanced up at the sky; some distant clouds floated on the horizon.

NOTES

Introduction

1. I have relied most heavily on the indispensable work of Branislava Susnik and Edgardo Cordeu for bibliographic sources. On certain occasions I even contacted them personally with questions they answered with constant good will and patience.

Chapter 1: The Great Myth

1. *Jútoro* signifies single, sexually free women. Susnik uses the term to refer to women who are not subject to the convivial restrictions of clan membership.

2. The *ahpora* (*Jacaratia corumbensis*) is a vine with tuberous root that stores water and that can become so large as to be disproportionate to the plant's thin stalks. (Personal communication of Jorge Escobar Argaña.)

3. The guayacan (*Caesalpinia paraguariensis*) is a tall tree whose wood is very dark and hard; the palo santo (*Bulnesia sarmientoi*) is a tree with a fragrant wood that burns with intense smell and luminosity.—Trans.

4. The caraguata or chaguar (*Bromelia hieronymi*) is a non-woody, edible forest plant historically used by all ethnic groups in the Argentine, Paraguayan, and Bolivian Chaco as fiber that is woven into ropes, bags, textiles, etc.—Trans.

5. What Escobar refers to by the term *avestruz* and what I have translated as "ostrich" is the *Rhea americana* or Greater Rhea, known in Guaraní as the *ñandú*. It is very similar to the ostrich but is about half its height at 1.5 meters, and has a feathered rather than bare neck. The *ñandú* is found from Brazil to the Patagonia and is considered near-threatened.—Trans.

6. Remember the Ishir principle of knowledge: knowing something's secret is acquiring power over the unknown, dominating the dark side. The secret of things, as the secret of all beings, must be conquered or must be revealed. Sometimes the object resists submitting itself to knowledge and opposes it with obstacles: deceit is an obstacle that must be negotiated or dismantled.

7. The New Tribes Mission is a fundamentalist Christian mission set up in 1942 to evangelize so-called tribal peoples. It is based today in Sanford, Florida.—Trans.

8. The carancha (*Caracara plancus*) is a long-legged vulturelike hawk known in English as the Crested Caracara for the dark tuft on its head; its body is dark and its neck light-colored.—Trans.

Chapter 2: Feathers and Featherwork

1. R. Otto (1958) calls states of terrified awe, seduction, and fear before the sacred *mysterium fascinans* and *mysterium tremendum*. These feelings require the structure of form to be channeled.

2. The carandá (*Copernicia australis*) is a tall palm tree.—Trans.

3. The *urutaú* (*Nyctibius spp.*) refers to seven species of this nocturnal bird; the wailing cry of some of its species has given it the name Potoo in English. When perched on a tree trunk it blends in through the patterns of its grey, black, and brown plumage.—Trans.

4. *Quebracho* is a common name for several trees—though it most often refers to the red quebracho (*Schinopsis lorentzii*) or white quebracho (*Aspidosperma quebracho-blanco*)—which are known for their hard tannin-rich wood. The name is derived from *quebra hacha,* "axe breaker."—Trans.

5. This account is developed in the narrative sources of Cordeu's "Aishtuwénte: Las ideas de deidad en la religiosidad chamacoco," published in various issues of *Suplemento Antropológico* (Asunción, Centro de Estudios Antropológicos de la Universidad Católica, 1989–1992). Sadly, these extensive narrations were not included in these publications, and I refer to the typewritten originals the author graciously provided.

6. The *samu'u* or *palo borracho* (*Chorisia insignis*) is known for its bulbous, thorn-covered trunk that stores water during dry weather.—Trans.

7. The chaja (*Chauna torquata*) or Southern Screamer (also Crested Screamer) is a waterfowl with black, brown, and grey feathers that can reach three feet in length. Their cries can be heard over three kilometers away.—Trans.

8. Author's free translation of the Portuguese original.

9. Yerba maté, or maté, is a caffeinated herbal tea originally consumed by the Guaraní and popular today in Paraguay, Uruguay, Argentina, and southern Brazil. It is prepared by steeping dry leaves in a hollow gourd and sipping through a metal straw.—Trans.

10. The *ahäporo* (*Thalia geniculata*) is an aquatic plant with leaves similar to the leaves of the banana tree.

11. *Pörkarro* is the Ishir name for *labón* (*Tabebuia nodosa*), a tree whose wood is used to obtain fire through friction. A piece of wood from this soft tree is rubbed against a piece of quebracho or palo santo hardwood until a spark ignites the *samu'u* cotton or the bird's nest provided to light the flame (Jorge Escobar Argaña, personal communication). The Ishir metaphorically speak of the *labón* as having a "soul of fire" and liken the dust obtained from its ground wood to gunpowder.

12. A species of acacia whose flowers give off a characteristic aroma; it is called *aromita* locally.

13. The jacana (*Jacana jacana*) is a black and brown bird with a yellow bill and red wattles on its head. It has unusually long toes that allow it to walk on the floating vegetation of its habitat.—Trans.

Chapter 3: Corporal Painting

1. *Jopará* refers to a mixture of Spanish and Guaraní.

2. The *surubí* (*Pseudoplatystoma coruscans*) is a large migratory species of catfish.—Trans.

3. Although Flores Balbuena respects these principles, in some of his tales the paths of the *konsaho* and gods cross each other briefly.

4. The *pririta* (*Guira guira*) is also known as the Guira Cuckoo.—Trans.

5. The *palo borracho* (*Chorisia insignis*) is a large bottle-shaped tree.—Trans.

6. *Urucú* (*Bixa arborea* and *B. arellana*) is also known as achiote or annatto and is used as a food dye.—Trans.

7. The genip (*Melicocca bijugatus*) is a small edible fruit with green leathery skin and sweet translucent pulp.—Trans.

8. The Colorado Party is identified with red and the Liberal Party with blue. (The Chamacoco do not find the distinction between blue and black to be relevant; according to them, black is simply the intensification of blue.)

9. The *pacú* (*Colossoma mitrei*) is a freshwater fish that resembles a large piranha.—Trans.

Chapter 4: The Rite

1. What the Ishir call *hopupora* is a nocturnal bird that the Ayoreo know as *asojná* and that plays a mythical and ritual function in the cultural context of both Zamuco groups: its cries herald the renewal of time and mark the beginning of the ritualized events. In a personal communication Jorge Escobar Argaña, who has investigated the ornithological equivalent of *asojná*, maintains that it corresponds to the *Caprimulgo parvulus,* a small nocturnal bird whose characteristic cries are heard in the months of September, October, and November. The fact that *hopupora* and *asojná* refer to the same bird permits some interesting parallels and intersections between Ashnuwerta, the maximum Ishir deity announced by the song of the *hopupora,* and Asojná, her Ayoreo equivalent, whose rite begins with the song of the same bird. This equivalence is also considered by Cordeu (2003, 263).

2. Note the rather arbitrary logic of the names that designate the play of colors: the Reds are painted with red and black stripes, and the Blacks are painted with black and white stripes.

Chapter 5: The Path of the Shamans

1. According to Cordeu (1986, 109), the Ishir shamans locate desire in the heart: "Intelligence [*eiwo*] determines the adequate course of action and communicates it to the mouth . . . where, transformed into volition, the sequence of desire and thought realizes itself finally in language."

2. Susnik (1957, 1995) has worked in detail on the classification of shamans according to categories.

3. The term *jila* means "inheritor of the power of"; it refers to the quality possessed by shamans of identifying themselves with a power, and of being protected by and instructed in this power. *Jilo* is the plural form.

4. Luciano's tale includes an episode in which the Moon's impatience provokes the death of the horse, which the Sun must then revive.

5. Emilio uses *jopará* ("mestizo" in Guaraní) to refer to the dowry.

6. The bloody Chaco War (1932–1935) was fought between Bolivia and Paraguay over the Grand Chaco: an arid, inhospitable region that was believed to hold oil reserves. It ended with a cease-fire and arbitration that granted Paraguay the largest piece of the disputed territory.—Trans.

7. Name of a prestigious Ebytoso sky shaman. Evidently, he adopted the name of Guido Boggiani, the famed Italian artist and anthropologist who came to Paraguay at the end of the nineteenth century and died at the hands of the Chamacoco.

8. Susnik refers to this contact, which takes place in dreams between sky shamans and the powerful souls of deceased shamans of the same category. Considered "stellar sons," the dead shamans lead the dreaming ones to their abode in the nebula and stare at them with "shining eyes" to initiate them in their deepest truths. The brilliant eyes of the dead shamans symbolize the capacity to "gaze and guard, gaze and persecute, gaze and worry" (Susnik 1984–1985, 127).

9. It is possible that the title "honeycomb eater" does not correspond to a register equivalent to the other categories. It seems that such a denomination refers to the procedure through which to access a high level of shamanic power, whatever the category. Logically, all "honeycomb eaters" should belong to the sky shamans, who have power over all flying creatures.

Chapter 6: The History

1. Usually the Great Ceremony takes place after September, sometimes after August. I never found out why those performances took place in San Carlos during our visit. It is possible that they knew we were going to be visiting: Clemente knew of our interest in the *debylyby* and could have convinced the Tomáraho to perform certain dramatic episodes

to theatrically support the presentation of a desperate circumstance. Hunting people know the tactics of seduction well, and speculating with their most solemn convictions is not a sacrilege to them. On the other hand, certain gods, like those of Hopupora, Ashnuwerta, Pohejuvo, etc., can occasionally make appearances outside the strict limits of the ritual calendar. This happens because their auspicious powers are required in extraordinary situations that do not coincide with the time of the ceremony.

2. In 1986 one dollar equaled approximately 660 guaranis.

3. According to Métraux, in 1928 there were about 1,500 Tomáraho in 301 families. Baldus gave the same estimate in 1930. In 1955 Susnik mentioned 1,000 Tomáraho (Chase-Sardi et al. 1990, 51). In 1986, Guillermo Sequera and I personally confirmed the existence of only eighty-seven people in San Carlos.

4. The name Puerto Esperanza designates both the territory of 21,300 hectares that belong to the Chamacoco, as well as a specific point of this territory located on the Paraguay River.

5. The Chamacoco of Puerto Diana were victims of a systematic process of ethnocide by the authoritarian and fanatic Salesian Mission and the New Tribes Mission. "From 1942," write Chase-Sardi et al., "the community [of Puerto Diana] has been completely detribalized and has lost its sense of identity" (1990, 56).

WORKS CITED

Baldus, Herbert. 1927. "Os indios chamacocos e sua lingua." *Revista del Museo Paulista* (São Paulo) 15.2:5–68.

———. 1932. "La mere commune dans la mythologie de deux tribus sudamericaines (Kagaba et Tumerahá)." *Revista del Instituto de Etnología de la Universidad Nacional de Tucumán* 2:471–79.

Boggiani, Guido. 1894. "I Ciamacocco." *Atti de la Societa romana di Antropología* (Rome).

———. 1900. "Compendio de Etnografía Paraguaya Moderna." *Revista del Instituto Paraguayo* (Asunción) 28:65–183.

Cazeneuve, Jean. 1971. *Sociología del rito*. Buenos Aires: Amorrortu.

Chase-Sardi, Miguel, et al. 1990. *Situación sociocultural, económica, jurídico-política actual de las comunidades indígenas en el Paraguay*. Asunción: Centro Interdisciplinario de Derecho Social y Economía Política (CIDSEP), Universidad Católica.

Cordeu, Edgardo. 1984. "Categorias básicas, principios lógicos y redes simbólicas de la cosmovisión de los indios ishir." *Journal of Latin American Lore* (Los Angeles) 10.2:189–275.

———. 1986. "Los atudendos shamánicos chamacoco del Museo Etnográficos. Un intento de interpretación simbólica." *RUNA: Archivo para las Ciencias del Hombre* (Buenos Aires) 16:103–36.

———. 1989a. "Aishtuwénte. Las ideas de deidad en la religiosidad chamacoco, Primera Parte." *Suplemento Antropológico* (Asunción, Centro de Estudios Antropológicos de la Universidad Católica [CEADUC]) 24.1:7–77.

———. 1989b. "Aishtuwénte. Las ideas de deidad en la religiosidad chamacoco, Segundo Parte." *Suplemento Antropológico* (Asunción, CEADUC) 24.2:51–85.

———. 1990. "Aishtuwénte. Las ideas de deidad en la religiosidad chamacoco, Tercera Parte." *Suplemento Antropológico* (Asunción, CEADUC) 25.1:119–211.

———. 1991a. "Aishtuwénte. Las ideas de deidad en la religiosidad chamacoco, Tercera Parte (Continuación)." *Suplemento Antropológico* (Asunción, CEADUC) 26.1:85–166.

———. 1991b. "Aishtuwénte. Las ideas de deidad en la religiosidad chamacoco, Cuarta Parte." *Suplemento Antropológico* (Asunción, CEADUC) 26.2:147–223.

———. 1992a. "Aishtuwénte. Las ideas de deidad en la religiosidad chamacoco, Quinta Parte." *Suplemento Antropológico* (Asunción, CEADUC) 27.1:187–294.

———. 1992b. "Aishtuwénte. Las ideas de deidad en la religiosidad chamacoco, Quinta

Parte (Continuación), Sexta Parte." *Suplemento Antropológico* (Asunción, CEADUC) 27.2:167–301.

———. 1999. *Transfiguraciones simbólicas. Ciclo ritual de los indios tomáraxo del Chaco Boreal.* Quito: Ediciones Abya-Yala.

———. 2003. *Transfiguraciones simbólicas. Ciclo ritual de los indios tomáraxo del Chaco Boreal.* Asunción: Centro de Artes Visuales/Museo del Barro.

Duvignaud, Jean. 1980. *El sacrificio inútil.* Mexico: Fondo de Cultura Económica.

Eliade, Mircea. 1959. *The Sacred and the Profane. The Nature of Religion. The Significance of Religious Myth, Symbolism, and Ritual within Life and Culture.* Translated by Willard R. Trask. New York: Harcourt, Brace, and World.

Escobar, Ticio. 1984. *Una interpretación de las artes visuales en el Paraguay,* 2 vols. Colección de las Américas. Asunción: Centro Cultural Paraguayo Americano.

———. 1986. *El mito del arte y el mito del pueblo.* Asunción: RP Ediciones/Museo del Barro.

———. 1988. *Misión: Etnocidio.* Asunción: Comisión de Solidaridad con los Pueblos Indígenas.

———. 1993. *La belleza de los otros (arte indígena del Paraguay).* Asunción: RP Ediciones/Museo del Barro.

Fric, A. V. 1946. *Indiáni Jizní Ameriky.* Prague: Jaroslav Prodrouzek.

Fric, Pavel, and Yvonna Fricova. 1997. *Guido Boggiani, fotógrafo.* Prague: Nakladatelství.

Geertz, Clifford. 1973. *The Interpretation of Cultures.* New York: Basic Books.

Jensen, Adolf. 1963. *Myth and Cult among Primitive Peoples.* Translated by Marianna Tax Choldin and Wolfgang Weissleder. Chicago: University of Chicago Press.

Métraux, Alfred. 1996. *Etnografía del Chaco.* Asunción: Centro de Estudios Antropológicos de la Universidad Católica (CEADUC).

Otto, Rudolf. 1958. *The Idea of the Holy.* Oxford: Oxford University Press.

Perrazo, José A. 1991. *Colección "Zamuco" B) Yshir-chamakoko.* San Lorenzo: Museo "Guido Boggiani."

Sahlins, Marshall. 1972. *Stone Age Economics.* Chicago: Aldine-Atherton.

Susnik, Branislava. 1957. *Estudios Chamacoco.* Asunción: Museo Etnográfico "Andrés Barbero."

———. 1970. *Chamacocos II. Diccionario Etnográfico.* Asunción: Museo Etnográfico "Andrés Barbero."

———. 1978. *Etnografía Paraguaya (Parte Primera).* 9th ed. Asunción: Museo Etnográfico "Andrés Barbero."

———. 1984–1985. *Los aborígenes del Paraguay VI (Aproximación a las creencias de los indígenas).* Asunción: Museo Etnográfico "Andrés Barbero."

———. 1995. *Chamacocos 1: Cambio Cultural.* 2nd ed. Asunción: Museo Etnográfico "Andrés Barbero."

Turner, Victor. 1967. *The Forest of Symbols: Aspects of Ndembu Ritual.* Ithaca, New York: Cornell University Press.

INDEX

Note: Page numbers in italic type indicate illustrations.